Racial and Ethnic Identity in School Practices

Aspects of Human Development

Edited by

Rosa Hernández Sheets
San Francisco State University

Etta R. Hollins
Wright State University

 LAWRENCE ERLBAUM ASSOCIATES, PUBLISHERS
1999   Mahwah, New Jersey   London

Published by Lawrence Erlbaum Associates, Publishers.

Lawrence Erlbaum Associates, Inc., Publishers
10 Industrial Avenue
Mahwah, NJ 07430

Cover design by Kathryn Houghtaling Lacey

Library of Congress Cataloging-in-Publication Data

Racial and ethnic identity in school practices : aspects
of human development / edited by Rosa Hernández
Sheets, Etta R. Hollins.
      p.   cm.
Includes bibliographical references and index.
ISBN 0-8058-2787-0 (cloth : alk. paper). — ISBN
0-8058-2788-9 (pbk. : alk. paper)
1. Education—Social aspects—United States.   2.
Minorities—Education—United States.   3. Race
awareness—United States.   4. Multicultural
education—United States. I. Hernández Sheets, Rosa.
II. Hollins, Etta R., 1942–
LC191.4.R336   1999
371.829—dc21
                                            98–48434
                                                 CIP

Books published by Lawrence Erlbaum Associates are
printed on acid-free paper, and their bindings are chosen
for strength and durability.

Printed in the United States of America
10   9   8   7   6   5   4   3   2

Contents

Preface

The purpose of this volume is to demonstrate and explicate the work of scholars and practitioners who are exploring the interconnectedness of racial and ethnic identity to human development in order to promote successful pedagogical practices and services. This volume presents a dual perspective that incorporates scholarship from the fields of psychology and education to empower practitioners and scholars to operationalize, interpret, contextualize, and bridge theory into practice.

By acknowledging that the racial and ethnic psychological experiences of individuals are consequential, this text (a) provides scholars in general psychology, educational psychology, counseling, and teacher preparation programs with current research on racial and ethnic identity formation and human development; (b) explains why traditional theories of human development, which are void of racial and ethnic dimensions and have evolved exclusively from a Eurocentric perspective, are problematic; and (c) documents current best practices from psychology, educational leadership, counseling, and teaching and classroom practices that support the claim that psychologists, counselors, and educators who are aware of racial and ethnic identity development (their own and others) are better prepared to respond to students from their own background, as well as with those from other racial, ethnic, and cultural backgrounds.

This text is divided into three sections. Part I explains why the relationship among racial identity, ethnic identity, and human development is critical to schooling and provides the conceptual framework guiding and unifying subsequent chapters. Theoretical models of racial and ethnic identities and their intersection with human developmental processes are explored. Current research in racial and ethnic identity are discussed in Part II. This scholarship includes examples from diverse racial and ethnic groups, makes linkages to human development, and suggests ways to apply these theories to school practices. Last, challenges and strategies for multicultural practices are the focus of Part III. This section presents the tenets of multicultural education and rubrics for training and practice in the areas of teaching, counseling, and administration.

This volume is designed to be interdisciplinary, demonstrating linkages between scholarship on racial and ethnic identity formation and human development to schooling by providing scholarship and research from respected scholars in the fields of psychology and education who are working in the area of racial and ethnic identity formation, classroom instruction, teacher preparation, counseling, and administration as well as providing documentation needed to directly challenge current Eurocentric notions of human development by including race, ethnicity, and culture as critical dimensions of identity.

Racial and ethnic identity issues are brought directly to schooling so that psychological services, counseling practices, and teaching–learning experiences can be most effective for a greater number of students in the educational process. We are speaking here not only of assumed privileges and advantages associated with race, or of ideals of equity and equality, but of psychoeducational experiences and actions that interfere with human development and, ultimately, affect the sociocognitive development of children.

This volume is intended for scholars, researchers, and practitioners in psychology and related fields, whose work directly intersects educational issues and the needs of children within the school environment. It is also intended for students on the graduate level in general psychology, educational psychology, and multicultural education. Students who are preparing to teach at the university level will find the information in this volume especially helpful in courses where the preparation of educational psychologists, counselors, and teachers is the major focus. This volume is also useful as a supplementary text for students of education and advanced students taking upper division psychology and educational courses on the undergraduate level who are examining the relationship between identity development and human development.

ACKNOWLEDGMENTS

The publication of this book began with a discussion in the lobby of the New York Hilton during AERA, 1997. Subsequently, Etta Hollins invited me to lunch and asked that I bring the book outline. I assumed book prospectus requirements and contract details would be major topics of conversation. Enjoying the friendly discourse, I waited throughout lunch; and, was a bit disappointed that little or no mention was given to the pending book. As we departed, Etta casually told Naomi Silverman (Lawrence Erlbaum Associates editor) that we would have the prospectus in by June. While the inception of this project appears low key, the guidance and mentoring from Etta throughout this process was extensive, supportive, and rewarding. I hope that I can, by helping others, repay in kind to Etta her infinite gifts of love, patience, and knowledge.

We are deeply indebted to the authors whose sustained commitment and excellent scholarship advance the literature and bring this book to completion. The superb editing skills provided by Kimberly Hollins, the support of our editor, Naomi Silverman, and release time provided by Dean

Jacob Perea of the College of Education at San Francisco State for Rosa, are especially appreciated. We also wish to thank members of our family, Karla Hollins, Kimberly Hollins, Joseph Sheets, Jaime Sheets, and Miguel Sheets for their feedback, patience, and inspirational support.

—*Rosa Hernández Sheets*
—*Etta R. Hollins*

I Racial and Ethnic Identity Theory and Human Development

Educators providing services in diverse settings must be able to interact effectively with students with whom they may or may not share racial, ethnic, and cultural heritages. The contributing authors of Part I describe trends in the research of racial identity, ethnic identity, and human developmental theory; review the literature on racial attitudes; provide information of racial and ethnic identity development and formation; discuss the critical roles of peers, parents, teachers, and society in the development of identity; explore the human developmental impact dimensions of identity across the life span; and make specific linkages between psychology and education.

In chapter 1, Branch distinguishes between race and ethnicity; provides a review of basic research assumptions on racial attitudes, racial identity formation, and human development; examines the influences that parents and teachers have on racial identity development among young children; and makes suggestions for using the classroom as a forum for the development of positive racial attitudes for parents and young children. He describes *race* as a genetic designation based on phenotypic characteristics and an *ethnic group* as people sharing a common heritage, practices, and beliefs. Branch contends that interchanging these concepts fosters confusion in the literature.

He identifies basic research assumptions that are problematic in the literature on racial attitudes at each stage across the life span. First, the study of racial attitudes among young children is based on assumptions that include the beliefs that young children's racial attitudes are constructed as unipolar entities, that young children understand the significance of race in U.S. society, and that children's racial attitudes are unidimensional and static. Second, the study of racial attitudes among adolescents is based on assumptions that include issues of self-definition and self-esteem as the most salient features of adolescent racial concerns; behavior in racially mixed settings is indicative of adolescents' underlying racial attitudes; racial identity as a developmental task is not intricately related to other issues of identity; and adolescents and childhood are discontinuous in the area of racial attitudes and behavior development. Third, the study of racial attitudes among adults is based on assumptions that include ideas such as: attitudes and behaviors observed among adults are discrete from the earlier developmental periods and are culminating and terminal; racial preferences tell the whole story of racial attitudes; race is a social construction and can be understood by simply subjecting it and related behaviors to intellectual analysis; and racial identity definable by physical dimensions can be measured by traditional instrumentation. These assumptions have led to errors in research designs, erroneous conclusions from research studies, and problems in the development of racial identity developmental theories in young children.

According to Branch, parents are critical for shaping the environments and experiences that children may have, yet they cannot account for all the variance in children's attitudes. He points out that teachers also influence the racial identity development of youngsters through perceptions of power and distance, which can create a sense of marginality and hence devaluation. Finally, Branch suggests that teachers learn about racial attitude development, develop a social curriculum that addresses children's racial attitudes, and construct a parent involvement project to engage parents in understanding the incorporation of these issues in classrooms.

The authors in chapter 2, Cross, Jr., Strauss, and Fhagen-Smith, focus on the development of racial identity in African Americans. First, they point out that African Americans evidence a wide range of social identities, which can be divided into two broad categories. According to Cross et al., African Americans operating with a group identity in which race and African American culture are central to their everyday lives have a social identity that is high in race salience (HS). When race and African American culture are not central to group identity, social identity is low in race salience (LS). These authors suggest that any discussion of Black identity must take into account both types of identities. Second, self-concept is composed of two components, a general personality and a referent group orientation, however, their discussion focuses on the referent group orientation. Third, they identify and describe five identity operations that are key to a multidimensional definition of Black identity—buffering, bonding, bridging, codeswitching, and individualism. Fourth, *Black oppositional theory*—a rejection of the dominant culture—is presented as a special case of behavior that is problematic during adolescence. These scholars maintain that this nihilistic psychology is also at odds with traditional African American values.

Cross et al. present the unfolding of Black identity in six sectors, each linked to a developmental phase: Sector 1, infancy and childhood; Sector 2, pre-adolescence; Sector 3, adolescence; Sector 4, late adolescence and early adulthood; Sector 5, adult nigrescence; and Sector 6, identity refinement during adulthood. Parents, relatives, friends, and peers, among others, lay the foundation for identity development during infancy, childhood, and preadolescence (Sectors 1 and 2), whereas adolescence (Sector 3) and early adulthood (Sector 4) mark the developmental periods when the individual tries to take ownership and responsibility for his or her self-identity. Sector

5 introduces a feature that is extremely unique to identity development in African Americans, the Nigrescence Process. *Nigrescence* is a five-stage process that results in a radical change of a person's racial identity. Sector 6 is called *Nigrescence Recycling*; it captures the ways in which racial identity continues to grow and be refined across the life span from early adulthood to mature adulthood. This chapter concludes with the types of guidance, support, validation, and sensitivity Black American students need in school settings to make possible the development and refinement of identity.

Chapter 3 provides an overview of White racial identity theory, shows the relationship between racial identity and other psychological models of development, and illustrates how racial identity development can enhance or limit personality growth. The discussion begins with Helms' (1990) Theory of White Racial Identity. This model describes two phases; unlearning racism and internalizing what it means to be White. Each phase encompasses three distinct racial identity statuses; Phase I, contact, disintegration, integration and Phase II, psuedo-independent, immersion/emersion, autonomy. The Helms' model is contrasted with Rowe, Bennett, and Atkinson's (1994) recent White racial identity theory which uses Helms' definition as a basis to reconceptualize White racial consciousness in two forms of identity status—achieved and unachieved—and seven attitude types—dominative, conflictive, reactive, integrative, dependent, avoidant, and dissonant. Ego and social identity models applicable to adolescents are presented; however, the authors point out that these models are either void of race and ethnicity or void of the role which racism and oppression plays in identity development.

The Helms' Theory of White Racial Identity is contrasted with two psychological theories of development—object relations theory and Maslow's (1987) self-actualization theory. Because object relations theory suggests that people develop a sense of self-identity within the context of relating to others, Richardson and Silvestri argue that this theory shares meaningful parallels with racial identity theory regarding the ways that optimal personal growth develops. The authors maintain that self-actualization, as defined by Maslow (1987), is incompatible with an unevolved White racial identity. In conclusion, the reader is reminded of the important role social context (such as, regressive vs. progressive families and peer norms regarding racist behaviors) plays in how individuals cope with potentially hostile environments and supportive social networks in their identity development journey.

According to Root (chap. 4, this volume), current racial and ethnic stage theory does not accommodate, capture, explain, or delineate the ways in which some multiracial individuals conduct and negotiate racial and ethnic spaces. In chapter 4, Root presents a cognitive–emotional process and discusses an ecological, interactional model of identity development to explain the evolution of racial and ethnic development over the life span for multiracial individuals.

The cognitive–emotional process, not necessarily sequential or stage-driven, contains a constructive and destructive differentiation within each cognitive–emotional process. Root refers to these processes as exposure/absorption, competition/stratification, and reflective/appraisal. In the exposure/absorption process, active or passive acquisition of information allows others to be constructed side by side with self rather than in competition or opposition (constructive) or prevents an understanding of differences in self and others and individual identity depends on maintaining distance from others (destructive). Competition/stratification is characterized by judgments retaining an open mind (constructive) or incorporating tactics that characterize self and others as inferior or superior (destructive). Reflective/appraisal is characterized by openness to new information and a willingness to suspend quick judgments. Change occurs as information is reconsidered over longer periods of time and within a contextualized framework (constructive) or prior conclusions are validated and retained as one processes more information in a slower more thoughtful response (destructive).

The ecological model includes interactive encounters of race and ethnicity with other salient aspects of identity (such as, gender, geographic history, class, and sexual orientation) in the development of identity. This integration of various dimensions of one's identity results in the deconstruction of traditional bipolar racial frameworks and, instead, places individuals in historical and geographical contexts. It is within these experiences and interactions with others across time and among changes in the environment that inherited influences (i.e., biological and environmental), traits (e.g., temperament, social skills, talents, and coping skills), and social interactions with the community (e.g., home, school, community, and friends) dynamically relate to one another changing at different times and in different contexts. Root theorizes that this ecological model accommodates the fluidity of identities in social contexts and provides a way to consider how multiple and significant aspects of identity components coexist and interact to inform a whole identity.

In chapter 5, Sheets explores the literature on ethnic identity theory to help understand why the relationship among ethnic identity theory, human development, and schooling has not been firmly established and begins the process of establishing these linkages. The chapter has four sections: a review of the literature in human development and ethnicity as it relates to ethnic identity; the development of an operational definition of ethnic identity; the role of schooling in the development of students' ethnic identity; and the implications for school practices.

Sheets points out that language usage and methodological issues in the research of ethnic identity are areas of concern. To understand the process of ethnic identity formation and development, she theorizes that at least four dimensions, which by nature, integrate, intersect, and overlap, are essential. These dimensions begin at birth and continue throughout the life span; they include content components, categorical ascription, situational and environmental context, and processual continuum. According to Sheets, changing teachers', administrators', counselors', and school psychologists' preparation to include understanding of ethnic identity formation and development (of self and others) is central to changing classroom and school practices.

REFERENCES

Helms, J. E. (Ed.). (1990). *Black and White racial identity: Theory, research, and practice.* New York: Greenwood.

Mazlow, A. H. (1987). *Motivation and personality* (3rd ed.). New York: Harper & Row.

Rowe, W., Bennett, S. K., & Atkinson, D. R. (1994). White racial identity models: A critique and alternative proposal. *The Counseling Psychologist, 22*(1), 129–146.

1 Race and Human Development

Curtis W. Branch
Columbia University

In an attempt to understand variations in human growth and development, social and behavioral scientists have identified a variety of categories that often serve as independent variables in empirical studies. Race is one such category. Despite its enormous popularity as a potential contributor to understanding behavioral outcomes, there is much confusion concerning the concept, its definition, and the ontogenic course that individuals follow in developing race-related attitudes and behaviors. Frequently, race is used interchangeably with ethnicity. On other occasions, the concept of race is used when researchers are studying ethnicity and vice versa. In my opinion, these two concepts are closely related but are two separate entities.

Race is a concept that is derived from a genetic designation based on phenotypic characteristics (i.e., physical features such as, skin color and hair texture). It is an idea that is clearly rooted in history. Race, as a category, may subsume several ethnic groups and in doing so, obliterates any uniqueness associated with more narrowly defined ethnic categories. An *ethnic group* can be thought of as a group of people with a common historical heritage, originating in the same place, and sharing cultural expressions such as manner of dress, art, music, food, literature, and other concrete manifestations. In this chapter, the interest is race, not ethnicity.

Discussions of individuals' sense of racial identity and their racial attitudes have occurred in the research literature within the contexts of childhood and adulthood. Very little has been written, comparatively, about racial attitudes and behaviors in adolescence. The notable exception to this is in the area of dating. In the case of children, discussions have typically focused on classification tasks in which children are asked to identify themselves and to place themselves or others into a racial category. Despite the fact that adolescence is seen as a transitory developmental period, little attention has been given to how children transition into adolescent racial attitudes or how adolescents transition into adult racial attitudes. Somewhat surprisingly, most of the literature on adult racial attitudes has been without a developmental framework that extends backward to take into consideration the early developmental experiences. Childhood, adolescence, and adulthood are treated as discrete periods. This state of discontinuity accounts, in part, for the absence of an understanding of how race and racial attitudes have different impacts across the life span. Branch and Carter (1996) suggested that this absence of continuity in theory contributes to the confusion about the influence of race on the human developmental process. They contended that the developmental stage of parents and adults needs to be addressed if researchers are to create a reliable model for understanding how children's racial attitudes are shaped. This chapter uses that idea as a thesis for exploring the roles that teachers and parents play in shaping young children's racial attitudes.

Conceptually, this chapter is divided into three sections: (1) a review of basic research assumptions on racial attitudes, racial identity formation, and human development; (2) a discussion of the roles of parents and teachers in shaping the emergence of racial identity among young children; and, (3) some brief thoughts about how the classroom can be used as a forum for the development of global and positive racial attitudes for parents and young children.

BASIC AND FAULTY RESEARCH ASSUMPTIONS

Racial Attitude Development Among Young Children

Racial Attitudes as Unipolar Constructions.   The approaches that researchers have taken when trying to measure racial attitudes seem to suggest an "either/or" perspective. The vast number of studies that rely on forced choice techniques as a way to assess racial attitudes attest to this observation. This tradition can be traced to the early doll studies conducted by Clark and Clark (1947). For many years after its creation, the either/or assumption of the doll studies characterized the approaches utilized by researchers. There have been methodological variations on this theme (e.g., Asher & Allen, 1969; Bird, 1952; Blake & Dennis, 1943; Goodman, 1964; Trager & Yarrow, 1952; Williams & Morland, 1976), but the basic assumption has remained the same. If children are placed in a situation of forced choice on the basis of race, choosing one stimuli means rejecting the other. The oversimplification of this logic was revealed by Branch and Newcombe (1986) when they showed that the results of the doll studies produce very different results when the subjects are given multiple-choice options. They created a variation of the Clark Doll Test, which allowed children to pick several dolls, black or white, in response to stimulus items. The result was that the commonly reported pattern of white preference and black rejection was not found. Inherent in the legacy of doll studies is a belief that the doll choices reflect children's real-life thinking and attitudes. This assumption has never been empirically validated.

Baldwin (1979) noted that the use of dolls has a serious limitation because of the novel quality of black dolls until well into the 1960s. He also pointed out that a doll choice is merely that, not necessarily reflective of real-world attitudes. It appears that part of the basis of the clinical inference of doll choices being representations of internal views can be traced to psychoanalytic thinking, which says that how individuals act in any situation is reflective of how they feel internally. This type of thinking has become so engrained in popular folk wisdom that many researchers and lay persons assume it to be true without questioning it. Of course, the only way to absolutely confirm that such is indeed the case would be to complete an extensive clinical interview with subjects. This rarely, if ever, happens in the research literature. Instead, researchers make assumptions about how and why children come to the decisions of their doll choices, as if there is only one interpretation for a doll choice. Additionally, choosing one doll is interpreted as proof that the other has been rejected. Such dichotomous thinking points to the need for an intermediate point of interpretation. How many things in life are absolutely either/or with no in between point?

Another assumption that is often not checked for its validity is that children's choices of dolls on the basis of race reflects a level of understanding regarding the significance of race in U.S. society. Again, this assumption often goes unchallenged and is regarded as being true. A closer look at this assumption, however, highlights how researchers have overinterpreted or miscalculated what children understand. For example, asking a child, Which is the bad doll? assumes a level of attribution that is not definable. How does the child define bad? Trager and Yarrow (1952) and Porter (1971) improved on this problem by operationalizing the words *bad* and *good* for the children. They read stories detailing the behavior of the dolls and then asked the children to make choices. Although this change represents a dramatic step forward, it is still tied to the dichotomous thinking that says a person is either bad or good. The logic of such questioning appears to be that a person can only have one set of descriptors for their behavior or that the child can only handle one chunk of information about a person at a time. In either case, it continues to assume that if a child describes a doll as bad, the opposite is true of the doll not chosen.

A personal experience that I had with a 4-year-old subject helped teach me this lesson very well. I was studying the racial attitudes of young African American children. The *Preschool Racial Attitude Measure II* (PRAM II; Williams, 1971), a forced-choice format that relies on stories about Black and White characters, and a detailed interview were parts of the battery. After making her choices on the PRAM II, the little girl said to me "Some Black people do bad things ... like that boy who lives down the hall. Some Black people steal and rob. They do bad, bad things, but I still like Black people." This was her way of saying that, despite having made many negative associations to the Black characters in the PRAM II stories, she still had positive regard for Black people as a whole. This response also helped illuminate another assumption that is nested in much of the historic racial-attitudes literature on children: Racial attitudes are potentially global and can be assumed to be transferable from one individual and one situation to all persons in all settings.

Racial Attitudes as Undimenisional and Static. A final assumption of the nature of children's racial attitudes has been that racial attitudes are undimensional and static. This is somewhat surprising given that much of the literature on racial-attitudes in developmentally-oriented journals (e.g., *Child Development, Journal of Research on Adolescence,* and *Journal of Early Adolescence*). A review of some of the articles shows that some authors carefully point out the limitations of their studies, but this seems to get lost among the readers. A classic example of this is the way in which studies of young children's racial attitudes note that the attitudes are emerging in the same way that language emerges among 4-year-olds. Despite that the findings are often extrapolated from the studies and treated as concrete fixed findings, the result are that ethnic minority children are described as being outgroup oriented, showing a white preference, and being confused about their heritage. This type of inflexible interpretation of results occurs for two reasons: Studies of children's racial attitudes have been overly simplistic in that they have not highlighted the changing nature of racial attitudes, secondary to cognitive and social development; and there is no comprehensive theory of racial attitudes against which child attitudes can be analyzed.

Efforts to understand the development of racial attitudes among children have focused almost exclusively on ethnic minority children. Such an exclusionary approach adds to the widely held folk belief that race is a "minority" issue. White children are frequently addressed in the literature only as an aside, as part of a racial comparison study. Their attitudes are taken as the implicit control group to which other subjects are compared. Studies examining the developmental course of racial attitudes among children tend to be one-time-only measurements that do not capture the dynamic nature of the attitudes or the influence of the context and nature of the task being asked of the children in the study. Longitudinal and cross-sectional research designs would help these problems. Two longitudinal studies in the literature are by McAdoo (1971) and Branch and Newcombe (1986). Both are concerned with racial attitudes among Black children. Some of the findings from the studies uncovered methodological and substantive assumptions that continue to be unchallenged (e.g., parental attitudes are critical predictors of children's attitudes, racial attitudes are unidimensional, and racial attitudes among children are fairly stable over time).

Racial Attitudes Among Adolescents

Self Definition and Self-Esteem. Studies of racial attitudes among adolescents are few in number (in comparison to studies of children), but they too suffer from some general assumptions thought to be true but are without empirical verification. Rosenberg and Simmons (1971) conducted one of the first studies to specifically address racial attitudes among adolescents. They were also concerned with the issue of self-esteem. The study was a Black–White comparison that led the researchers to conclude that the Black subjects felt better about their physical characteristics than their White counterparts. In some ways this pioneering work may have established a precedent for subsequent adolescent studies to focus very heavily on self-appraisals along racial lines. Indeed, much of the research on adolescents and racial attitudes has concerned self-esteem and physical characteristics (e.g., attractiveness and dating preferences) and very little attention to psychological characteristics inherent in racial attitudes. The assumption that follows from this parochial focus is that issues of self-definition and self-esteem are the most salient features of adolescent racial concerns. However, in other areas of research with adolescents, it is fairly common practice to have adolescents generate a list of their concerns or "hot topics," from which the researcher then selects items for further exploration.

Behavior in Racially Mixed Settings Is Indicative of Private Attitudes. Another common assumption is that behavior in racially mixed settings is indicative of adolescents' underlying racial attitudes. This is demonstrated by studies that interpret interracial friendships among adolescents as an indicator of racial attitudes toward others. Folk wisdom suggests that with the tremendous increase in the rate of public school education, there would also be a parallel increase in the rate of friendships that extend across racial boundaries. It appears that researchers and the general public assume that there has been a significant shift in the racial U.S. society and the outcome is more racial mixing among children and adolescents, evidence that they, too, are more liberal in their thinking and behavior than past generations. The logic supporting all of these assumptions seems to be related to a misinterpretation of the impact of school integration on the psychological dynamics of adolescent culture.

Atwater (1996) suggested that:

. . . merely attending an integrated school does not necessarily foster interracial friendships. A lot depends on the climate of learning in the classroom. When minority students are competing with Caucasian students, especially when many of the latter have more advanced skills and higher socioeconomic status, racial prejudice is increased on both sides. (p. 219)

The specific dimensions of school climates that are conducive to social and interpersonal development have not been identified in the literature. The often cited Rutter, Maughan, Mortimore, Ouston, and Smith (1979) study provides a very detailed account of how school affects children's development. Unfortunately, they did not explore interpersonal relationships within schools; racial and ethnic concerns were not addressed at all by Rutter and his colleagues.

In the area of interracial friendships among school children, Hallinan and her colleagues (Hallinan & Teixeira, 1987a, 1987b; Hallinan & Williams, 1987) started to identify structural effects in school settings that may be causative factors. Much of their research has been with elementary and middle school children. Hallinan and Teixeira (1987b) noted that:

A series of individual characteristics that previous research has found to be relevant to children's same-race friendships are also relevant to cross-race friendships. That is, the likelihood that a child will form cross-race friendships is very much affected by gender, age, social status, friendliness, and reciprocity, just as same-race friendships are. (p. 580)

Their findings strongly suggested that structural characteristics, such as class size, racial proportions, and the presence of different races in the same ability groups and activities, are also causative factors. The focus of their work—Black–White friendships—allowed them to point to racial differences in perceptions of friends. They were not, however, able to address the substantive questions of dynamics of the friendships or identify the processes that underlie them.

Hallinan and Williams (1987) concluded that individual characteristics are the most salient determinants of interracial friendship stability. Despite this conclusion, they added a cautionary note, indicating that "schools can adopt policies and practices that promote stable friendships between Black and White students" (p. 653). Such factors qualify as school climate variables. A curious omission from the Hallinan studies is the roles parents play in preparing their children to function in the school climate and to be responsive to the possibility of cross-racial friendships.

The foregoing paragraphs are offered as substantive evidence of the complexities associated with understanding interracial friendships. Cross-racial friendships are not just an index of adolescents' racial attitudes nor are they simply an index of subjects' openness about relating to others different from themselves. To interpret cross-racial friendships primarily as racial attitudes transformed into concrete behaviors is an oversimplification. The beginning and persistence of cross-racial friendships are the result of multiple systems interacting, including parents and teachers.

Many researchers are misled about the utility of cross-racial friendships as an index of racial attitudes and conclude that superficial relationships are deep and meaningful friendships. The superficial mixing of adolescents in extracurricular school activities, such as athletic teams and clubs, should not be construed as a statement that there is racial harmony or an openness to interracial friendships.

Racial Identity Development Is Unrelated to Other Identity Issues. Another faulty assumption of racial-attitudes research in the period of adolescence is that racial identity, as a developmental task, is not intricately related to other issues of identity. This is nowhere more evident than in the voluminous research that has grown out of the Eriksonian (1959) tradition. Specifically, the ego-identity literature (Marcia, 1966) proposed that there are four identity statuses—diffused, foreclosed, moratorium, and achieved—through which all individuals pass, in interpersonal and ideological matters. Each status is characterized by a different level of autonomy and independence. *Diffused individuals* have not found an identity, are not actively seeking one, and are not particularly concerned about their lack of movement toward resolving the ultimate question of adolescence (e.g., "Who am I?"). *Foreclosed individuals* have assumed an identity that has been created for them by others (such as, parents, friends, and teachers). Persons in a state of *moratorium* have not settled on an identity but are actively looking for one. At the end of the continuum are adolescents who have achieved an identity with which they are comfortable. This conceptualization of adolescence as a transitory developmental period has enjoyed a high level of acceptance among theorists. It has been the object of much research and theory building (Adams, Bennion, & Huh, 1989; Adams & Shea, 1979; Berzonsky, 1992; Branch, 1996; Bruer, 1973; Clancy & Dollinger, 1993; Cross & Allen, 1970; Donovan, 1975; Flum, 1994; Ginsburg & Orlofsky, 1981; Mallory, 1989; Orlofsky, 1978; Read, Adams, & Dobson, 1984; Rowe & Marcia, 1980; Waterman & Waterman, 1974). Yet, nowhere in this body of literature (and related 12 studies) was there any mention of the role that race plays in helping to shape the identity of adolescents. Questions regarding racial attitudes were not included on the two major questionnaires (Adams et al., 1989; Marcia, 1966) that have risen from this research tradition. Perhaps researchers did not believe race to be a significant contributor to the social environments from which adolescents receive messages about who they are or who they may become. Perhaps the omission of race as a contributor to the identity development process can be understood as an extension of the Eriksonian omission of race.

In critiquing the limitations of developmental theory as an approach for understanding the impacts of race on human development Carter (1995) criticized Erikson's avoidance of the topic.

> Erikson tended to focus on culture broadly defined and did not deal with the issue of race for all people. Erikson (1968) did discuss race in his book *Identity: Youth and Crisis*; in the final chapter, he noted that racial categories have effects on all members of society wherein those who are denigrated are used by those who denigrate to project negative aspects of themselves. He argued that members of all racial groups need to evolve wider identity structures that include positive and negative elements of all groups. It should be pointed out that Erikson was at that time attempting to reconcile the identity metamorphosis of Black people. He was, in part, explaining the civil rights and Black Power movement, not necessarily altering in any fundamental way the basic ideas presented in his classic book *Childhood and Society*. None of his observations was incorporated in subsequent editions of his classic work. Nevertheless, his stages of psychosocial development were thought to be universal, with a differential emphasis for individuals from different cultures. (p. 75)

Race is a critical factor in shaping the environments of adolescents. Because of that, it has a continuous influence on the ecological niches that shape the lives of adolescents. Branch and Carter (1996) devised a theory that contends that all of the systems to which adolescents look for definition are overwhelmingly influenced by racial factors.

Discontinuity of Childhood and Adolescent Racial Development. It is not an assumption in the usual sense of the word, but it appears that researchers have assumed that adolescence and childhood are discontinuous in the area of racial attitudes and behavior development. A casual reading of the literature shows that many scholars do not connect the skills and emerging cognitive capacities of childhood to the tasks of adolescence. It is almost as if childhood and all of the development in the areas of classification of individuals (including self) on the basis of race; growing individuation from parental racial attitudes, and a capacity to articulate an understanding of racially driven realities like racism, never occurred. Despite that denial or disconnective type of behavior, race exerts a major influence in the lives of adolescents, starting with the onset of puberty and the types of expectations and fears that others have for them. Brooks-Gunn (1987) documented many of the pressures of puberty and also demonstrated that racial differences in sexual behavior during adolescence is real (Brooks-Gunn & Furstenburg, 1991).

There are several faulty assumptions that some researchers tend to make concerning racial attitudes and behavior among adults. The first is that attitudes and behaviors observed among adults are discrete from the earlier developmental periods. I do not know if this is a conscious effort, but the aforementioned disconnect that is made between adulthood, childhood, and adolescence periods seems to suggest that they are viewed as unrelated. In addition to this cardinal error, there are other conceptual problems that render many studies of race in the lives of adults suspect. For the purposes of this chapter I comment on three: adulthood as a culminating and terminal point in the human developmental process, preference and identity as dimensions of racial thinking, and the nature of measurement procedures and problems inherent in them, especially when dealing with a very volatile subject such as race.

Racial Attitude Development in Adulthood

Attitudes in Adults Are Discrete From Earlier Development. The journey into adulthood is often thought of as completing the quest for resolution of issues related to race. Adult racial attitudes are discussed as if they represent the final piece of the puzzle, metaphorically speaking, but more amazingly, they are discussed without any systematic treatment of the contexts out of which they arose. Personal histories of subjects are frequently discussed, especially if the researcher is employing an ethnographic approach. Even then, there is often an absence of any significant discussion of the chronosystemic influences, such as, points in history and participants place in their own personal developmental progression. Ethnographers may ask participants a sample question such as "What was it like growing up Black in a predominately White neighborhood?" That type of direct probing obviously gets to the heart of the issue of personal history quite directly. It also seems to imply that the influence of racial minority status for such individuals is a matter that is behind them. The reality of the matter really is that in American society the influences of race continue to exert influence on individuals even into adulthood and old age. In a lot of ways, the impacts are greater in adulthood because most individuals do not have someone who takes the role of protector as did their parents. If anything, the participants now have to be protectors of their own children.

Closure, as in being finished with the struggle about race, does not occur in the ways that researchers suggest. Continuously changing social environments, economics, and governmental policies about things related to race means that the struggle is never over. For example, the recent trend toward the dismantling of affirmative action programs will have ramifications for many persons who might otherwise regard themselves as having achieved a final state of resolution concerning racial attitudes and even their own racial identity and how it gets expressed. Changes in the political climate of this country undoubtedly usher in a period where lots of people have to reevaluate their philosophical positions. On another level, it also means that many who benefited from affirmative action policies will have unconscious reactions to its disappearance. The dynamic and reciprocal relationship between individuals and their environments has not found wide acceptance among scholars interested in racial matters, evidenced in part by the near absence of systematic analysis of the ecologies in which people function simultaneously as the subjects are studied. Rather, adults are viewed as representing racial attitudes that are the termination point of an evolutionary process. I think that is not the case.

Adult racial attitudes are a temporary resting place on a continuum of growth and development. As adults become more resolved about their own life issues (i.e., occupation, choice of mate, and completing childrearing functions) they shift their views. Some may call the point at which the shift occurs a midlife crisis. The exact quality of life when the change occurs is open to debate. What is less open to debate is the fact that the changes do occur.

Significant life events that are racial in nature have the potential of spawning new racial attitudes or causing adults to regress to attitudes and behaviors that they employed at earlier points in their lives. A common example of this regression is what happens when many parents learn that their child is involved in a romantic interracial relationship. Radicalized thoughts that many adults believed they had long ago discarded suddenly resurface. This leads one to believe that in adulthood, many individuals do not fully resolve their issues with race, but they merely become more skillful at disguising them than they were in childhood and adolescence. Developmentally, this makes sense. Ego defense mechanisms and the ways in which they get activated are more sophisticated among adults than younger people.

Racial Preference Plus Physical Identity Equal Racial Attitudes. The belief that racial preference and identity tell the whole story of racial attitudes is also a common myth that is perpetuated among adults, including researchers. Althoguh both of the dimensions of race are important, they do not speak to the issues of affective reactions to the reality of race. In fact, to date, most of the discourse on race has focused on the intellectual and cognitive components. There have not been many, if any, studies attempting to link racial thinking or responses to racialistic situations with psychological changes, as has been the case with clinical research that is attempting to teach male batterers to recognize their threshold of arousal. I think the assumption that race is a social construction that can be understood by subjecting it and related behaviors to intellectual analysis is faulty. Thus, we do not appreciate the debilitating effects of continuous stress of being subjected to racialized environments many adults of color experience. The connection between stress and levels of social support has been made by Sarason and his colleagues (Sarason, Johnson, & Siegal, 1978; Sarason, Levine, Barsham, & Sarason, 1983; Sarason, Sarason, Potter, & Antoni, 1985) as well as blood pressure readings differing along racial lines (Roberts & Rowland, 1981). The role of race in precipitating stress and eroding social supports has not been directly addressed.

One final area in which faulty assumptions about studying race and its impact on adults are perpetuated is that of instrumentation. Pencil-and-paper techniques can capture the essence of some dimensions of race and identity. Racial identity is assumed to be definable by physical dimensions. This assumption applies to all of the developmental periods noted here, but it has special ramifications for adults. Perhaps the best index for identification is a measurement of how internalized the issue becomes with an increase in age, assuming again that the issue has been recognized by the subject for an extended period of time. External expressions such as racial labeling and affiliation with groups (i.e., friends and neighbors), merely become concrete evidence of an abstract internal process. The assumption that objective procedures can fully examine racial attitudes is a cardinal and pervasive tenet of researchers. Despite its centrality to the research enterprise it just may not be true.

Stevenson (1996) made a similar observation in his studies of racial socialization techniques employed by Black mothers. Specifically, he commented that many subjects complain that pencil-and-paper techniques are too limiting, making it difficult for mothers to tell their story in an authentic and comprehensive way. Likewise, I think racial attitudes are the source of such strong emotions that it is difficult, if not impossible, to reduce the most critical part of a subject's revelations to an objective data point. This is not to say that because of the emotional component in measuring racial attitudes the task should be abandoned, but rather that researchers should acknowledge it as a potential source of variance in the performance of subjects.

Racial Identity Is Definable by Physical Characteristics. Assumptions related to the nature of racial attitudes do not fully reflect the complexity of the society in which we live. Nowhere is this more evident than in the area of racial identity. Increasingly biracial identity is becoming a reality in our society, but research on racial identity still persists in classifying people in an either/or fashion.

These ideas represent some of the issues that permeate the racial literature. The presentation is not comprehensive. Other significant factors that are noted to be the object of significance include race of the experimenter, setting of the research, and the modality of presentation of stimuli. They will not be addressed here except to say that the reader should note that they too influence the outcome of studies and the eventual theoretical constructions arising from empirical investigations. Another set of

influential factors in the outcome of measurements with children and adolescents are parents and teachers. What and how they contribute to the development of racial attitudes among young people is explored in the
following section.

PARENTS AND TEACHERS SHAPE RACIAL IDENTITY

The emphasis in this section is on how parents and teachers of young children provide racial socialization experiences. Some comments will be offered about the same practices with adolescents for purposes of
illustrating psychological continuity in an area that has been discontinuous as far as researchers are concerned. Think of these comments on adolescents as a statement of the sequel to childhood socialization
experiences.

Parents as Contributors to Identity Development

Most researchers agree that parents are significant contributors to the development of attitudes and behaviors regarding intergroup relations
among children. The relationships very heavily among Black parents and
their children have been explored (Branch & Newcombe, 1986, 1988;
McAdoo, 1971, 1988; Spencer, Brookins, & Allen, 1985; Wilson, 1984).
There is a comparable body of literature, focusing on cognitive developmental tasks concerning Latino children, produced by Bernal and her associates (Bernal & Knight, 1993; Bernal, Knight, Garza, Ocampo, & Cota,
1990). Both literature focus primarily on the preschool years. However,
there is precious little work available on the relation between racial attitudes and behavioral congruence between parents and adolescents. Yet,
there is a host of anecdotal accounts of how parents have acted to influence
their teenagers' behavior relative to intergroup relations, most notably
dating.

Shaping the Environment and Experiences

The way in which the literature has evolved continues to give credence to
the idea that racial attitudes and racial socialization are exclusively people
of color issues. Because of this belief, virtually no attention is given to understanding how White parents conduct themselves in these matters.
Hirschfeld (1996) noted that for many White children discussions of race
and ethnicity mean someone else's race and ethnicity. He also believed that
the role of parents in creating racial attitudes among children is not critical.
According to him, the pervasive nature of racial attitudes in this society
causes children to get significant racial socialization experiences, sometimes even in the absence of any parental indoctrination.

Aboud (1988) utilized a cognitive-developmental framework to explain racial prejudice among White children. She noted that children as young as 5 years old exhibit racially prejudiced thinking. By age 8 or 9, Aboud noted, there appears to be a decline in prejudicial thinking. She attributed this decline to social–cognitive development. White children under the age of 12 seem to have racial prejudice thinking patterns that are unlike those of their parents and friends. Despite the dissimilarity, Aboud thought parents and friends could be enlisted as catalysts for changing the attitudes of children. Specifically, she recommended open discussions as a way of counteracting prejudice; "Tolerance may also be promoted through school curricula that strengthens role taking and differentiation skills" (p. 229).

Other empirical studies that highlighted the importance of parents to the development of racial attitudes among different populations of children and adolescents include Banks (1984), Gopaul-McNicol (1988), Mather and Kalia (1984), and Winn and Priest (1993). All note that parents are an important but that the relation between children's attitudes and parental attitudes is not simple, linear, or direct.

Banks (1984) studied the self-concepts of ability, general self-concepts, levels of externality, and attitudes toward physical characteristics, neighborhoods and schools. His subjects were 8 to 18-year-old Black students from middle-class families. According to Banks (1984), "Results show that the predominantly White suburban communities in which the subjects were socialized had not prevented them from developing positive attitudes toward themselves, their communities, and their schools" (p. 3). This pattern is, however, only part of the finding. He further noted that:

> Black children socialized within predominantly White suburban communities are likely to become highly attitudinally assimilated into White society and … this kind of assimilation may have complex effects on their racial attitudes toward Blacks and their level of ethnocentrism. (p. 3)

These findings reported by Banks suggest that the movement away from their original socialization of positive self-regard and a sense of connectedness with other Black individuals may become more tenuous as the youth get older and experience more attitudinal assimilation as the influence of parents decreases and the young person has to respond to more environmental messages, many of which indicate that assimilation is the preferred route of social conduct.

The works of Gopaul-McNicol (1988) and Mather and Kalia (1984) also highlight the importance of parents in the development of racial attitudes among children, but in a slightly different way. Both studies are concerned with preschoolers. The doll choice technique is used in both investigations. Gopaul-McNicol (1998) reported that both the Trinidad and New York subsamples preferred the white doll. She explained the results as being a function of parental attitudes, media influence, and favoritism in school. In all situations white appeared to be more valued than black. Mather and Kalia (1984) used an Asian sample, but found results similar to those of Gopaul-McNicol. Most of the 30 preschoolers in their study preferred the white doll. Gender and socioeconomic status (SES) were found to moderate prejudice toward the black doll. The overall finding was that there was a nonsignificant relationship between color consciousness and parental attitude toward color. The combination of these two studies make a couple of critical points regarding the contribution of parents as shapers of children's racial attitudes.

Social Cognition.   Parents are critical for shaping the environments and experiences that children may have, but they cannot account for all of the variance in children's attitudes. Gopaul-McNicol (1988) suggested that it is the attitudes that parents probably espouse regarding racial matters that influence the children to exhibit a preference for White people. Yet, Mather and Kalia (1984), using an Asian sample, noted that the relationship of the parental attitudes toward color concepts is not significantly related to that of their children. Branch and Newcombe (1986) demonstrated that children and parental attitudes regarding race are closer when the children are older. They interpret the increase in the strength of the relationship between the two as evidence that children start to hear and internalize larger cultural messages differently than they did at an earlier age. The relationship between the two is not a simple and straight forward matter. Branch and Newcombe (1986) indicated that the type and strength of parental social approach is related to the family type and gender of the child:

> Parents were found to express different attitudes about teaching their children about race according to the gender of the child; parents of male children were found to have more extreme attitudes about ethnocentrism and race-related childrearing issues than were parents of female children. This difference was particularly true among one-parent families. (p. 146)

A similar pattern of marital status of the mother being a significant variable in explaining her approach to racial socialization of her children is reported in a more recent study by Branch (1996). Married mothers are more likely to directly teach their children about race than are single mothers.

Aboud's (1988) finding of the shift in the strength of the parental and child racial attitude congruence was consistent with the other findings reported here. As White children get older, they seem to develop attitudes that are reflective of the social experiences they have had, unlike their younger counterparts who demonstrate a high level of prejudice, which often does not match their parents' attitudes. An essential difference in Black and White subjects appears to be that as the Black children get older, their attitudes become more like those of their parents. Hirschfeld

(1996) thought that as children get older, they will express attitudes that run counter to those of their parents as a way of asserting their autonomy and independence, even if they do not believe what they are saying to be true.

Congruence of Parent and Child Racial Attitudes. A large survey of parent–child pairs adds additional information to the question of similarity versus dissimilarity between parental and child racial attitudes. Griffure and Schweitzer (1983) obtained data from 2,065 parent–child pairs. The children were between the ages of 8 and 18. The researchers were interested in knowing the degree to which children's racial attitudes were related to their parents' racial attitudes and how the age of the child might affect such a relationship. Pearson showed that parent and child attitudes were positively correlated, regardless of parent's sex or child's age. More detailed analyses, however, revealed that "beginning at age 12 females' attitudes became progressively more liberal and males' attitudes more conservative than those of their parents" (p. 9).

A few comments about biracial parents and parents of biracial children is necessary here, lest we be found guilty of the assumption of the dichotomous nature of racial identity discussed earlier. Root (1990) has been one of the most prolific researchers in this area. She asserted that parents are of critical importance for biracial children, perhaps more important than in monoracial families, for helping children discern the importance of their two racial identities. How well the parents have resolved their identity issues dramatically affect their ability to be helpful to their children. She insisted that if parents are to be helpful to the children, there must be an egalitarian position in what the parents teach. Pride in both racial heritages must be overt and pronounced.

The absence of such a proactive teaching strategy can easily lead to some of the difficulties uncovered by Winn and Priest (1993) in their study of 34 children, between 8 and 20 years old, from 15 biracial families. Using a semistructured interview, they discovered that the children consistently felt torn between selecting one parent's racial identification over the other's. The majority of the children felt obligated to assume a monocultural racial designation, but others felt that they were being a traitor to the parent with whom they did not racially identify. A very large percentage of the children felt that their parents had not sufficiently prepared them for the realities of prejudice and racism.

What we can say is that the state of knowledge concerning parents as contributors to children's racial attitudes is probably less than one would imagine. Logic says that parents are important because they provide for children until they become independent and self-sufficient. The exact mechanisms of how parents provide for children in the areas of social cognition are not clear or absolute. On one hand, parents serve as role models, but they are not the only source of information. This is borne out in the area of racial attitudes by the studies that suggest that children are aware of racial differences as early as 5 years old, but their attitudes differ some-what from those reported by the parents. Yet, there are at least a couple of other interpretations for this finding. The parents may be more skillful in masking their true racial attitudes from the researcher than the children, or it could be that the racial attitudes that the children express are their unso-phisticated attempts at imitating parents. In the process of trying to pat-tern their lives after their parents, the children have misinterpreted or misread the parental signals. On the other hand, it may be that the par-ent–child racial attitude similarity is not a linear progression because of competing messages from other sources.

Sanders-Thompson (1994) reported that racial socialization for many Black subjects in her study primarily occurred through contact with adult family members other than parents. In this regard, the impact of media and friends should not be overlooked. The recent work by Branch (1996) also indicates that many parents are keenly aware of the importance of teaching children about the reality of race, but they are reluctant to ap-proach the task directly. Often, they report concerns about not placing their issues on their children.

Despite all of the caveats and possible alternative interpretations, par-ents are important contributors to the racial socialization of children, overtly and covertly. Sometimes it is what is left unsaid that conveys the greatest message. Not discussing race as a matter of social importance gives the message that it is of little relevance or it is such a monstrosity that it should be ignored. Root (1990) thought the same to be especially true of biracial children whose parents model indifference or ambivalence to the dual racial identity of their children by not talking openly, frankly, and honestly about their feelings. No comments or guidance for children in this matter of racial attitudes contributes to the destructive power that race has over many lives. Not talking about race simply reinforces the idea that it is a taboo topic.

Another way in which parents contribute to the racial socialization of young children is through the ways in which they construct social ecolo-gies for the children. Research in this area typically includes the type of neighborhood a parent chooses for the family as well as the type of school-ing. The latter may be less a matter of choice than neighborhood. However, the level of participation the parents have within the school community has the potential of sending powerful messages about race and intergroup relations. Perhaps the primary relationship the parents have within the school is with the teacher. It is through this relationship that parents and teachers model very powerful lessons about racial matters, especially if there is a racial incongruence between the teacher and the parent.

Teachers as Contributors to Racial Identity Development

The significance of teachers in the lives of many young children cannot be overestimated. Schools and teachers often are the first out-of-family con-

tact some young children experience. Because of that, the nature of the interactions with the teachers has far-reaching implications for how
children and parents come to regard future extrafamilial relationships. In
addition, teachers are the first persons to make critical assessments about
children and their ability to respond to the demands of the environments
in which they will be expected to function. Teachers represent a vital link
between the child's home environment and the outside world. Social attitudes and behaviors exhibited by teachers in classrooms are standards for
children, implicitly and explicitly. This occurs in a variety of areas including racial socialization.

There are three ways in which teachers significantly influence the racial
identity quests of young students: the perceptions of power distance and
how it creates a sense of marginality and devaluation; teacher attitudes regarding diversity; and the other curriculum which gets introduced into the
classroom on a daily basis. These points can be understood by thinking of
the school as an ecological niche that is good or bad for learning. There is a
supportive environment and new ideas are introduced in a way that stimu-
lates interest and curiosity among students and parents. In addition there
is an openness to new ideas, especially those that emanate from creditable
sources (i.e., teachers and administrators).

Perceptions of Power, Distance, and Devaluation.   The climate of a
classroom is often taken as an index of the teacher's attitudes toward cultural diversity. Iadicola (1983) extended this idea by suggesting that perceptions of power differences contribute to creation of symbolic violence
among Hispanic students. He studied the relationship between two mechanisms of symbolic violence (i.e., power difference and curriculum factors)
among a group of Hispanic sixth graders (n = 118). *Power difference* was defined as student power differences (i.e., percent Anglo and SES in the
school), parent power differences, and staff power differences. *Curriculum
factors* were operationalized in terms of the level of multicultural curriculum in the school. Overall, his findings show that the greater the power
difference, the more powerless the subjects perceived themselves to be.
Iadicola interpreted these differences as symbolic violence against the Hispanic students.

Teacher Attitudes Toward Diversity.   Iadicola's (1983) study represents one approach to examining the impact of teachers' attitudes and behavior on the internal processes of students. The problem of school as an
agent of socialization is often subtle. What happens in situations in which
the messages of racial socialization are more covert? Examples of covert socialization include the common practice of highlighting minority cultural
expressions as "special" rather than as part of the ongoing life of the school

community. This happens with such frequency that many of the perpetrators are blind to the offensive nature of their behavior. An extreme, but real, example of this practice is the frequency with which Martin Luther King Jr. only gets talked about in connection with civil rights activities or as a part of Black History Month celebrations. Despite having good intentions, this practice only serves to continue to isolate the legacy and accomplishments of African Americans, not to synthesize it into the mainstream of the school's curriculum.

The foregoing examples may appear to be oversimplifications, but they occur with such frequency that it is alarming. The fact that they represent very real occurrences seems to point out the need for teachers to be more cognizant of their own attitudes toward racial and cultural matters and how they find expression through lessons taught, procedurally, and content wise.

Implications for School Practices.   The question that arises from the previous discussion concerns the utility of racial attitudes developmental literature to persons involved in the education of children. There are at least three major ways in which this information can be of use to teachers and educators. Racial attitudes are not a unidimensional construct. Because children develop racial attitudes in a variety of settings, teachers and administrators should be careful not to assume that the attitudes children express in school are reflective of all of their thinking in this area. Rather, the probability that school comprises on setting, which provides limited opportunities for racial attitudes to be expressed, should be considered. Racial attitudes may find expression in the form of interracial friendships. Such alliances provide a wonderful way for children of all ages to learn about others whom they perceive to be different from themselves. The teacher can do a great deal to foster exchanges across cultural lines. This, of course, assumes that the teacher shares in the belief that intergroup relations are necessary. However, care should be taken to ensure that intergroup relating is done in such a way that all parties participating in the exchange are seen as equals. Minority children should not be showcased in a way to teach others, without requiring the others also teach and engage in some level of personal self-disclosure.

The idea that children can serve as catalysts for racial attitude expansion should be considered very carefully and with consideration that some parents may not favor such mixing. Parental resistance toward this type of social interaction may take several forms and may never be expressed directly. Again, the teacher can be helpful in overcoming such resistance by carefully constructing projects that involve parents from multiple ethnic and racial groups. Differences among parents should be readily acknowledged and talked about when necessary. The differences should be respected and treated as desirable rather than merely being tolerated. The atmosphere of intergroup dynamics can serve as a model for children to interact with others different from themselves. Indeed, the practice transforms an ideal into a concrete behavior. Teachers should also recognize that childrens' racial attitudes undergo developmental changes similar to other emerging skills. Perhaps more importantly, the racial attitudes verbalized by young children often do not match those exposed by their parents. Over time, children come to be more like their parents. In this regard, schools can create a setting in which children acquire a viewpoint that is inconsistent with that of their parents. The result may be that some parents will become concerned and upset that the school is changing their child in ways that make them feel uncomfortable. Teachers, who decide to approach critical social issues, such as racial and ethnic attitudes, as part of their social curriculum, are encouraged to regard children's attitudes in this area as emerging, not fixed. The literature seems to suggest that racial attitudes among children are fairly fluid until about late childhood.

Finally, teachers should consider the reality that everyone has a racial and ethnic designation. The literature clearly shows that these dimensions of self are apparently more important for ethnic minority individuals than for majority group persons. This points to the need to help nonminority children and their parents examine their lack of valuing racial and ethnic salience in their own lives. It also highlights the need for parents to think about how they can talk to their children about the realities of race in American society without being defensive or apologetic.

REFERENCES

Aboud, F. (1988). *Children and prejudice.* New York: Blackwell.

Adams, G., Bennion, L., & Huh, K. (1989). *Objective measure of ego identity status: A reference manual.* Available from Gerald Adams, Department of Family Studies, University of Guelph. Guelph, Ontario, Canada.

Adams, G., & Shea J. (1979). The relationship between identity status, locus of control and ego development. *Journal of Youth and Adolescence, 8*(1), 81–89.

Asher, S., & Allen, V. (1969). Racial preference and social comparison processes. *Journal of Social Issues, 25*(1), 157–166.

Atwater, E. (1996). *Adolescence* (4th ed.). Upper Saddle River, NJ: Prentice-Hall.

Baldwin, J. (1979). Theory and research concerning the notion of Black self-hatred: A review and reinterpretation. *The Journal of Black Psychology, 5*(2), 51–77.

Banks, J. (1984). Black youths in predominantly White suburbs: An exploratory study of their attitudes and self-concepts. *Journal of Negro Education, 53*(1), 3–17.

Bernal, M., & Knight, G. (1993). *Ethnic identity: Formation and transmission among Hispanics and other minorities.* Albany: State University of New York Press.

Bernal, M., Knight, G., Garza, C., Ocampo, K., & Cota, M. (1990). The development of ethnic identity in Mexican American children. *Hispanic Journal of Behavioral Sciences, 12*(1), 3–24.

Berzonsky, M. (1992). A process perspective on identity and stress management. In G. Adams, T. Gullotta, & R. Montemayer (Eds.), *Adolescent identity formation: Advances in adolescent development* (Vol. 4, pp. 193–215). Newbury Park, CA: Sage.

Bird, C. (1952). Studies of group tensions. The effect of parental discouragement of play activities upon the attitudes of White children toward Negros. *Child Development, 23*(4), 295–306.

Blake, R., & Dennis, W. (1943). Development of stereotypes concerning the Negro. *Journal of Abnormal and Social Psychology, 38*(4), 525–531.

Branch, C. (1996). *The relationship between ego-identity status and ethnic identity: Transitioning from adolescence to adulthood*. Unpublished manuscript.

Branch, C., & Carter, R. (1996). *Race and racial identity across the life span*. Unpublished manuscript.

Branch, C., & Newcombe, N. (1986). A longitudinal and cross-sectional study of the development of racial attitudes of Black children as a function of parental attitudes. *Child Development 57*(3), 712–721.

Branch, C., & Newcombe, N. (1988). The development of racial attitudes in Black children. In R. Vasta (Ed.), *Annals of child development* (Vol. 5, pp. 125–154). Greenwich, CT: JAI.

Brooks-Gunn, J. (1987). Pubertal pressures: Their relevance for developmental research. In V. B. Hasselt & M. Hersen (Eds.), *Handbook of adolescent psychology* (pp. 110–130). New York: Pergamon.

Brooks-Gunn, J., & Furstenburg, F. (1991). Adolescent sexual behavior. *American Psychologist, 44*(2), 249–257.

Bruer, H. (1973). *Ego-identity status in late-adolescent college males as measured by a group administered incomplete sentence blank and related to inferred stance toward authority*. Unpublished doctoral dissertation, New York University, New York.

Carter, R. (1995). *The influence of race and racial identity in psychotherapy*. New York: Wiley.

Clancy, S., & Dollinger, S. (1993). Identity, self, and personality: I identity status and the fire-factor model of personality. *Journal of Research on Adolescence, 3*(3), 227–245.

Clark, K., & Clark, M. (1947). Racial identification and preference in Negro children. In T. M. Newcomb & E. L. Harley (Eds.), *Reading in social psychology* (pp. 169–178). New York: Holt Rinehart & Winston.

Cross, J., & Allen, J. (1970). Ego identity status, adjustment, and academic achievement. *Journal of Consulting and Clinical Psychology, 34*(1), 228–239.

Donovan, J. (1975). Identity status and interpersonal style. *Journal of Youth and Adolescence, 4*(1), 37–56.

Erikson, E. (1959). Identity and the life cycle. Monograph 1. *Psychological Issues*. New York: International Universities Press.

Flum, H. (1994). Styles of identity formation in early and middle adolescence. *Genetic, Social, and General Psychological Monographs, 120*(4).

Ginsburg, S., & Orlofsky, J. (1981). Ego-identity status, ego development and locus of control in college women. *Journal of Youth and Adolescence, 10*(4), 297–307.

Goodman, M. (1964). *Race awareness in young children.* Reading, MA: Addison-Wesley.

Gopaul-McNicol, S. (1988). Racial identification and racial preference of Black preschool children in New York and Trinidad. *Journal of Black Psychology, 14*(2), 65–68.

Griffure, R., & Schweitzer, J. (1983). Child–parent racial attitude relationships. *Psychology: A Quarterly of Human Behavior, 20*(1), 9–13.

Hallinan, M., & Teixeira, R. (1987a) Opportunities and constraints: Black-White differences in the formation of interracial friendships. *Child Development, 58*(5), 1358–1371.

Hallinan, M., & Teixeira, R. (1987b). Student's interracial friendships: Individual characteristics, structural effects, and racial differences. *American Journal of Education, 95*(4), 563–583.

Hallinan, M., & Williams, R. (1987). The stability of interracial friendships. *American Sociological Review, 52,* 653–664.

Hirschfeld, L. A. (1996). *Race in the making: Cognition, culture, and the child's construction of human kinds.* Cambridge, MA: MIT Press.

Iadicola, P. (1983). Schooling and symbolic violence: The effects of power differences and curriculum factors on Hispanic students' attitudes toward their own ethnicity. *Hispanic Journal of Behavioral Science, 5*(1), 21–43.

Mallory, M. (1989). Q-sort definition of ego identity status. *Journal of Youth and adolescence, 18*(4), 399–412.

Marcia, J. (1966). Development and validation of ego-identity status. Journal of *Personality and Social Psychology, 3*(3), 551–558.

Mather, S. S., & Kalia, A. K. (1984). Color consciousness among nursery school children in relation to sex and income level. *Asian Journal of Psychology and Education, 13*(1), 30–33.

McAdoo, H. (1971). Racial attitudes and self-concepts of Black preschool children. *Dissertation Abstracts International, 31*(8- A), 198–213.

McAdoo, H. P. (1988). *Black families* (2nd ed.). Beverly Hills, CA: Sage.

Orlofsky, J. (1978). Identity formation, achievement, and fear of success in college men and women. *Journal of Youth and Adolescence, 7,* 49–62.

Porter, J. (1971). *Black child, White child.* Cambridge, MA: Harvard University Press.

Read, D., Adams, G., & Dobson, W. (1984). Ego-identity status, personality, and social influence style. *Journal of Personality and Social Psychology, 46*(1), 169–177.

Roberts, J., & Rowland, M.(1981). Hypertension in adults 25–74 years of age: United States, 1971–1975. *Vital Health Statistics, Series 11, 11*(221), 1–107.

Root, M. P. P. (1990). Resolving "other" status: Identity development of biracial individuals. In L. Brown & M. P. P. Root (Eds.), *Diversity and complexity in feminist therapy* (pp. 185–205). New York: Harrington Park Press.

Rosenberg, M., & Simmons, R. (1971). *Black and White self-esteem: The urban school child.* Washington, DC: American Sociological Association.

Rowe, I., & Marcia, J. (1980). Ego identity status, formal operations, and moral development. *Journal of Youth and Adolescence, 9*(2), 87–100.

Rutter, M., Maughan, B., Mortimore, P., Ouston, J., & Smith, A. (1979). *Fifteen thousand hours: Secondary schools and their effects on children.* Cambridge, MA: Harvard University Press.

Sanders-Thompson, V. L. (1994). Socialization to race and its relationship to racial identification among African American. *Journal of Black Psychology, 20*(2), 175–188.

Sarason, B., Johnson, J., & Siegel, J. (1978). Assessing the impact of life stress: Development of life experiences survey. *Journal of Consulting and Clinical Psychology, 46*(5), 932–946.

Sarason, I., Levine, H., Barsham, R., & Sarason, B. (1983). Assessing social support: The social support questionnaire. *Journal of Personality and Social Psychology, 44*(1), 127–139.

Sarason, I., Sarason, B., Potter, E., & Antoni, M. (1985). Life events, social support, and illness. *Psychosomatic medicine, 47*(2), 156–163.

Spencer, M. B., Brookins, G. K., & Allen, W. R. (1985). *Beginnings: The social and affective development of Black children.* Hillsdale, NJ: Lawrence Erlbaum Associates.

Stevenson, H. C. (1996). Kinship social support and adolescent racial socialization beliefs: Extending the self to family. *Journal of Black Psychology, 22*(4), 498–508.

Trager, H., & Yarrow, M. (1952). *They learn what they live.* New York: Harper Brothers.

Waterman, C., & Waterman, A. (1974). Ego identity and decision styles. *Journal of Youth and Adolescence, 3*(1), 1–6.

Williams, J., & Morland, J. (1976). *Race, color, and the young child.* Chapel Hill: University of North Carolina Press.

Williams, J. E. (1971). *Preschool racial attitude measure II: General information and manual of directions.* Bethesda, MD: National Institute of Child Health and Human Development.

Wilson, M. (1984). Mothers' and grandmothers' perception of parental behavior in three generational Black families. *Child Development, 55*(4), 1333–1339.

Winn, N. N., & Priest, R. (1993). Counseling biracial children: A forgotten component of multicultural counseling. *Family Therapy, 20*(1), 29–36.

2 African American Identity Development Across the Life Span: Educational Implications

William E. Cross, Jr.
University of Massachusetts, Boston

Linda Strauss
Peony Fhagen-Smith
Pennsylvania State University, University Park

Not too long ago, any discussion of Black identity focused almost exclusively on issues of low self-esteem and self-hatred; however, the last 20 years has seen an explosive expansion of this discourse (Akbar, 1985; Clark, 1983; Cross, 1991; Cross & Fhagen-Smith, 1996; Early, 1993; Gordon, 1980; Lawrence-Lightfoot, 1994). Beyond self-hatred, internalized racism, and oppositional identity, contemporary discussions highlight the broad range of identities to be found among African Americans. The identity of any particular Black person lays claim to multiple identity reference points; therefore, future explanatory models will further seek to understand the identity dynamics of, for example, a Black person who is female, lesbian, biracial, and disabled, or a German-born Black male who now lives in Chicago, believes in an East Indian concept of god, heads a school of futuristic modern dance, and is an accomplished cyclist.

Not all Black people place race and Black culture at the center of their identity (Cross & Fhagen-Smith, 1996). For many, their sense of well-being, personal worth, self-esteem, and personal efficacy are derived from something other than race or ethnicity. Perhaps it is true that any Black person with a positive general personality has an equally positive social identity; however, the focus or content of that social identity may be racial or nonracial. For some, social identity or reference group orientation may be grounded in religious ideas or the fact that they are gay or lesbian, whereas for others, race, ethnicity, and Black culture are at the core of their existence (Cross, 1991). For discussion purposes, *low salience* identities

29

(LS) refer to Black social identities or reference-group orientations that accord only minor significance to race and African American culture in determining what is, and is not, important in one's everyday life; *high salience* identities (HS) characterize Black social identities for which race and African culture are of central significance. These labels help avoid a common problem in discussing Black identity development; the assumption that African Americans who score high on a measure of Black identity enjoy psychological and social health, and those who score low on the same measure are dysfunctional. The perspective advocated in this work is that persons who score *high* on Blackness operate with a social identity that gives considerable salience to race and Black culture, whereas persons who score *low* on Blackness have other frames of reference, for which race and Black culture play a less prominent role.

The following discussion describes LS and HS social identity development in African Americans, from the ontogeny of identity during infancy and childhood through social identity refinement at early and late adulthood. The discussion emphasizes race salient identities, although our comparative approach sheds light on the LS social dynamics as well. Furthermore, we show how the two stances become linked during an identity metamorphosis. Persons who start out with a LS type of identity, may have an encounter or racial epiphany that impels them to convert to a HS frame of reference. This identity conversion process–*Nigrescence*–depicts the four or five stages Black people traverse during transformation from a social outlook that minimizes race to a Black identity for which race and African American culture are highly central.

Self-concept has two components: a general personality or personal identity dimension and a reference-group orientation, group identity, or social identity component (Cross, 1991; Porter & Washington, 1979; Spencer, 1988). Self-esteem, aggression, ability to receive and impart affection, introversion–extroversion tendencies, shyness propensities, and other general personality traits and dynamics fall under the personal identity or general personality component. This discussion focuses on the second self-concept component labeled cultural identity, group identity, social identity, and reference-group orientation. Current research (Cross & Fhagen-Smith, 1996; Sellers et al., in press) suggests that African Americans show great variability across both components. For example, African Americans evidence a spectrum of personality profiles and an equally broad range of social identities. Although self-esteem level, degree of shyness, or other general personality traits are universal personality dynamics found in all groups, this chapter focuses on the social identity configurations unique to Black psychology.

DEFINING BLACK IDENTITY

Most modern observers depict Black identity as a complex construct (Cross, 1991; Gordon, 1980; Sellers et al., in press). There are multiple ways in which Black identity operates or functions in one's daily life. Rather than using a single trait to define Blackness, one must envision an identity profile formed by drawing a line between a series of points, each representing a discrete identity operation. Assume that five operations or functions go into the making of a Black identity profile. One person's identity development may accentuate the growth and refinement of operations 1, 3, and 5, whereas another person's pathway highlights operations 2, 4, and 5. These differential configurations underscore the phrase *identity profile*. The five key identity operations for conducting a functional analysis of Black identity include: buffering; bonding; bridging; code-switching, and individualism (Clark, Swim, & Cross, 1995; Cross, 1991; Cross, Parham, & Helms, 1995).

Buffering Function

The *buffering identity function* refers to those ideas, attitudes, feelings, and behaviors that accord psychological protection and self-defense against everyday encounters with racism. The person either anticipates that which might be avoided or employs a buffer to blunt the sting and pain arising from an unavoidable or unsuspecting racist encounter. Optimally, buffering prepares one for racist encounters, leading to greater personal control; however, applied too heavy-handedly, it may limit opportunities for growth and development. Consequently, one's buffering capacity must be able to filter out racist information, and to let nonracist experiences, relationships, transactions, and opportunities flow through.

HS African Americans tend to recognize potential racist encounters in everyday American life and consider the development and constant refinement of the buffering mechanism to be crucial to their psychological integrity. Conversely, LS African Americans stress a colorblind perspective and tend to see less racism in everyday American life. They associate buffering with a victimization perspective that results in negativism and lack of motivation. For them, missed opportunities result from being too careful and overly sensitive about race. Consequently, LS African Americans diminish, and in some extreme cases, deny the need for buffering.

Bonding Function

The *bonding function* addresses the degree to which the person derives meaning and support from an affiliation with or attachment to Black people and Black culture. HS African Americans place importance to their attachment to Black people and Black culture. LS African Americans tend to exhibit less attachment and affiliation to Black culture. This lack of attachment may be misinterpreted as evidence that LS African Americans are without an identity, or even worse, that they are ill and psychologically dysfunctional. Although LS Black persons evidence less bonding to the Black experience, they find meaning in life through other connections and affiliations.

Bridging Function

The *bridging function* refers to those competencies, attitudes, and behaviors that make it possible for a Black person to immerse himself or herself in another group's experience, absent of any need to suppress one's sense of Blackness. The person moves back and forth between Black culture and the ways of knowing, acting, thinking, and feeling that constitute a non-Black worldview. During these bridging transactions, no demands are made on either party to deny his or her cultural frame of reference. Part of the joy associated with this exchange is derived from being able to immerse oneself in the other person's social construction of reality, while never losing site of one's point of departure. Difference becomes the object of intimate sharing.

Some HS African Americans who embrace a Black nationalist or Afrocentric perspective may not place much value in bridging, preferring to concentrate their time and energy on Black (in-group) tasks and problems. Some HS African Americans, who are as comfortable by that which makes them American as that which makes them Black (biculturality) or who relish sharing experiences with a range of other groups (multiculturality), are more likely to use the bridging function. LS African Americans may have experiences across racial and cultural divides, not out of a sense of cultural or ethnic bridging, but because their colorblind philosophy makes out-group friendships and experiences possible. For example, a LS Black person may have a friend who happens to be Jewish, but may make neither race or religion a key dimension of their friendship.

Codeswitching Function

The buffering, bonding, and bridging functions of Black identity have been identified by Cross (1991) as well as Cross et al., (1995). More recently, Clark et al., (1995) extended the list to include codeswitching and individualism. The *codeswitching function* allows a person to temporarily accommodate to the norms and regulations of a group, organization, school, or workplace. Codeswitching, or *fronting,* may occur when an organization or group shows signs of discomfort with explicit expressions of difference, especially race. In situations that foster codeswitching, African Americans act, think, dress, and express themselves in ways that maximize the comfort level of the person, group, or organization toward which the communication is focused. In some ways, fronting makes it possible for a Black person to be seen as just another person, employee, shopper, or schoolmate. Fronting escapes being categorized as a form of buffering because the individual, group, or workplace to which one is adjusting is not necessarily racist or unaccepting of African Americans. Nor is this categorized as bridging because transactions avoid sharing race and cultural interests. Both LS and HS African Americans use this function; however, HS individuals are more likely to make greater use. Black nationalists may employ fronting in most of their interactions outside of the Black community.

Individualism Function

Finally, *individualism* is the expression of one's unique personality. It may drive one's identity dynamics when a person acts in a race-neutral fashion in accord with the whims and dictates of the unique aspects of one's self-concept. Both HS and LS African Americans employ this identity strategy. However, LS Black individuals, who interpret their own behavior from a humanistic, individualistic, and colorblind perspective, disavow the need for a social identity and may stress that they always act, think, and express themselves in accordance with their individual perspectives and personalities.

In summary, the authors of this chapter share a multidimensional and multifunctional conceptualization of Black identity. By *functional,* we mean a dynamic, rather than a static, interpretation of Black identity. In racist situations, a Black identity may function as a psychological buffer or filter (buffering), whereas in searching for meaning in life, it can function as a sense of bonding, connection, and affiliation (bonding). In negotiations, experiences, and transactions with people, places, and things outside of the Black community, it can function to help achieve intimate sharing and intensely authentic reciprocity (bridging) or it can make possible temporary accommodation or situation-specific assimilation (codeswitching). Last, it can help a person understand when he or she is acting as an individual or in a race-neutral manner (individualism).

To appreciate the totality of a Black person's social identity, one must have information about each of the functional modes that construct an identity profile. African Americans with LS social identities tend to place great emphasis on individualism and less reliance on the other functional modes. African Americans with HS social identities may have profiles that differ in accordance to their ideological orientations. Those who are extremely race-focused and Black-culture-focused have profiles that stress buffering, bonding, and codeswitching, but certainly not bridging. HS African Americans, who are either bicultural or multicultural in their reference-group orientations, also stress buffering, bonding, and codeswitching, but, in addition, their identities may embrace bridging operations that facilitate friendship patterns, associations, workplace interactions, and social interests that simultaneously transcend and engage difference.

Space limitations prohibit a discussion of all possible combinations or permutations of the five functions, but it might be helpful to give one negative and one positive example. Persons who are self-hating and alienated from both Black and White people may have paranoiac racial filters (buffering to the extreme), shallow connections to other Black people (weak bonding or a pattern of internalized racism), weak or poorly developed bridging and codeswitching competencies, and, in their social isolation, extreme self-involvement tendencies (individualism). Persons who use all five operations in a positive manner, may buffer selectively, negating any need for a rigid identity shield (buffering); may partake in any number of Black cultural events that sustain and affirm their connection to other Black people and Black institutions (bonding); may have long standing and deeply felt transracial friendships (bridging); and may codeswitch any number of times during the day, depending on the situation (codeswitching). Last, they may experience prolonged moments when they think and act as an individual (individualism).

BLACK SOCIAL IDENTITY DEVELOPMENT ACROSS THE LIFE SPAN

As shown in Fig. 2.1, the unfolding of LS and HS identities is divided into six developmental sectors: Infancy and Childhood, Preadolescence, Adolescence, Late Adolescence and Early Adulthood, Adult Nigrescence, and Identity Refinement During Adulthood (Cross & Fhagen-Smith, 1996).

Sectors 1 and 2: Infancy and Childhood and Preadolescent Social Identities

The social niche (Bronfenbrenner, 1979) into which each African American child is born is shaped by a number of factors, such as family and kin networks, inclusive of family traditions and histories; family socioeconomic status and family material resources; local institutions, such as schools, churches, and cultural organizations, influenced by the quality and dynamics; and macroinfluences reflecting national and local political trends, social policy debates, and overarching historical drifts. Threads from these and other factors produce a tapestry that defines a child's social context (Spencer, 1994). Variations in context, in conjunction with a child's distinctive temperament, result in unique behaviors and attitudes, inclusive of precursors to what will become the child's social identity.

Yet, if variability in social context were not enough to explain differences in early Black social identity development, Tatum (1987) reminded us that Black parents employ a range of child-rearing strategies, differing, among other things, in racial and cultural emphasis. According to Tatum, some Black parents avoid discussions of race with their children (race

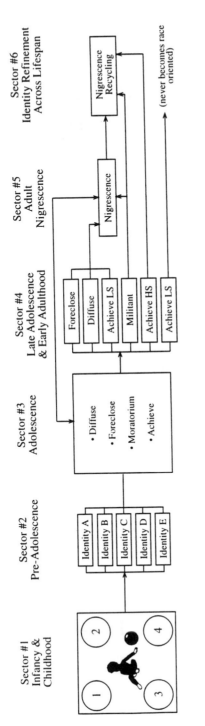

FIG. 2.1. Model Depicting the Relationship Between Ego Identity Development and Nigrescence (Cross & Fhagen-Smith, 1996).

avoidant), and, when possible, guide their children in the construction of a worldview that diminishes the significance of race. Others take a neutral stance (race neutral) and discourage any militant thinking about race. A third group is very race- and culture-conscious (race conscious) and constantly seek ways to inject race and ethnic information into the child's everyday exchanges, learning events, and social activities. Stevenson (1995) found a similar range of strategies in his study of Black adolescent recollections of race-related child-rearing strategies employed by their parents; Boyd-Franklin (1989) recorded nearly the same strategies in her clinical work with Black families.

The combination of contextual variation and divergent child-rearing strategies results in Black children who differ in social identity development. The range in emergent social identities linked to preadolescence is captured in Sector 2 of Fig. 2.1 by the series of identities labeled A through E. This list is merely symbolic, and a more realistic listing might run A to Z, 1 to 100, or 1 to 1000. The outlines of the five identity functions take on more than a skeletal form at this growth period, but the young person's ability to formulate an identity that orchestrates the different functions into a coherent identity is the work of the next growth period, adolescence.

Sector 3: Adolescence

In modern Western societies, such as the United States, adolescence is the time when young people ritualistically scrutinize their own personality and self-concept dynamics, the contours for which have been greatly influenced by parents, significant others, and social circumstances. Adolescents seek to determine whether the self that has been partially sculptured for them (by others) is the self they want to take ownership of and carry forward into adult life. Erikson's four-part model (1968; Marcia, 1966) has greatly influenced the discourse on this phase of identity development (see Sector 3 of Fig. 2.1). Identity moratorium is an active and aggressive self-examination phase. Should the self-criticality of this period result in a sense of identity clarity, focus, and self-motivation, an achieved identity evolves. Rather than moving from a moratorium to achieved identity, some youths shift from one identity to another, leading to a confused, unsettled, perhaps even negative, state of affairs to which Erikson applied the label, *diffused identity*. Finally, evidence of the absence of contemplation, reflection, and self-examination, wherein the young person seems to accept, somewhat uncritically, the negative or positive identity brought forward from the preadolescent period is called *foreclosed identity*.

When Erikson's ideas are applied to African Americans, there is a tendency to assume that the social identity focus of all Black youth is, or should be, race and Black culture (Phinney, 1989). However, in the Cross and Fhagen-Smith (1996) developmental perspective, it is not automatically assumed that youths with LS identities are developmentally stunted or deviant. Let us glance back at Sector 2 of Fig. 2.1, which depicts the diversity of LS and HS identity development at the preadolescent period. Assume that Identities A and B are different types of LS identities and Identities C through E are different types of HS identities. The focus of A might be one's homosexuality, more so than race and Black culture, and accomplishing an achieved gay identity may be the work of one's moratorium experience. For those Black youths whose parents have steered them toward an American or assimilated and class-conscious identity, they may aspire to an achieved assimilated identity. In another instance, understanding and attaining a religious worldview may occupy the attention of some Black youths.

Shifting to the HS identity patterns, the focus on diversity continues, for HS identities are not all the same. Looking at Sector 2 once more, one notes that Identity C might represent young people raised by parents with very strong Black nationalist attitudes and given a continuation of this trajectory after moratorium, their achieved Black identity profiles may stress the buffering, bonding, and codeswitching functions, but not bridging. Identity D could represent biracial youths, some of whom may strive for buffering, bridging, codeswitching, and individualism, along with a complicated dual-bonding function in which attachments to both the White and Black aspects of their social histories are sought. Identity E could be that of a Black youth, who, while race-focused, is moving in the direction of gang membership, school alienation, and a macho male image, all highlighted by buffering and bonding dynamics that are as much homophobic, sexist, and anti-White, as pro-Black. These LS and HS scenarios suggest that the great majority of Black youths do, in fact, go through an Eriksonian identity struggle at adolescence; however, each young Black person's identity agenda likely varies in race and cultural content, inclusive of agendas for which race is minimally salient.

Having made the point about identity diversity, we note that in a large sample of Black youth, race, and culture can be expected to be of considerable significance. Born to and raised by Black families who live in Black communities, most Black children become vessels for African American culture. Balancing these more positive familial presses are negative ecological constraints, such as employment discrimination against Black youths, the resurgence of raw racism and public discussions of Black inferiority, continued housing segregation that often leads to the hyperisolation of poor African Americans, the demonization of Black males as well as the denigration of the image of Black adolescent females in the mass media, and the ubiquity of racial hate crimes that target Black Americans. These positive and negative factors combine to increase the probability that race and Black culture will be key socializing themes in the early development of many Black children (Sectors 1 and 2) as well as adolescence (Sector 3). During early development, parents, relatives, friends, and peers, among others, help Black youth lay the foundations and skeletal frameworks for the five functions that define Black identity. In turn, the period of adolescence finds Black youth examining the racial frame imparted to them by significant others; moving toward the expression of an explicit worldview or ideology (nationalist, biculturalist, or multiculturalist frame of reference), which makes possible the integration of the five identity functions; and in accordance with their ideological frame, working to refine all or some of the five identity functions. Should they go the nationalist route, refinement of their buffering, bonding, and codeswitching functions will be underscored; should they express comfort with and acceptance of both American and African components of their identity, in addition to buffering, bonding, and codeswitching, they will stress the refinement of bridging functions to make possible effective social intercourse with White Americans and White institutions. For Black youths with multicultural inclinations, their Black identity profile will closely follow that of biculturalists, however, with a greater refinement and elaboration of the bridging function.

Note that a line connects Sectors 3 and 5 (Adolescence and Nigrescence). We have already made it clear that a person may be socialized into a LS identity and that this frame of reference could stay with the person across the life span. However, through a process known as Nigrescence, a person may change from a LS to HS social identity (Cross, 1991; Helms, 1990). The Nigrescence Process incorporates five developmental stages: Pre-Encounter, Encounter, Immersion–Emersion, Internalization, and Internalization–Commitment. The process begins with a description of the identity to be changed (*Pre-Encounter*). The person has an epiphany (*Encounter*), which causes the person to see for the first time, the racial gap in his or her current social identity and to comprehend the necessity for an identity conversion. From the Encounter stage, the person enters an intense transition phase (*Immersion–Emersion*), during which the existing and emergent identities battle for psychological dominance. Stereotypically, this is the period of Black militancy. The transition period is characterized by frequent emotional swings, an intense, militant orientation, and an ideology that is rigid, categorical, simplistic, and highly romantic. In addition, the person's perceptions of White people and White American society may become truncated, negative, and somewhat racist. If the person is able to work through the challenges of transition, markers of the old social identity are expunged, and the new social frame becomes habituated or achieved (*Internalization*). In taking ownership of the new identity, the person becomes more relaxed, flexible, open-minded, and accessible. *Internalization–Commitment,* the final stage, symbolizes the continuation and refinement of the new identity across the remainder of one's life.

With Nigrescence in mind, recall that some Black youths enter adolescence with a LS social identity and in the absence of an encounter, move forward into adulthood with an achieved LS identity. However, should they have a racial epiphany, their moratorium will take on strong Nigrescence characteristics. Other African Americans enter adolescence with an identity that is already very African American culture-oriented because that is how they have been raised. Their moratorium or taking ownership period may also reflect Nigrescence or Black militant dynamics, not as a sign of change, but as evidence of the contestation-to-acceptance shift that is typical of moratorium. This means that at adolescence, Black militancy can either be a sign of profound change and conversion or the combative embracement of extant, developmental tendencies.

The Special Case of Adolescence and Black Oppositional Identity.
Over the last 30 years, the American economy has changed drastically. Many well-paying, blue-collar and factory jobs have disappeared, especially in and around locations generally accessible to Black inner-city residents (Coontz, 1992; Massey & Denton, 1993; Wilson, 1996). This has generated a new type of Black poverty in which entire Black neighborhoods consist of a large percentage of working-aged adults who are either continuously unemployed or underemployed with jobs that cannot sustain marriage and family life (Wilson, 1996). Housing policies have hyperconcentrated the so-called Black underclass within specific areas of Black neighborhoods. Children socialized under these conditions eventually discover for themselves that a large number of the adults, including, sometimes, their parents, have no value, connection, or role in the larger society. Their communities look and are policed like warzones. Drawing from these observations, many youths conclude that their future, their destiny, is that of their parents and the surrounding adults: The life of an economically redundant worker about which society could care less. These perceptions are accorded all the more credibility when Black youths learn of the public debates about Black IQ inferiority or the passage of welfare laws that point not to the absence of good-paying jobs as the culprit in today's poverty dynamics, but the psychology and values orientation of the people themselves (e.g., poor people, Black people in particular, are poor because they want to be). The image of Black males receives particular demonic treatment in this campaign of racial denigration (e.g., Black males are depicted as crime-prone, sex crazed, and intellectual misfits, best contained by imprisonment; Glasgow, 1981). The picture is further complicated by the fact that a critical percentage of the underclass has created, and/or has been drawn into, an alternate economy based on illegal drugs, an involvement that practically guarantees lifelong stigmatization as either an addict, exaddict, pusher, or excon (Oliver, 1994).

Many Black children living under these circumstances embrace a nihilistic psychology that encourages the development of attitudes, feelings, and behaviors which make possible the rejection of society (before society has a chance to reject them). The resulting oppositional identity (Fordham & Ogbu, 1986) draws a line between so-called authentic Black behavior and so-called White behavior. The list covers concerns such as speech patterns, dress styles, body language, friendship patterns, ways to act in school, sexual attitudes, and gender relations. If White Americans are perceived to act one way, Black identity is its reverse. If to study and express high academic achievement is White, not studying and poor achievement is cool; if White Americans speak Standard English, African Americans must speak Ebonics and resist learning Standard English. If showing an attachment toward one's teachers and an interest in mainstream school clubs or afterschool activities is White, then rejecting teachers as role models and avoiding school extramural affairs is Black. Furthermore, if White people say that life is hopeful, positive, and worthy of future planning and high expectations, Black people counter that nothing about Black life is connected to the healthy parts of the larger society; consequently, one must learn to live hard, fast, and for the moment. It is not uncommon for Black nihilists to believe they will be dead before the age of 25.

It is ironic that at an early age, practically all Black preschool- and elementary-aged children enter school with enthusiasm and hope (Spencer, Brookins, & Allen, 1985). However, over time, the children of dislocated workers discover the redundancy of their parents, the propaganda about White beliefs in Black inferiority, and schools that seem intent on tracking them into academic oblivion (Anderson, 1990; Massey & Denton, 1993). In turning to nihilistic oppositionalism, their buffering functions become premised on the belief that all White people and every White institution are hopelessly racist, and a bonding function that, besides being anti-White, greatly circumscribes what is authentic Black behavior. Given their ideology of nihilism and rejection, their bridging and codeswitching capacities are practically nonexistent, and while they stress individualism, it is heavily constricted by in-group expectations.

From the turn of the century to the early 1960s, the percentage of Black nihilists was contained by the larger number of Black people, who, due to employment, were able to sustain family and community life (Coontz, 1992; Cross, 1995). In school settings, Black children with a nihilistic psychology were the minority and they were pressured by the majority of traditionally raised Black children to change and become more hopeful (Anderson, 1988). Even if the nihilists remained unphased, their small numbers meant that the moral tone and achievement aspirations of the school were dictated by children operating with the more traditional Black psychology. The Black identity of the traditional Black Americans stressed a buffering mechanism that saw racism as situational rather than omnipresent, and thus subject to manipulation; a bonding function that was proactive and pro-Black, rather than anti-White, inclusive of strong academic achievement and hope for the future themes; a bridging function that, even under circumstances of segregation, never dismissed the possibility of White and Black connections; sophisticated codeswitching functions that made it possible to work, play, or attend school in racially circumscribed settings; and a powerful emphasis on the dignity of one's individuality and the potential to make a difference.

It becomes evident that the Black nihilistic identity was, and continues to be, at odds not only with that which is perceived as White, but also with that which is traditionally African American. As long as traditional African Americans had the upper hand, numerically speaking, nihilistic oppositionalism was an important but minor theme in Black life, from as far back as the early 1900s and up to the late 1960s (Cross, 1995). Today, in the 1990s, economic conditions in the Black community have regressed to the point that in some inner-city schools, there are more Black children who have developed in accordance with the nihilistic psychology than the traditional (Wilson, 1996). Consequently, nihilists, rather than traditionalists, set the academic and social climate in such schools (Cross, 1995). Although middle-class White Americans are generally spatially isolated from poor White people, who may also develop oppositional frames of reference, such is not the case for middle-class and blue-collar Black families. African American residential patterns are still shaped by racist housing policies. Although not sharing the exact residential addresses, middle-class and working-class Black families may find their children attending schools that draw students from nearby underclass enclaves and housing projects (Massey & Denton, 1993). At the junior high and high school levels, this mix can be quite volatile, as traditional conceptions of buffering, bonding, bridging, codeswitching, and individualism are challenged by the nihilist perspective that relies heavily on paranoiac buffering and extreme, reactionary bonding (Fordham & Ogbu, 1986).

In summary, adolescence is the period during which a broad range of LS and HS social identities come to fruition. It is also the point at which LS identities may be changed by a Nigrescence conversion. The more recently evolved Black oppositional identity may also bellow its presence, as the progeny of the Black underclass win a small victory by exiting society before society has a chance to communicate its utter indifference.

Sectors 4 and 5: Early Adulthood and Nigrescence

After adolescence, the general personality and social identity profiles for human beings become well-established, taking on very distinct patterns. If a person exhibited neurotic tendencies, at earlier points in development, continuation of this pattern into early adulthood is likely to result in a neurotic classification as an adult. The reverse would be true of someone evidencing more normative personality characteristics, resulting in a nonneurotic or healthy classification. The same is true of the way we classify a person's social identity. If a person exhibited diffusion identity behavior during adolescence, his or her social identity as an adult will be classified as diffuse in nature. Likewise, a person who never shows a hint of

self-criticality during adolescence is likely to embrace an adult social identity that is foreclosed. Sector 4 of Fig. 2.1 shows the various LS and HS social identity classifications associated with African Americans moving
into early adulthood; Sector 5 shows how many of these adult patterns
may become linked to a Nigrescence experience (Cross, 1991; Cross &
Fhagen-Smith, 1996). Moving back and forth (from Sector 4 and Sector 5),
we note that Black adults with a foreclosed (unexamined) social identity
may go through Nigrescence as a way of finally experiencing
self-criticality and self-ownership of their sense of Blackness. Black adults
with a diffused social image may go through Nigrescence as a way of gaining focus, self-clarity, and commitment, or in the case of the diffused
self-hating person, to achieve a positive as well as focused identity. A Black
adult who has accomplished an achieved identity that is low in race salience (achieve LS), may experience Nigrescence as a way of converting to
an achieved identity that is HS. Black militants, or perpetually angry Black
people, may need Nigrescence to better work through their issues. At the
bottom of Sector 4 in Fig. 2.1 is the classification *Achieve LS,* which represents those African Americans who live their entire lives with a social identity that gives very limited significance to race and culture. Finally, there is
no line connecting someone with an Achieved HS identity at Sector 4,
with *Nigrescence* at Sector 5 because a person raised by parents to have a
Black focus will not need a Nigrescence conversion at early adulthood.
Nigrescence is not a developmental cycle required of every Black person. It
is designed for those who are not fully developed (foreclosed and diffused
identities) or for those who ave evolved, to date, with a healthy but LS social identity. If, by early adulthood, a person has already achieved a solid
and fulfilling sense of Blackness, there is no developmental requirement
for conversion.

Sector 6: Identity Refinement Across the Life Span

Figure 2.1 has lines that connect anyone who has gone through *Nigrescence*
at Sector 5 with *Nigrescence Recycling* at Sector 6 (Parham, 1989). There is a
line connecting the *Achieved HS* identity from Sector 4, with *Nigrescence
Recycling* at Sector 6. *Nigrescence Recycling* stands for continued development of one's Black social identity. Whether one was raised to identify
Black or whether one was converted to Blackness through Nigrescence,
there are always going to be new questions, new challenges, and new trag-
edies that reveal gaps in one's thinking about what it means to be Black.
For example, the questions and issues that drive a person's Black identity
at age 21, are going to change or be different at ages 30, 40, and 50. These
new encounters cause the person to recycle through some of the stages of
Nigrescence, for the purpose of bringing resolution to the new issues. Mar-

riage, divorce, changing jobs, moving to new locations, being racially harassed at work, and witnessing the roll back of affirmative action programs are examples of personal and public events that can challenge one's social identity. Perhaps there is need to further refine one's buffering function or a joyous turn of events may energize one's lack of bonding to an overlooked Black organization. Positive mentoring from a White supervisor may give one pause to rethink some rather rusty bridging capacities; a new job may stress the limits of one's codeswitching abilities or the death of a loved one may bring one closer to concepts, ideas, and feelings that transcend race (humanism and individualism). If the question at hand represents a modest challenge, the recycling may be felt as a mild cognitive restructuring, but if it takes the form of a jolting, traumatizing event, recycling may be as volatile as one's initial conversion experience. With each recycling, greater insight into Blackness comes, bringing a sense of wisdom within reach (Parham, 1989).

IMPLICATIONS FOR SCHOOL PRACTICES

Single-Factor Versus Multidimensional Perspective

Educators should determine, through self-examination, whether they tend to operate with a single-trait or multidimensional perspective on Black identity. The authors favor a complex frame of reference and are leery of single-factor models. Furthermore, although we grant that there are a variety of ways in which one may approach or define this multiplicity, we argue for the efficacy of a functional approach that asks the question: "What are the different ways in which Black identity operates or functions in the everyday life of the person?"

The Five Functions of Black Social Identity

Buffering, bonding, bridging, codeswitching, and individualism are the five identity functions associated with Black social identity development. These situationally sensitive and interaction-oriented psychological mechanisms are crucial to the everyday adjustment of African Americans. Black parents and teachers must provide guidance to Black children, which makes possible the development and refinement of these life-enhancing functions. Black children need to learn the difference between a sledgehammer approach to buffering, in which all White people and all White institutions are seen as threats to one's integrity, versus a buffering mechanism, which filters out racism, while letting in nonracist experiences and information. Likewise, parents and teachers have the task of helping Black youths learn the distinction between myopic, ethnocentric, and nihilistic in-group bonding, compared to bonding and ethnic attach-ment that is pro-Black, proactive, and achievement oriented. Black youths need to feel confident and competent in their bridging capacities. Recipro-cal cultural sharing does not just happen and schools must find explicit ways to teach bicultural and multicultural competence, whether children attend a monoracial or multiracial school. Competent codeswitching is a fundamental requirement of everyday Black life. Not every situation, workplace, school, or social setting is governed by a Black or multicultural ethos, and Black children must learn to enter, function, and exit all situa-tions with grace, confidence, sophistication, and a sense of efficacy. Finally, Black youth must feel free to explore and develop individual quali-ties, traits, habits, and personal proclivities unique to one's innermost sense of self.

LS and HS Social Identities

A Black identity operates with a social identity that gives high salience to race and Black culture, especially with regard to the buffering and bonding functions. However, not every Black person is raised to have a Black iden-tity, and educators must develop the sensitivity to know when the absence of a Black identity is a deficit or when it is an indication that something other than race is central to a child's sense of joy and everyday living. The range of LS and HS social identities among Black youth is directly related to variability in the social contexts within which Black children are social-ized and variations in the parental attitudes on how best to raise a Black child (race avoidant, race-neutral, and race-conscious strategies). Black people are not stereotypically Black, and educators must be prepared to nourish the full range of LS and HS identities that Black children bring to the classroom.

Ideology and Black Identity Profiles

If Black social identities differ in being either HS or LS, it is just as impor-tant to note that not all HS identities share the same profile. During ado-lescence, Black identities become organized around ideological concerns, and one's ideology can determine which identity functions will be high-lighted in everyday life. Black nationalism stresses strong buffering and bonding functions, whereas interactions with people and institutions out-side the Black community are carried out through codeswitching opera-tions. Black biculturalists—Black people who see themselves as American and African—as well as African Americans who hold to a multicultural worldview stress the development of a very refined and sophisticated bridging function, in addition to buffering, bonding, codeswitching, and individualism. It should not be the objective of educators to direct Black youth down one ideological path or another; but understanding the functions method of defining Black identity, teachers can guide and challenge students to think through the strengths and pitfalls of each frame. Educators can help students self-reflect on the functions, allowing the students to discover how extreme buffering can block one's ability to see an opportunity in situations being categorically rejected and/or how the absence of moderate buffering skills may lead to unnecessary hurt and pain.

Nigrescence and Identity Change

If coming to terms with the evolution of one's social identity was not a challenge in and of itself, many, but not all, African Americans find it necessary to reinvent themselves through Nigrescence. Educators may expose children to significant events in Black history that may act as an encounter and trigger militancy in the youth. Although the Black bravado associated with militancy can be disarming, educators must realize that adolescents are not yet adults and that they can use positive adult feedback and direction. Anger, rage, and militancy are common reactions to an in-depth study of Black history, and adult guidance can help young people find constructive outlets for their perturbation.

Oppositionalism and Traditional Black Identity

Perhaps the most pressing challenge for educators who work with Black youth from the homes of economically redundant Black workers is finding ways to inspire hope. Society would have us believe that the answer must come from better education. The senior author challenges this perspective, suggesting that the first step is not in the manipulation of the children, but in the meaningful employment of their parents (Cross, 1995; see Coontz, 1992; Wilson, 1996). Employed working-class and poor Black parents have traditionally found ways to inspire hope in their children, which has made it easier for educators to advance their children beyond their parent's social status. Today, we are confronted with Black poverty stemming from unemployment and under these circumstances, hope is quickly changed to despair and nihilism. It is one thing to help youth look beyond societal limitations that can reasonably be transcended through personal effort, but how can educators replace the examples and role modeling of parents whose very lives constantly communicate to their children that society does not care? From our vantage point, such answers lay beyond the pale of a work on identity.

REFERENCES

Akbar, N. (1985). *The community of self.* Tallahassee: Mind Productions.
Anderson, A. (1990). *Streetwise.* Chicago: University of Chicago Press.
Anderson, J. (1988). *The education of Blacks in the south, 1860–1935.* Chapel Hill: University of North Carolina Press.
Boyd-Franklin, N. (1989). *Black families in therapy.* New York: Guilford.
Bronfenbrenner, U. (1979). *The ecology of human development: Experiments by nature and design.* Cambridge, MA: Harvard University.
Clark, L., Swim, J. K., & Cross, W. E., Jr., (1995). *Functions of racial identity in everyday life: A daily diary study.* Unpublished manuscript.
Clark, R. M. (1983). *Family life and school achievement.* Chicago: University of Chicago Press.
Coontz, N. (1992). *The way we never were.* New York: Basic Books.
Cross, W. E., Jr. (1991). *Shades of Black.* Philadelphia: Temple University Press.
Cross, W. E., Jr. (1995). Oppositional identity and African American youth. In W. D. Hawley & A. W. Jackson (Eds.), *Toward a common destiny* (pp. 185–204). San Francisco: Jossey-Bass.
Cross, W. E., Jr., & Fhagen-Smith, P. (1996). Nigrescence and ego identity development. In P. B. Pederson, J. G. Draguns, W. J. Lonner, & J. E. Trimble (Eds.), *Counseling across cultures* (pp. 108–123). Thousand Oaks, CA: Sage.
Cross W. E., Jr., Parham, T. A., & Helms J. E. (1995). The stages of Black identity development. In R. L. Jones (Ed.), *Black psychology* (2nd ed., pp. 319–338). Berkeley, CA: Cobbs & Henry.
Early, G. (1993). *Lure and loathing.* New York: Allen Lane.
Erikson, E. (1968). *Identity: Youth in crisis.* New York: Norton.
Fordham, S., & Ogbu, J. (1986). Black students' school success: Coping with the burden of acting White. *The Urban Review, 18*(3), 176–206.
Glasgow, D. (1981). *The Black underclass.* New York: Vintage Books.
Gordon, V. (1980). *The self-concepts of Black Americans.* Washington, DC: University Press of America.
Helms, J. E. (1990). *Black and White racial identity development.* New York: Greenwood.
Lawrence-Lightfoot, S. (1994). *I've known rivers.* New York: Addison-Wesley.
Marcia, J. (1966). Development and validation of ego identity status measure. *Journal of Personality and Psychology, 3*(5), 551–558.
Massey, D., & Denton, N. (1993). *American apartheid.* Cambridge, MA: Harvard University Press.
Oliver, W. (1994). *The violent social world of Black men.* New York: Lexington.
Parham, T. A. (1989). Cycles of psychological nigrescence. *Counseling Psychologist, 17*(2), 187–226.
Phinney, J. (1989). Stages of ethnic identity development in minority group adolescents. *Journal of Early Adolescence, 9*(1–2), 34–49.

Porter, J. D. R., & Washington, R. E. (1979). Black identity and self-esteem: A review of the studies of Black self-concept, 1968–1978. *Annual Review of Sociology, 5,* 53–74.

Sellers, R. M., Shelton, J. N., Cooke, D. Y., Chavous, T. M., Rowley, S. A. J., & Smith, M. A. (in press). A multidimensional model of racial identity: Assumptions, findings and future directions. In R. L. Jones (Ed.), *African-American identity development: Theory, research and intervention.* Hampton, VA: Cobb & Henry.

Spencer, M. B. (1988). Self-concept development. In D. T. Slaughter (Ed.), *Perspectives in Black child development* (pp. 59–72). San Francisco: Jossey-Bass.

Spencer, M. B. (1994). Old issues and new theorizing about African-American youth: A phenomenological variant of ecological systems theory. In R. L. Taylor (Ed.), *African American youth: Their social and economic status in the United States* (pp. 37–69). New York: Praeger.

Spencer, M. B., Brookins, G. K., & Allen, W. R. (1985). *Beginnings: The social and affective development of Black children.* Hillsdale, NJ: Lawrence Erlbaum Associates.

Stevenson, H. C., Jr. (1995). Relationship of adolescent perceptions of racial socialization to racial identity. *Journal of Black Psychology, 21*(1), 49–70.

Tatum, B. D. (1987). *Assimilation blues.* Northampton, MA: Hazel- Maxwell.

Wilson, W. J. (1996). *When work disappears: The world of the new urban poor.* New York: Knopf.

3 White Identity Formation: A Developmental Process

Tina Q. Richardson
Timothy J. Silvestri
Lehigh University

Although race is a salient dimension by which all people in the United States are categorized, there has been limited discussion of the developmental processes that occur across the life span for White Americans regarding their racial identity formation. Nevertheless, there is a growing body of literature on models of White racial identity (e.g., Hardiman, 1982; Helms, 1984, 1990; Ponterotto, 1988; Rowe, Bennett, & Atkinson, 1994; Sabnani, Ponterotto, & Borodovsky, 1991; Sue & Sue, 1990). *White racial identity consciousness,* as discussed in this chapter, refers to awareness of one's own racial group membership, underlying race-related cultural values, and an understanding of the sociopolitical implications resulting from membership in a particular racial group. *Racial identity* refers to a sense of group or collective identity based on one's perception that he or she shares a common racial heritage with a particular racial group. Membership in this country's dominant racial group (White) neither exempts White people from developing a racial identity nor makes exploration of White racial consciousness a moot issue. Erikson (1968) pointed out that a person's individual identity is linked to a communal or group identity and highlighted the necessity of examining the concepts of racial identity and racial consciousness. Thus, because the United States is a race-conscious society, it is likely that race is a significant part of the total identity development process for White Americans throughout the life span. This chapter provides an overview of White racial identity theoretical frameworks, integrates racial identity with other psychological models of development, and provides examples of how racial identity is applicable as a dynamic developmental phenomenon.

OVERVIEW OF WHITE RACIAL IDENTITY FRAMEWORKS

Helms' Model of White Racial Identity

Fuller (1974) and Welsing (1974) defined *racism* as a White person's belief in White supremacy. Jones (1981) defined racism as the transformation of race prejudice and/or ethnocentrism through the exercise of power against racial minority groups by White individuals and institutions with the intentional or unintentional support of White culture. Jones' concept of racism emphasized ideology (*ethnocentrism*) and attitudes of racial superiority (*individual racism*), institutional power as a means of implementing ideological biases (*institutional racism*), and a broad-based cultural support of an ethnocentric and culturocentric ideology (*cultural racism*). According to Helms (1992), the process of developing a healthy White identity means unlearning racism and internalizing what it means to be White without the aid of racial inequity and inequality.

One of the most influential models in research has been Helms' (1984, 1990) model of White racial identity. Helms described a variety of ways in which White people may choose to identify with other White people as a membership group and develop racial and cultural identities, as well as realize the political implications resulting from their racial group membership. According to Helms (1990, 1992), developing a healthy White racial identity is a two-phase process: Phase I, abandoning racism and Phase II, developing a nonracist identity.

Each phase in Helms' model encompasses three distinct racial identity statuses. Development through the statuses occurs as individuals encounter critical incidents or significant relationships that cause them to explore racial identity issues. The first status in Phase I is *Contact Attitudes,* during which a person is oblivious to the existence of racism and is naive, concerning the significant role race plays in American society. Therefore, that person judges others from a White cultural perspective. The second status, *Disintegration,* is characterized by confusion and guilt from realizing the implications of being White and the moral dilemmas associated with such a privileged racial membership. In an attempt to resolve the discomfort associated with this identity status, the individual may begin to assume characteristics of the *Reintegration Identity status* in its passive or active form. The Reintegration Identity status reflects an underlying belief in the superiority of White people and inferiority of people of color. Any previous awareness of societal restrictions and limitations for people of color are thwarted by the belief, "People get what they deserve." In addition, a Reintegration Identity status can be expressed in passive or active forms. The passive Reintegration person assumes, without question, that there are elements of truth in racial stereotypes and, consequently, avoids interacting with people of color. An active Reintegration Identity status person may outwardly treat people of color as inferior by committing violent acts and supporting exclusion designed to protect the White privilege system (Helms, 1990).

The remaining three racial identity statuses (Pseudo-Independent, Immersion/Emersion, and Autonomy) are associated with the conflict inherent in developing a positive nonracist White identity (Phase II). Although the *Pseudo-Independent* individual is beginning to abandon the belief in White superiority and the inferiority of people of color, this individual's affect, thoughts, and behaviors still unintentionally perpetuate these attitudes. In addition, the Pseudo-Independent person approaches racial issues from an intellectualized stance characterized by emotional distance.

The Immersion/Emersion status involves an active search for personal meaningfulness in being White in the United States and the world in general (Helms, 1990). The focus of this identity status shifts from attempting to change people of color toward a commitment to encouraging other White people to explore their own Whiteness and to abandon racism.

Last, in *Autonomy,* the individual continues to internalize a positive White identity and appropriately integrates knowledge and experiences dealing with racial issues. The individual endeavors to abandon racism on a personal, institutional, and cultural level. In addition, a person who has reached autonomy psychologically and behaviorally commits to the elimination of oppression. Although Autonomy is the most evolved White racial identity status, maintaining this identity is an ongoing process requiring continuous openness to learning about racial, cultural, social, and political issues as well as integrating proactive behavior.

Rowe, Bennett, and Atkinson White Racial Identity Theory

In contrast to Helms' (1984, 1990) model, another White racial identity theory has recently developed (Rowe et al., 1994). Rowe et al. (1994) used Helms' (1984) definition of White racial consciousness as the basis for their model and conceptualized racial consciousness in terms of two forms of identity statuses (achieved and unachieved) which, in turn, encompass seven attitude types. In general, achieved statuses require an exploration of racial issues and a concomitant commitment to these beliefs. Unachieved statuses lack exploration, commitment, or both of these components.

Achieved statuses are characterized by four relatively stable internalized attitude types. *Dominative* attitudes refer to strong ethnocentric perspectives that justify the oppression of minority groups. *Conflictive* attitudes reflect opposition to discriminatory practices and opposition to programs designed to reduce or eliminate such discrimination. *Reactive* attitudes entail a recognition that White society wrongly benefits from and promotes discriminatory practices. *Integrative* attitudes refer to comfort with one's Whiteness and with minority groups.

Within the unachieved status, the three attitude types share a noninternalized set of expressed racial attitudes. *Dependent* attitudes reflect the reliance on others to define one's own racial attitudes. *Avoidant* attitudes are characterized by a lack of interest in one's own White identity and a lack of concern for issues surrounding race. Last, *Dissonant* attitudes entail uncertainty about one's sense of racial consciousness and racial issues. Moreover, a person experiences dissonance between previously held beliefs and recent personal experiences.

Ego and Social Identity Models

In contrast to the two aforementioned racial identity models are ego identity theorists who are primarily based in developmental adolescent psychology. In addition, the research generated from the ego identity models has emphasized ethnic identity as opposed to racial identity, although the differentiations between these two constructs are not always clear.

As an extension of Erikson's work (1968), Marcia (1966, 1980) suggested four ego identity statuses based on whether individuals have explored their identity options and whether they have made a decision about these options. *Diffusion* occurs when individuals have not made a commitment or engaged in exploration. *Foreclosed* status entails the person who makes an identity commitment without exploration, usually on the basis of external influences (e.g., parents). *Moratorium* involves the exploration of an identity without having made a commitment. Finally, *achieved* status is characterized by the person making a firm commitment after having explored their options. One of the primary problems with Marcia's ego identity theory is that issues of racial and ethnic identity, for the most part, have not been addressed (Phinney, 1990; Ponterotto & Pedersen, 1993).

Phinney and her colleagues applied Marcia's (1980) ego identity theory to ethnic (racial) issues among adolescents (Phinney, 1989, 1990; Phinney & Alipuria, 1990; Phinney & Chavira, 1992; Phinney, DuPont, Espinosa, Revill, & Sanders, 1994; Phinney, Lochner, & Murphy, 1990; Phinney & Tarver, 1988). In spite of the fact that Phinney's discussion of ethnic identity is usually applied to "minority" groups (Phinney, 1996), it is important to acknowledge the significance of ethnic identity development of White people as well. In many respects, the general model that Phinney described has some relevance for White people also. Phinney (1989, 1990) proposed a three-stage progression, ranging from an unexamined ethnic identity, through a period of examination, to an achieved or committed ethnic identity. Stage 1, *Unexamined Ethnic Identity,* is characterized by the lack of exploration of one's ethnicity. Essentially, the adolescent is ignorant of and/or may not be interested in ethnic issues. This stage is comparable to Marcia's (1980) Diffusion and Foreclosure ego identity statuses.

Stage 2, *Ethnic Identity Search/Moratorium,* is triggered by a traumatic encounter that forces individuals to think about the meaning surrounding their ethnicity. Therefore, individuals actively undergo the process of learning more about their respective ethnic cultures. This stage is similar to Marcia's (1980) Moratorium ego identity status.

Last, in Stage 3, *Ethnic Identity Achievement,* individuals attain a deeper understanding and appreciation of their ethnicity. That is, adolescents have internalized a clear sense of what their ethnicity is or means to them. Stage 3 corresponds to Marcia's (1980) Achieved ego identity status. It is important to note that the ego identity research (e.g., Adams, Ryan, Hoffman, Dobson, & Nelson, 1984; Adams & Shea, 1978; Jones & Hartman, 1988; Marcia, 1966; Phinney, 1989, 1990; Phinney & Alipuria, 1990; Phinney & Chavira, 1992; Phinney et al., 1990; Phinney & Tarver, 1988) examined ethnic identity issues primarily among adolescents and not adults. However, the White racial identity theories were applied to primarily adult populations in order to examine racial identity development. The sociopolitical underpinnings of these models differ greatly as, for example, the racial identity models were based on mapping out how racism and oppression imposed by White Americans impact the person's sense of self; yet, the dynamics of racism and oppression are not, implicitly or explicitly, addressed in the ego identity models. The dynamics of race and one's relationship with and status in the dominant culture are not ignored in Phinney's (1989, 1990) work.

RACIAL IDENTITY AND OBJECT RELATIONS

White racial identity models first appeared in the literature in the 1970s and, two decades later, very little has been done to incorporate these essential models into general psychological theories of development. Existing models of development (e.g., object relations and self-actualization theory) are not only incomplete without the integration, but reflect the racist social and/or political context in which many theories were created. Thus, they uphold the status quo that minimizes the significance of race in the psychological development process of White people rather than taking a progressive approach to identity development. One profound consequence of White identity theory appearing in the professional literature (independent of general developmental theories) is that a salient dimension of identity for White people gets ignored in much of the psychological discourse where it is most needed.

For example, object relations theory provides a full discussion on how people develop a sense of self-identity within the context of relating to others (see Hamilton, 1990 for details). This theoretical perspective provides a viable framework for how an individual can develop and emerge a unique and separate self that is simultaneously connected to external objects or social contexts. In object relations terms, the *self* refers to conscious and unconscious mental representations that pertain to one's person, whereas *object* means an external person, place, or thing and some-

times, an internal image (Hamilton, 1990). White racial identity development is particularly relevant to the discussion of formation of self and the
separation and individuation process described by object relations theory.
The self forms as a result of interactions with internal or external objects
and evolves from initial states of symbiotic or fused relatedness to differ-
entiated states of relatedness. In Phase I, *Contact Identity* status, a symbiotic relationship exists wherein Whiteness is undifferentiated from
racism. In addition, obliviousness to the meaning of being White is possible because other objects (e.g., racial minorities) are not knowable or are irrelevant. *Disintegration* is characterized by development toward more
differentiation in that the self is able to acknowledge external objects (e.g.,
racial minorities) as relevant and point out differences in racial behaviors,
as well as issues of inequality, injustice, and immorality directed at racial
minority groups. In many respects, it may be the very process of differentiation that is achieved in the Disintegration status that solidifies White
identity development because as object relations theory points out, in order for a meaningful identity to form, with respect to race in this case,
there must be acknowledgment of some external object(s) with which to
compare one's self; without it, there is no self and no stable sense of reality
(Hamilton, 1990). Hamilton went on to say that "our very selves will dis-
integrate without external as well as internal objects, for the self is nothing
except half of the self-object duality" (p. 18). This duality is illuminated
with more clarity in the Reintegration status of White racial identity that
is characterized by a conscious and/or unconscious need to be distinguished along racial lines and to attribute values to the distinction in the
form of good–bad splitting (e.g., superior–inferior and us–them). In fact,
the process of abandoning racism, which is the central Phase I developmental task for White identity formation, can be likened to the early stages
of differentiation described in object relations theory, whereas the Phase II
developmental task of developing a nonracist identity is more reflective of
advanced differentiation processes.

When White racial identity development is described in terms of the
separation-individuation process, it is easy to see why these two theoretical frameworks of psychological development are strengthened by integrating them in an interdependent manner. According to object relations
theory, the *separation and individuation processes* refer to a series of psychological processes that lead the individual to an increased sense of separateness and individual integrity (or autonomy), while simultaneously
acknowledging the importance of connection with others. According to
Mahler, Pine, and Bergman (1975), the *psychological birth process* that provides the foundation for later identity development evolves out of a state
of *autism* or psychological insulation and *symbiosis* or total unity with an
external object. As previously stated, this state of identity development is
consistent with the psychological processes of the Contact individual.
However, in order to develop what Helms (1990) described as a Phase II
identity (Pseudo-Independence, Immersion/Emersion, Autonomy), one

must be able to master certain object relations tasks with various degrees of interdependence with external objects (e.g., other people). In object relations theory, the process of achieving interdependence or *Separation–Individuation* is described as a continuous cycling through the following phases: *Hatching,* which refers to the initial physical and psychological separating of self from primary object; *Practicing,* which is characterized by exercising autonomous ego functions and mobility used to explore the external environment; *Rapprochement,* which refers to increased cognitive awareness of vulnerability and separateness; and *Object Constancy,* which is characterized by individuality and an increasingly stable sense of self across social contexts (see Hamilton, 1990, pp. 35–57 for a detailed description).

With respect to White racial identity formation, the Phase II developmental task of achieving a nonracist White identity requires competence in negotiating the psychological skills associated with Separation–Individuation. One cannot achieve a nonracist White identity without having mastery of the Hatching, Practicing, and Rapprochement phases (see Table 3.1). According to Helms (1990), Pseudo-Independence is characterized by relinquishing societal-sanctioned White superiority, at least on the intellectual level. This requires, in object relations terms, that the individual engage in Hatching and Practicing processes to abandon previously internalized beliefs. The active search for personal meaningfulness of Whiteness, which is reflected in the Immersion/Emersion status, requires Practicing and Rapprochement processes. Last, Autonomy, in the authentic sense, requires what object relations theory refers to as *Object Constancy* (Hamilton, 1990).

The integration of these two conceptual perspectives on identity formation allows for greater understanding of the task of identity development throughout the life span. They incorporate the salience and significance of race in the identity process. According to Cross, Parham, and Helms (1991), a life span perspective to the study of White racial identity emphasizes the following: "Within the context of normal development, racial identity is a phenomenon which is subject to continuous change during the life cycle" (p. 331). Although they were initially discussing Black identity development, Cross et al. (1991) described how statuses of racial identity are manifested at three phases of life—late adolescence/early adulthood, midlife, and late adulthood. They emphasized that manifestations of identity during childhood are most often a reflection of parental attitudes or societal stereotypes that are incorporated more than integrated into a complex cognitive identity structure. It is during adolescence and early adulthood that an individual may start the process of exploring his or her White identity beyond the teachings of parental influences. In many respects, racial identity exploration may occur simultaneously with other aspects of self-explorations, such as gender identity, sexuality, and career. In late adulthood, White racial identity formation will be influenced by distinctive developmental tasks associated with each phase of the adult life span (Cross et al., 1991).

TABLE 3.1
Separation–Individuation and White Racial Identity

Psychological Birth	Share Processes Achieved/Unachieved	White Racial Identity Statuses
Autism and Symbiosis • no distinction made between self and external object • self in total unity with external object	•limited ability to make distinctions between self and experiences of other	Contact • obliviousness and/or naiveté about racial issues and injustice • racial egocentrism
Hatching • initial physical and psychological separating of self from primary object	• a sorting through of self experiences and the experiences of others	Disintegration • initial awareness of racial differences in the treatment people
Practicing • exercise of autonomous ego functions and mobility to explore external environment	• full understanding of external objects but person explores own superiority over others	Reintegration • acceptance of White racial superiority in a passive or active manner
Rapprochement • cognitive awareness of vulnerability and separateness	• understanding the cognitive and emotional effects of racial separateness	Pseudo-Independence • initial process of abandoning racial prejudice • intellectual understanding of the negative impact of racism
Object Constancy • individuality • increasingly stable sense of self across social contexts	• a highly evolved individual who maintains a sense of connectedness to others but behaves in an appropriate interdependent manner with regard to race	Immersion/Emersion • active pursuit of the meaning nonracist Whiteness
		Autonomy • integrated sense of self as White person • incorporation of proactive nonracist behavior

Cross et al. (1991) also indicated that the demanding characteristics of each status of racial identity in adult development may cause most people to recycle through the identity process. They defined *recycling* as "reinitiation into the racial identity struggle and resolution process after having gone through the identity process at an earlier stage in one's life" (p. 332). Theoretically, a person could achieve identity resolution by completing one cycle through the White identity model (e.g., Autonomy) and as a result of life challenges for which the initial cycle did not address, recycle through the statuses again (Cross et al., 1991). In addition, Cross et al. (1991) introduced the notion that racial identity development does not have to start with the first status of racial identity (e.g., Contact) if a child or adolescent is exposed to and indoctrinated with parental and social messages that are characteristic of later statuses (e.g., Disintegration and Pseudo-Independence). Thus, racial identity theory and object relations theory share some meaningful parallels regarding the manner in which development occurs, specifically in terms of what it takes to reach optimal growth and the notion or recycling through developmental processes.

WHITE RACIAL IDENTITY AND SELF-ACTUALIZATION

This section describes how the combination of White racial identity development (Helms, 1990) and personality development, as defined by Maslow's concept of self-actualization, provide a better understanding of identity development. Maslow (1987) viewed the healthiest and most psychologically mature individuals as those who are self-actualized. He defined the self-actualized person as one who has:

> full use and exploitation of talents, capacities, potentialities, and the like. Such people seem to be fulfilling themselves and to be doing the best that they are capable of doing ... they are people who have developed or are developing to the full stature of which they are capable. (p. 126)

Maslow divided self-actualization into 19 individual traits:

1. *Perception of Reality.* An unusual ability to detect the spurious, the fake, and the dishonest in personality, and in general to judge people correctly and efficiently.

2. *Acceptance.* Acceptance of the self and the absence of a neurotic style.

3. *Spontaneity.* A developed natural style which can interact appropriately with one's surroundings while keeping intact one's ethical and moral considerations.

4. *Problem Centering.* Central foci on external problems rather than being ego centered.

5. *Solitude.* Although the problem centering is focused on the outside, the self-actualized individual retains the ability to detach from the environment and function autonomously.

6. *Autonomy.* Independence and the ability to be self-contained especially when faced with adversity. They seek knowledge and growth and can ascertain the same from an internal mechanism.

7. *Fresh Appreciation.* The ability to appreciate the simplicities of life repeatedly.

8. *Peak Experiences.* A subjective, mystic experience which usually greatly effects the individual's daily life.

9. *Human Kinship.* "A deep feeling of identification, sympathy, and affection for human beings in general." (Maslow, 1987, p.138).

10. *Humility and Respect.* A self-humility along with a respect for all others. Also, a strong democratic ideology.

11. *Interpersonal Relationships.* Deeper and more profound interpersonal contacts albeit a smaller circle of close friendships. The difference is qualitative, rather than quantitative in nature.

12. *Ethics.* A certainty about right and wrong. Self-assured regarding issues of ethics.

13. *Means and Ends.* A higher focus on the ends rather than the means.

14. *Humor.* Humor transcends that which is at the expense of another, but rather that which is closely allied to philosophy.

15. *Creativity.* Special creativity and originality which is less common among the general population.

16. *Resistance to Enculturation.* Detachment from mainstream culture with an emphasis on being grounded in one's own philosophies.

17. *Imperfection.* Harbor imperfections in a healthy manner.

18. *Values.* Guided by a well-developed value system which structures their daily life events.

19. *Resolution of Dichotomies.* In favor of a continuum approach to conceptualization and thought.

The authors of this chapter suggest that the possibility of achieving self-actualization is significantly diminished in individuals who have not adequately addressed issues of racial identity as part of the complex range of identity formation processes.

According to Dennis (1981), there are many negative consequences of an identity based on a racist worldview for White people, whether the biases are conscious or unconscious. A brief summary of some of the consequences when racism has not been abandoned are highlighted in the following—in conjunction with Maslow's traits of self-actualization. First, Dennis (1981) suggested that racism creates an ignorance of others based on prejudices. Yet, Maslow's self-actualization trait, *Perception of Reality,* emphasizes the ability to perceive reality, one's environment, and people correctly and efficiently. However, the ability to perceive people correctly, especially those of another race, cannot fully occur if one is unaware of the internalized biases held as a result of the identification with the mainstream cultural, institutional, and individual racism that dominate the Phase I racial identity statuses (e.g., Contact, Disintegration, and Reintegration).

The second consequence of racism is the development of moral confusion and a double sociopsychological consciousness, due to the ego-dystonic nature of racism when compared to one's perceived moral and ethical beliefs, which are significant characteristics of the Disintegration status. The moral confusion of the Disintegration status conflicts with Maslow's traits of *Spontaneity*—interactions with one's surroundings while keeping intact one's ethical and moral considerations—and *Ethics*—certainty about right and wrong—because they both assume a resolution of one's internalized moral beliefs. Also, the trait of *Values*—guided by a well-developed value system that structures one's daily life events—is disrupted by the double social consciousness that often accompanies racial situations.

A third consideration of Dennis (1981) is the propensity toward group conformity (*submission of the self*) in order to receive social support and acceptance. Such conformity, in the context of daily experiences of racism, is in direct contrast to Maslow's trait of *Autonomy*—independence and the ability to be self-contained especially when faced with adversity—because an autonomous individual has the ability to stand alone with less regard for the implications from the group. A fourth consequence of racism is the threat to one's capacity for intellectual complexity and growth. *Racism,* which engenders irrationality, inhibits intellectual growth, and negates democratic thought, is mutually exclusive with Maslow's traits of *Acceptance*—acceptance of the self, and the absence of a neurotic style or irrationality—and *Humility and Respect*—a self-humility along with a respect for all others; also, a strong democratic ideology.

Another important aspect of racism that has particular implications for self-actualization is the symbolic (or *aversive*) form of racism. Dovidio and Gaertner (1986) demonstrated that although individuals denied harboring racist beliefs or prejudices, they demonstrated racist tendencies in daily interactions. This lack of awareness of the racism that exists in individuals can be explained by the moral confusion that racism engenders (Dennis, 1981; Helms, 1990). Religious and ethical morality dictates the fair treatment of all individuals, yet society teaches White people to fear and be prejudicial toward large racial minority populations. Thus, an individual who has yet to resolve personal racist beliefs is unable to fully explore and transcend the cultural, institutional, and individual worldview constraints that have developed. Such individuals may have partially internalized the traits consistent with self-actualization, but will be unable to be identified with all of the traits. For example, the traits of *Human Kinship*—a deep feeling of identification, sympathy, and affection for human beings in general—and *Humor*—humor that transcends that which is at the expense of another—are constructs that are unattainable for one who unknowingly harbors racism. Thus, it is the authors' contention that complete self-actualization for White people, which encompasses a connection with all Americans (and more generally, all the people of the world), must contain, as a prerequisite, the working through of one's internalized racism in favor of a fully developed White racial identity (Helms, 1992).

Maslow described two other traits that are particularly relevant to White racial identity. The first is *Problem Centering*—central foci on external problems rather than being ego-centered. Part of the developmental process of White racial identity is gaining the ability to critically analyze the many realities possible from a single event, depending on the individual's viewpoint. Also, a person with a more developed White racial identity will begin to see his or her actions (intentional or unintentional) in terms of how they may be impacting others. Likewise, a self-actualized individual will be better able to identify the sociopolitical implications that racism has on people in general. The second trait is *Solitude*—although the problem centering is focused on the outside, the self-actualized individual retains the ability to detach from the environment and to function autonomously. This is a crucial element for a more advanced Phase II White racial identity status (e.g., Immersion/Emersion and Autonomy) because this individual will be in direct contrast to the mainstream oppressive viewpoint. Thus, the ability and, in fact, necessity, to detach from one's surroundings is an essential survival tool when repeatedly exposed to an environment in complete disagreement with one's belief or worldview. This concept of solitude is intertwined with White racial identity because neither can be fully realized without the other.

Research by Tokar and Swanson (1991) reported a significant positive relationship between White racial identity and self-actualization. They used the Personal Orientation Inventory (Shostrom, 1964) to assess self-actualization traits consistent with Maslow's theory. The positive correlation between White racial identity statuses and self-actualization is significant because it demonstrates the influence that the abandonment of racism, in favor of a healthy White racial identity, has on the overall functioning and growth of an individual. By dissecting White racial identity into its various components, we can begin to understand the relationship between White identity and self-actualization.

Personality constructs such as self-actualization, that discuss identity development are limited because they do not effectively incorporate issues of race and racial identity into the identity formation process. As we demonstrated, self-actualization is incompatible with an unevolved White racial identity due to the limitations of racism and monoculturalism. The authors of this chapter contend that the interdependence of racial identity and other personality developmental models can be seen as an attempt to strengthen existing theories by adding the necessary and relevant racial identity and cultural components to create a more inclusive and holistic theory.

IMPLICATIONS FOR SOCIAL INTERACTIONS

Development toward a nonracist (healthier) White racial identity requires Object Constancy and is associated with self-actualization. As Pedersen (1994) highlighted, we are born into and handed certain cultural and sociopolitical beliefs based on cultural, institutional, and individual racism. In other words, the social context can provide the appropriate environment for positive racial identity development or provide a context that will limit personality growth. The implications for a person who strives to achieve a healthy, nonracist, self-actualized identity versus someone who does not are quite varied. Healthy identity development, which reflects greater responsiveness to the sociopolitical dynamics of race and principles of cultural socialization with regards to racism and autonomy of thought and action, will have an impact on family, peer, and collegial relations.

Helms (1990) proposed a racial identity interaction model that described the type of dynamics that occur intraracially when people interact from different racial identity worldviews. She classified relationship types in the following two categories: *Parallel relationships,* which refer to interactions in which participants represent similar types of racial identity attitude statuses. In parallel social relationships, the dynamics for interactions related to racial issues are relatively smooth because common worldviews are shared. *Cross interactions* are characterized by participants who represent identity statuses that differ by at least one status. Crossed relationships can be progressive in nature, wherein the more influential person in the relationship has achieved an identity status that is more advanced than the other person or regressive, wherein the reverse is true. Thus, intraracial relationships vary from smooth to tumultuous, depending on the combination of racial identity statuses represented.

For example, because the family is the place where individuals are initially indoctrinated with much of their cultural and sociopolitical beliefs, growth toward a nonracist worldview and personal racial identity has a significant impact on the family. Separation–individuation issues concerning family teachings (norms) about race, and the development of a more autonomous race relevant identity based on independent observations and cross-racial interactions, may result in family conflicts and confrontations. In regressive situations, where a family's core beliefs are anchored in racism and are invested in the proliferation of ingrained prejudicial ideology, any attempts to discuss or challenge the status quo will be met with negative reactions, such as hostility, anger, impatience, or rejection. In this context, striving to achieve a healthy racial identity will be viewed as a negative gesture of political correctness, immature and naive, disruptive, argumentative, and/or self-righteous by the larger family unit.

The incongruence of statuses between the family members may cause frustration, friction, and even turmoil as each member begins to sift through their differences. A renegotiation of boundaries may ensure the safety of the family's original beliefs from this new inside threat. Unless the family structure itself begins to renegotiate its philosophical orientation and racial identity, this friction will be unresolved and will mirror much of the negative interactions that occur in American society today. However, in progressive family situations, a positive consequence may be that the family will begin to experience growth toward a nonracist White identity through exposure and experiences initiated by an individual.

Peer group interactions will also be influenced by growth toward a healthy nonracist identity when cross-racial identity dynamics are prevalent. For example, an individual who is striving to achieve a White racial identity equivalent to Helms' (1992) Autonomy status is acutely aware and highly responsive to racism and the sociopolitical implications of race and culture as they exist in peer interactions. Yet, exposing individual viewpoints to friends may be in direct contrast to peer group norms, therefore, the person may risk a level of social rejection from friends for confronting racial issues ranging from "harmless" jokes with racist overtones (e.g., unintentional acts of racism) to intentional racism creating isolation and discomfort for the individual. The individual is faced with the constant battle of whether to expose oneself and fight racism or stay quiet and give up one's ideals.

IMPLICATIONS FOR SCHOOL PRACTICES

Regardless of whether the challenging dynamics come from the family, peer group, or some other social context, such as in school settings, what is clear is that White racial identity development will only occur in relationships where there is a press or object with which to interact. However, school settings often provide a broader range of exposure to racial groups or stimuli necessary to initiate White racial identity than family. Educators are in a prime position to facilitate growth in this area of identity development. Thus, when conflicts arise related to racial issues, teachers and administrators can use the incidents to promote healthy racial identity among students. For example, it is not uncommon for students to form social subgroups based on racial similarity and consequently, out-groups related to differences. Teachers and administrators can help students examine their attitudes and beliefs about other races and their own Whiteness and challenge them to explore more appropriate relationships across racial boundaries in order to encourage positive racial identity development beyond the naiveté and obliviousness of the Contact status or the negativity of other status of White identity. In situations in which individual or institutional racism is expressed in the school context in ways that characterize Disintegration, Integration, or Pseudo-Independence statuses, professional staff can help students understand the impact of such behaviors in oppressing human potential (e.g., developing an Autonomous identity). It is through the process of exposure to racial issues, examination of beliefs and attitudes, and practicing new behaviors that positive outcomes can occur and lead individuals to initiate the elimination of racism and develop a nonracist identity that reflects Object Constancy and self-actualization. Helping students begin this growth process at a young age may increase the likelihood of people successfully completing the process of healthy racial identity formation. It is for these reasons that issues described in this chapter referring to the developmental processes, such as Separation–Individuation and self-actualization, are so important and inextricably intertwined with racial identity. In light of the isolation the (Autonomous) individual may experience, it is extremely important that the individual has the internal fortitude and strength to effectively cope with a hostile environment and creates a new support network that understands and shares the individual's worldview because we all need a place where we can stop fighting (at least momentarily) and simply enjoy being alive. With the helpful intervention of teachers and administrators, the school setting can be such a place.

REFERENCES

Adams, G. R., Ryan, J. H., Hoffman, J. J., Dobson, W. R., & Nelson, E. C. (1984). Ego identity status, conformity behavior, and personality in late adolescence. *Journal of Personality and Social Psychology, 47*(5), 1091–1104.

Adams, G. R., & Shea, J. H. (1978). The relationship between identity status, locus of control, and ego development. *Journal of Youth and Adolescence, 8*(1), 81–89.

Cross, W. E., Parham, T. A., & Helms, J. E. (1991). The stages of Black identity development: Models. In R. L. Jones (Ed.), *Black psychology* (3rd ed., pp. 319–338). Berkeley, CA: Cob & Henry.

Dennis, R. M. (1981). Socialization and racism: The White experience. In P. B. Bower & R. G. Hunt (Eds.), *The impact of racism on White Americans* (pp. 71–85). Beverly Hills: Sage.

Dovidio, J. F., & Gaertner, S. L. (Eds.). (1986). *Prejudice, discrimination, and racism.* New York: Academic Press.

Erikson, E. H. (1968). *Identity: Youth and crisis.* New York: Norton.

Fuller, N. (1974). *Textbook for victims of White supremacy.* Washington, DC: Library of Congress.

Hamilton, N. G. (1990). *Self and others: Object relations theory in practice.* Northvale, NJ: Aronson.

Hardiman, R. (1982). *White identity development: A process oriented model for describing the racial consciousness of White Americans.* Unpublished doctoral dissertation, University of Massachusetts, Amherst.

Helms, J. E. (1984). Toward a theoretical explanation of the effects of race on counseling: A Black and White model. *The Counseling Psychologist, 12*(3–4), 153–165.

Helms, J. E. (Ed.). (1993). *Black and White racial identity: Theory, research, and practice.* New York: Greenwood.

Helms, J. E. (1992). *A race is a nice thing to have.* Topeka, KS: Content Communications.

Jones, J. M. (1981). The concept of racism and its changing reality. In B. P. Bowser & R. G. Hunt (Eds.), *Impact of racism on White Americans* (pp. 27–49). Beverly Hills: Sage.

Jones, R. M., & Hartman, B. R. (1988). Ego identity: Developmental differences and experimental substance use among adolescence. *Journal of Adolescence, 11*(4), 347–360.

Marcia, J. (1966). Development and validation of ego-identity status. *Journal of Personality and Social Psychology, 3*(5), 551–558.

Marcia, J. (1980). Identity in adolescence. In J. Adelson (Ed.), *Handbook of adolescent psychology* (pp. 159–187). New York: Wiley.

Maslow, A. H. (1987). *Motivation and personality* (3rd ed.). New York: Harper & Row.

Pedersen, P. (1994). *A handbook for developing multicultural awareness* (2nd ed.). Alexandria, VA: American Counseling Association.

Phinney, J. S. (1989). Stages of ethnic identity development in minority group adolescents. *Journal of Early Adolescence, 9*(1–2), 34–49.

Phinney, J. S. (1990). Ethnic identity in adolescents and adults: Review of research. *Psychological Bulletin, 108*(3), 499–514.

Phinney, J. S. (1996). When we talk about American ethnic groups, what do we mean? *American Psychologist, 51*(9), 918–927.

Phinney, J. S., & Alipuria, L. (1990). Ethnic identity in older adolescents from four ethnic groups. *Journal of Adolescence, 13*(2), 171–183.

Phinney, J. S., & Chavira, V. (1992). Ethnic identity and self-esteem: An exploratory longitudinal study. *Journal of Adolescence, 15*(3), 271–281.

Phinney, J. S., Dupont, S., Espinosa, C., Revill, J., & Sanders, K. (1994). Ethnic identity and American identification among ethnic minority youths. In A. Bouvy, F. van de Vijer, P. Boski, & P. Schmitz (Eds.), *Journey into cross-cultural psychology* (pp. 167–183). Berwyn, PA: Swets & Zeitlinger.

Phinney, J. S., Lochner, B. T., & Murphy, R. (1990). Ethnic identity development and psychological adjustment in adolescence. In A. R. Stirman & L. E. Davis (Eds.), *Ethnic issues in adolescent mental health* (pp. 53–72). Newbury Park, CA: Sage.

Phinney, J. S., & Tarver, S. (1988). Ethnic identity search and commitment in Black and White eighth graders. In A. Bouvy, F. Can de Vijver, P. Boski, & P. Schmitz (Eds.), *Journeys into cross- cultural psychology* (pp. 167–183). Berwyn, PA: Swets & Zeitlinger.

Ponterotto, J. G. (1988). Racial consciousness development among White counselor trainees: A stage model. *Journal of Multicultural Counseling and Development, 16*(4), 146–156.

Ponterotto, J. G., & Pedersen, P. B. (1993). *Preventing prejudice: A guide for counselors and educators.* Newbury Park, CA: Sage.

Rowe, W., Bennett, S. K., & Atkinson, D. R. (1994). White racial identity models: A critique and alternative proposal. *The Counseling Psychologist, 22*(1), 129–146.

Sabnani, H. B., Ponterotto, J. G., & Borodovsky, L. G. (1991). White racial identity development and cross-cultural counselor training: A stage model. *The Counseling Psychologist, 19*(1), 76–102.

Shostrom, E. L. (1964). An inventory for the measurement of self-actualization. *Educational and Psychological Measurement, 24*(2), 207–218.

Sue, D. W., & Sue, D. (1990). *Counseling the culturally different: Theory and practice* (2nd ed.). New York: Wiley.

Tokar, D. M., & Swanson, J. L. (1991). An investigation of the validity of Helms' (1984) model of White racial identity development. *Journal of Counseling Psychology, 38*(3), 296–301.

Welsing, F. (1974). The cress theory of color confrontation. *The Black Scholar, 5*(8), 32–40.

4 The Biracial Baby Boom: Understanding Ecological Constructions of Racial Identity in the 21st Century

Maria P. P. Root
University of Washington

In this chapter, a discussion of the cognitive–emotional process that engages racial socialization over the life span within a psychosociopolitical framework is presented. This discussion provides the foundation for understanding the processes that are present throughout the ecological model of racial identity that is subsequently presented (see Fig. 4.1). This model considers the evolution of ethnic and racial identity development in relationship to other statuses. Whereas race and ethnicity are salient aspects of identity in this stratified society (Phinney, 1990), which are historically and geographically defined (Root, 1997b; Waters, 1990), they are coconstructed with other salient aspects of identity, such as gender (Ossana, Helms, & Leonard, 1992; Stoler, 1995), class, generation (Padilla, 1995), and sexual orientation (Allman, 1996; Kich, 1996). The existing psychological models have not explicitly considered the interactive role of geographic history, gender, class, sexual orientation, or generation on the construction of racial or ethnic identity (Root, in press).

My critique and proposal of racial identity theories are meant to entertain the possibility that we have limited our constructions of racial identity because we are not exempt from the insidious influences of racial assumptions inherent in everyday life in this country. My proposal offers an ecological framework that allows for the following three possibilities: (a) there may be many different outcomes of racial identity and it will become increasingly harder to evaluate these outcomes in a stratified way; (b) racial construction, although historically rooted, is dynamic; and (c) many persons live with multiple secondary statuses

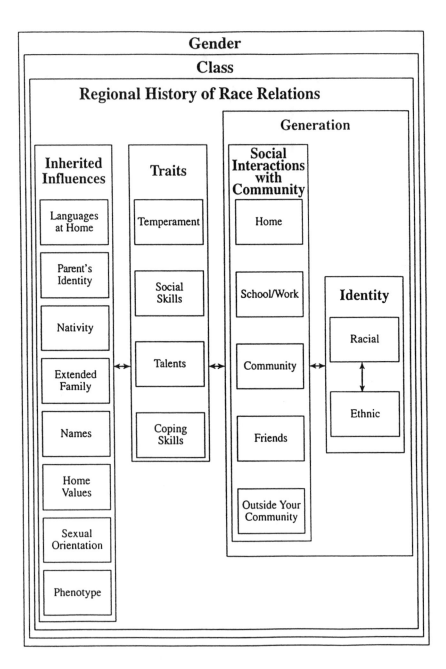

FIG. 4.1.   Ecological Influences on Racial Identity Development.

that interact with race and necessarily influence the salience of race and the formation of racial identity.

COGNITIVE EMOTIONAL PROCESS AND THE CONSTRUCTION OF THE SELF

The Construction of the Self

A discussion of the process of identity cannot proceed without some discussion of assumptions and frameworks within which the self is socially constructed. Conflicting notions of the self appear to rest in sociocultural differences and matrices of power. Eurocentric originated theory assumes the necessity of individuation operationalized at its extreme (Erikson, 1968; Mahler, 1963). These models have been depicted as being founded on male socialization within European and American cultures. Feminist theorists (Collins, 1991; Miller, 1986; Surrey, 1991) suggest that the models of development and maturation of the self rooted in patriarchal models are also rooted in values of individualism. In contrast, the socialization of women emphasizes the realization of self in relationship to other people. Healthy adult functioning requires interdependence (e.g., input and reflection from others). This model is rooted in a more collectivistic orientation. Furthermore, autonomy and maturity might be redefined through the individual's capacity for and quality of relationships with multiple people.

Cross-cultural considerations of the self emphasize the self that is defined relative to interdependency (Markus & Kitayama, 1991). Different ethnically identified communities have emphasized the collective over the individual. Thus, the notion of self in relation to others has been a foundational concept for understanding the choices of many persons who are viewed as culturally different.

Discussion of the self is relevant to examining some of the assumptions of the process of racial identity development. It is possible that because the majority of racial identity theories were developed by men, unwittingly, the privileged position of males in this society informed the models. Without alternate prevailing models of psychosocial development around identity available in training experiences, theorists developed models necessarily bounded and influenced by the psychodynamic models of personality development that prevailed in the 1960s and 1970s.

Theories of the self rooted in interdependence suggest that the self must necessarily be attached to some referent group, although not necessarily a group that holds a dominant position. Cross and Fhagen-Smith's (1996) reexamination of data for revision of Cross's earlier stage work suggests this strongly in his example using data from Johnson's (1981) dissertation on gay Black men and identity. Some of the men seemed to find their primary identity in being Black; other men found their primary identity in being gay. Both groups showed good psychological adjustment, to Cross and

Fhagen-Smith's initial surprise. However, this was not a surprising result if the third possibility mentioned in my ecological framework operates. Gay and lesbian people of color have not experienced welcome receptions in communities of color. Furthermore, multiple aspects of identity can be dynamic with one another and orthogonal. For multiracial people, they may identify as multiracial in order to have a referent group, even if a psychological one (Weisman, 1996), given the racial politics that often scrutinize multiracial persons' belonging and create conditional experiences of belonging and acceptance.

Cognitive Development

Regardless of the cognitive theory of intellectual development that one subscribes to, they all posit that our ability to categorize emerges in the preschool years and becomes increasingly complex. Furthermore, we are supplied with schemata for categorization. For example, initially we may be able to categorize blocks of different shapes and color by a single category—shape or color. It takes further complexity, usually accomplished in the early grade-school years, to simultaneously categorize an object along two dimensions (e.g., red cubes or blue pyramids).

Initially, children do not have schemata for racial categorization. Children are repeatedly taught through the racial labeling of persons based on real and imagined physical features. Jacobs (1992) described how children must learn to distort the colors by which they perceive skin color in order to make accurate racial self-identifications. This is a learned process. Thus, the accuracy of racially identifying people in this country requires a learned vigilance for the gestalt of racial features, which include phenotype.

Emotional Development

Emotional schemata are in part informed by our emotional experiences in bonding and our relationships with those to whom we look for security. Psychological injuries can span a lifetime and co-inform cognitive schemata. Emotional development is also influenced by repeated messages about self-worth and the valuation of people with whom an individual identifies or is identified. Because trauma has usually been thought of as a single, definable, unusual, and horrific event, racial identity theories have not typically framed the process as a response to trauma (Root, in press). However, most models discuss a definable incident that impacts an individual, shattering assumptions about the way race operates in the world and in relationship to themselves. Trauma fragments the self and can disconnect an individual from their community and at its extreme, humanity.

Healing, following trauma, necessitates an integration of reorganized meaning and connection to others in mind, body, and spirit (Root, 1992b).

In reviewing racial identity theories, there is a distinct possibility that these theories are capturing and describing a race-specific response to the accumulation of trauma (Root, in press). One option is to move the conceptualization of trauma beyond the individual to a larger systemic framework rooted in the sociopolitical system (Root, 1992a). In order to do this, we must redefine what constitutes the nature of trauma that changes schemata by which we organize the meaning of events and interactions.

Three types of traumatic experiences suggest the severity with which racial construction and racism injure individuals and communities (Root, 1992b). *Direct trauma* includes rape, war experiences, kidnapping, dislocation, and internment. In addition to direct traumas, two other traumas are relevant to the lives of persons who occupy secondary statuses: *indirect trauma* and *insidious trauma*. *Indirect trauma* reflects the vicarious impact of observing or hearing about another person's experience (e.g., hate crimes, someone else's torture, and rape). *Insidious trauma* tends to be cumulative and its effects are often directed toward a devalued group of people or an individual based on their group membership (e.g., race, gender, and sexual orientation). Although not necessarily including physical violence, insidious trauma poses a distinct threat to psychological safety, security, and survival through various forms of debasement and disenfranchisement. All three types of trauma may be transgenerationally transmitted as unresolved trauma, particularly when remnants of conditions or actions that fueled the original trauma still exist, serving as cues for cognitive or affective flashback experiences. However, through time, the transformation of symptoms may no longer be recognizably attached to the original traumas.

Furthermore, Root (1992b) suggested that the meaning of trauma is mediated by "(1) the *perceived intent* of the source of the trauma (for example, malicious or accidental); and (2) the *interpersonal context* within which the trauma is experienced (for example, whether the experience occurred in isolation or with companion victims)" (p. 242). These distinctions are important because recipients of accidental traumas are usually not blamed for their misfortunes, whereas recipients of malicious ones are often blamed. Perloff (1983) suggested that belief in an individual's *unique vulnerability* is a defensive position taken by others to disavow the possibility that these irrational events could happen to them.

Developmental age is also significant in how intent is experienced. The preencounter stage may reflect an individual's organization of meaning by a *just world hypothesis*—you get what you deserve—as described by Lerner (1980). To operate outside of this belief system requires more energy and vigilance as well as belief and acceptance of the malevolence of human beings. Interestingly, the event that precipitates an encounter and eventually leads one to immersion in one's racial group suggests a shattering of cognitive assumptions about how the world works (Atkinson, Morten, & Sue, 1979; Cross, 1991).

When the trauma is experienced in isolation, this further contributes to a sense of unique vulnerability. Immersion stages in racial identity theories point out the value of companionship in reviewing experience and making meaning out of experience in community. Furthermore, in this stage, the individual manifests many of the characteristics symptomatic to trauma (Root, 1992b). Root (1992b) notes:

> Trauma permanently changes a person. In contrast to a stressful experience, which challenges an individual's capacity to cope, trauma destroys multiple dimensions of security and exceeds the limits of human capacity to process and integrate horrible experiences into a coherent perception of self and self-in-relationship to others and the world. The disorganization created by this upheaval motivates the individual to attempt to find meaning in the experience so that she or he can reorganize the experience and integrate it into her or his perceptions of self, and self in relationship to others and the world. (p. 260)

Emotional schemas for coping are further influenced by the complexity of thinking and language we have for issues. Two topics that our country has connected, but about which we cannot comfortably converse, are race and sex (Collins, 1991; hooks, 1984; McClintock, 1995; Stoler, 1995; Young, 1995). Both topics are often deemed inappropriate for "mixed" company. The morality of this process is complex.

The U.S. Constitution provides a template of fairness as a standard for moral development in this country. However, fairness has not been equally applied in the lives of persons with secondary status, women, people of color, and sexual minorities (e.g., gay, lesbian, or sexual transgendered; Stoltenberg, 1989). Thus, like the U.S. Constitution, many individuals may possess moral codes infused with much integrity, but exempt their discriminatory attitudes and behaviors from their moral code due to their cognitive and emotional development as well as social identity.

All three of these areas of our development—cognitive, moral, and emotional—may become stifled because of race education in this country. For example, White parents advocating for multicultural celebration who place their children in school environments that are racially and ethnically diverse find themselves caught in exposing the following dilemma: It is a great opportunity for their children to have friends from various backgrounds. Dating interracially may be acceptable, but proposals of marriage hit some cognitive and emotional limitations, which place these parents in a bind.

COGNITIVE PROCESSES ACROSS THE LIFE SPAN

I suggest that different cognitive processes across the life span guide the way in which we assimilate and process information. There are three processes: Exposure/Absorption, Competition/Stratification, and Reflective Appraisal. Within each of these three processes, the processes of constructive and destructive differentiation may occur, which shape the meaning of differences. These two concepts provide a framework for understanding how different organizing schema develop around similar material, resulting in different conclusions.

Constructive Differentiation

Fearlessness of differences creates tolerance for ambiguity. Consequently, differences are neither immediately stratified nor avoided out of anxiety, and the individual has a better chance for acquiring a greater context within which to understand difference—and even to find oneself in part of the difference. If she or he is able to suspend stereotyping or to refrain from rigidly applying conceptual frameworks that do not fit the situation, the person who is *other*—different from oneself—may be constructed side by side with self rather than in opposition or competition. Such a construction allows for connection while recognizing differences.

Destructive Differentiation

Ironically, one of the pivotal songs of the film, *South Pacific* (Rogers & Hammerstein, 1958), set during World War II, captures the cognitive process that orients us to understanding race in this country. Sung by a White officer, Lt. Cable grapples with his bigoted attitude toward marrying the Polynesian woman with whom he had a love affair in the South Pacific,

you've got to be taught
before it's too late
before you are six, or seven, or eight
to hate all the people your relatives hate

These few lines from the song capture the brainwashing that almost guarantees that the other will be interpreted as threatening. Indeed, studies have shown that by 7 and 8 years old, children have internalized the stratified racial system and overgeneralized the meaning of physical differences (cf. Jacobs, 1992; Johnson, 1992). Destructive differentiation employs reductionistic strategies that prevent contextualized understanding of difference. Racial epithets, flung between children, operationalize this process, often before the children cognitively understand the words they are saying. They understand, however, the emotional valence of the intended words. With a few words, an overtly hostile act of differentiation connotes the intent to hurt and to depict the other as inferior. The identity of the instigator is fragilely defined through opposition and superficial understanding of difference from the other. Subsequently, a convoluted process of rationalization becomes necessary to hold onto this interpretation of difference and a moral stand of rightness. Because all three systems—cognitive, emotional, and moral—become entwined in this process, it is difficult to extricate oneself from the beliefs and attitudes that support a superior definition of self (Allport, 1954). Thus, negative differentiation results in self-definition by what one is not and is dependent on maintaining distance from the other. For example, the literature on White identity development (Helms, 1990) suggests that many White people do not think about what it means to be White and have not consciously and constructively defined self as a White person. This state in part comes about through the usurped privilege of skin color, but also by keeping distance so that one is not confronted daily with difference. Unfortunately, destructive differentiation leaves little room for exploration on the very dimensions one might use to expand one's worldview.

The contemporary multiple allegiances and affiliations of multiracial people have been distorted through a process of negative differentiation (Root, 1996). Ironically, Freire (1970) and others noted that political consciousness pertaining to racial and ethnic identity is a response to negative differentiation in which being the *other* has simultaneous negative meaning and invisibility. Historically, racially mixed people have been negatively constructed through a mythological pseudoscience (Provine, 1973; Young, 1995), religion, and law (*Lovings v. Virginia,* 1967). These people have been defined as biological aberrations that should eventually be infertile to justify miscegenation statutes (cf. Young, 1995) and are infantilized in terms of morality or cognitive capacity, as in the stereotype of the tragic mulatto.

I propose that three processes guide the way in which we assimilate and process information: Exposure/Absorption, Competition/Stratification, and Reflective Appraisal. These processes are differentially salient across the life span. However, I am not suggesting that they are sequential; they may all exist at any point in the life span once we have the capacity for thinking and expressing ourselves coherently in words. Each of these processes is discussed.

Exposure/Absorption

Although the process of acquiring new information may be passive or active, neither process is superior to the other. Often passive, the individual takes the world in by observing and noting differences without initially conferring a value judgment. This process is subsequently impacted by accepting others' interpretations of the meanings of differences and organizing information into existing or new schemas. This process is active when people seek out information or experience purely for stimulation or curiosity. This process becomes interactive with input from others who help to differentiate and place meaning on differences. This differentiation can take a constructive or destructive path.

Competition/Stratification

Formal schooling in this country rewards competitiveness. Furthermore, most educational systems orient students to stratify the meaning of differences. In patriarchally driven cultures, competition must result in stratification—a winner and a loser—whether in the academic setting, social interactions, work settings, or even intimate relationships. This sparring, often gender and culturally prescribed at its simplest, stratifies according to right and wrong. From a moral development perspective, right and wrong, as a way of evaluating differences, is a stage of thinking achieved in preadolescence; many adults do not transcend this stage. In the least complex version of this schema, right is positioned with the individual with more ascribed social status. One who differs with him or her is wrong (Allport, 1954). Thus, the ability to grasp and assign valence and order to one's experiences and observations is a central organizing theme in this process. With recognition and even acceptance perceived to be at stake, combined with the individualistic orientation this country rewards, competition can take on meanings by which a person evaluates their self-worth and the worth of others. *Self-in-relation theory* is applicable to this process, by which the individual depends on the status of another to determine the individual's value.

Although there is nothing inherently wrong with making judgments that someone's behavior or skill set is superior or inferior to someone else's, it becomes a problem in two situations. First, it is problematic when a quick decision is made in the absence of contextual background for situating an individual. Second, this instantaneous judgment often leads to erroneous overgeneralization of a possible situational characteristic or behavior of the individual or group.

In the process of competition, if one retains an open mind to new information and does not extend one's conclusions beyond the data, the process of differentiation may embody a constructive process. In contrast, competitions that lead to positioning of the self in the most favorable light by disassociating with the object of their competition—the other—are destructive. This dehumanizing process allows individuals to justify and commit atrocities against other individuals (Root, 1992b). Dysfunctional conflict resolution skills typically employ competitive strategies that determine superiority or inferiority of individuals in generic ways. Such competition requires the conclusion that someone is inferior and the other superior.

Reflective Appraisal

This process reflects on the self in relationship to its connectedness with other people. It promotes questions about priorities in life, utilizes hindsight, and attempts to resolve regrets and mistakes. Compassion exists for persons different from oneself. Ability to admit wrongdoing and mistakes suggests a constructive use of the Competition/Stratification process. Connections are sought in the face of differences. There is necessarily a renewed openness to new information and a willingness to suspend quick appraisals or judgments. This process often includes a self-identified spiritual component. In contrast to the process captured by Exposure/Absorption, one already has organizing schemata, hindsight, and a morality to guide behaviors and evaluation of actions—past, present, and future. Although this process is derived from a process reported in later stages of life, the way in which I describe it allows for young children to have the capacity to reflect on their actions and use these reflections for making ethical decisions.

Because this process necessarily slows down the evaluation process, enough time may be allowed for contextualizing others' responses, which may lead to constructive differentiation. Without resolution of fears and anxieties about difference, one's ability to open one's mind to information that conflicts with past information is still limited.

AN ECOLOGICAL MODEL OF RACIAL IDENTITY DEVELOPMENT

In my original proposal on biracial identity (Root, 1990), I suggested that there were at least four possible outcomes to identity. The first was the *acceptance of the ascribed identity*. This meant that rules of hypodescent would be applied. However, one's identity may be constructed differently in different parts of the country at this point in time. The second possibility was to *identify with both racial groups*. This option included responses that could be coded as two racial labels ("I'm White and Asian") or a mixed label ("I'm Creole; I'm biracial," or simply, "I'm mixed"). This strategy requires that the individual have coping mechanisms in place to be able to defend the core of this racial identity in light of the general rules of hypodescent. The third option resembles that of the first option: *identification with a single racial group*. This option utilizes an active strategy, however. This is a difficult strategy to maintain in parts of the country that have a history that precludes an understanding of such an identity. Again, the biracial person needs to have coping strategies for the discrimination or authenticity tests one might experience. The last option was *identification as a new group*. This individual may be marginal to all groups of their heritage, but not feel marginalized because their referent group is biracial or multiracial people.

Thus, they move in and out of groups with some resilience despite their racial identity being misunderstood.

I also suggested that identity resembles a spiraling and circular process (akin to Parham's cycling process, 1989) by which one resolves tensions and accomplishes identity. The systemic forces driving one toward resolution are embedded in political, social, and familial environments. Thus, identity is a political process that cannot be separated fully from the nation's sociopolitical history of race (Daniel, 1992; Fernandez, 1992; Nash, 1995; Spickard, 1992; Wilson, 1992) and one's personal history around other critical core components of identity such as gender, ethnicity, and class (Espin & Gawelek, 1992). In our attempt to grasp a fuller understanding of identity, it may ultimately be important to consider how different secondary statuses in identity interact with the process of coming to know and declare who we are in this world privately and publicly. For example, how does being a woman affect the racial identity process or how does being biracial affect one's sense of self as a woman? What if she is poor versus well-to-do? How does being lesbian or gay interact with racial identity development or race as an organizing factor (Allman, 1996; Kich, 1996)? Both Miller (1992) and Stephan (1991) have previously offered ecological frameworks for understanding multiracial identity. Many possible outcomes of racial identity can be anticipated—and perhaps even more positions as the constructions of race, gender, and sexuality are contemporarily questioned. Increasingly, scholars are pointing out how race and gender are coconstructed (Zack, 1997) as statuses that are defined by dominant–subordinate dynamics.

The proposed model breaks away from bipolar racial frameworks (Black–White), but encompasses this experience. It places individuals in historical, geographical, class, gender, and generational contexts. Environments are discerned as learning places for corroboration and challenges to one's identity. This is particularly important for racially ambiguous people whose identity may be negotiated or known in their community. What happens when a 24-year-old Japanese African American man, who asserts himself as such and has lived all his life in a racially diverse city such as San Francisco, California moves to a less racially diverse place such as Raleigh, North Carolina? How is racial identity reformulated by the multiracial and multiethnic person born and raised in Honolulu, Hawaii (where this status has a positive connection) who moves to the mainland to attend a West coast university where there are many Asian Americans? In both experiences, geographical history is going to have a tremendous impact on the rules of race and their new communities' perceptions of who they are, perhaps how they should act, and even who they should befriend.

All boxes in the model (see Fig. 4.1) may be construed as lenses through which experiences are filtered. Interpreted through a symbolic interactionist perspective, these lenses are dynamic in relationship to one another, shifting from prominent foreground to the most recessive background filter. The lenses layer on one another, shifting in relationship to one another through nuanced changes in interpersonal interactions, changes in age, and changes in environment. These lenses recognize the influences of the individual, family, and community through both private and shared realities. Because these factors exist dynamically in experiential time rather than only in linear clock and calendar time, historical influence and experience can transcend generations, particularly when unresolved trauma is involved as is the case with much of our secondary statuses (e.g., race, gender, and sexual orientation; Root, 1992b). Each of the three core grouped lenses are discussed: *Inherited Influences, Traits,* and *Social Contexts With Community.* Within each grouping, the lenses dynamically relate to one another, changing at different times and in different contexts within the context of gender, class, and regional history of race relations.

Inherited Influences

The inherited influences include both biological and environmental inheritance. Biological inheritance, such as sexual orientation (Allman, 1996; Kich, 1996) and phenotype (Arce, Murguia, & Frisbie, 1987; Russell, Wilson, & Hall, 1992), significantly influence one's reception among family, community, and strangers. Other inherited influences that have been associated with ethnic or racial identity (Phinney & Rotheram, 1987) are languages spoken in the home; parent's ethnic; racial; and national identity; nativity; given names and nicknames; and the presence or absence of influence from extended family members for reflection of self, acceptance, and socialization (Johnson, 1992; Miller, 1992; Root, 1990). Home values may be more or less ethnically specific.

Using the variables from this group of lenses in the broader framework of history and gender, consider the different experience and social location the following two young people will have encountered by 15 years old. Consider their social class location as similarly middle class. The differences in their experiences will influence the saliency of different lenses in different situations. Angie was born in Seoul, Korea in 1954. Her mother is Korean and her father is a third generation White American who is disconnected from his ethnic roots. She and her mother joined her father in San Francisco, California in 1959. Angie started school shortly after her arrival in the United States without speaking English, although she was fluent by the end of the school year. Her parents subsequently had three more children. Her mother's English was not very proficient; she spoke to her children primarily in Korean mixed with some English. Although initially proficient in Korean, Angie gradually became less so. By the time she was a teenager, she spoke to her mother almost exclusively in English with some Korean occasionally mixed in. In the home, her mother cooked Korean food, and gradually learned to cook American food with a Korean flair. By 8 years old, Angie was making her own lunches to take to school because she dreaded lunch time with her schoolmates who teased her about the contents of the lunch packed by her mother. In her school, people knew she had a Korean mother, but had no framework for understanding what being Korean meant. Her mother always identified herself as Korean, never Korean American. Angie seldom saw her American grandparents because they disapproved of the marriage. Her father's siblings lived across the country. She has only met them twice. Phenotypically, Angie is often mistaken for Chicana when in Los Angeles.

Contrast Angie's story with that of Michael's. Michael was born in 1980 in Oakland, California to a Chinese American mother and African American father, both fourth generation. Michael's family has raised him to appreciate both sides of his ethnic heritage. Icons of African American culture reside right next to a family heirloom of Chinese tapestry. Michael, at 15 years old, has never been asked what country he is from, and people are often disbelieving when he says he is Chinese and African American, although he frequently notices strangers looking at him. He is used to his teacher's surprise on the first day of school when the classroom roster of names lists him with a Chinese middle name. Thus, his body is more saliently marked Black by this country's rules of racial classification, although his name is ethnically marked with his Chinese heritage, too. He is not alone in his multiracial heritage. Although an only child, five of his many friends are of racially mixed heritages. Recently, he has expressed an interest to his mother that he would like to learn Cantonese and Swahili.

These two young people, born in different times with vastly different inherited influences, will go through this world differently. Angie was born at a time when multiracial Asians were almost always the product of international marriages and associated with war; Michael was born at a time when multiracial Asians were primarily the result of two American parents. The perception of Asians has also changed from Orientals to Asians. Much meaning accompanies this change. Angie is likely to encounter more confusion about nationality, ethnicity, and race than Michael. Nationality is not an issue in Michael's home either by parental nativity, language, or parental identity. That Korean is spoken in Angie's home suggests the likely transmission of Korean values through Angie's mother. In contrast, Michael comes from an all-American family where he possibly seeks more cultural connectedness through the exploration of languages, neither of which his parents speak. The racial ambiguity of Angie's phenotype may exotify her in some people's eyes as women's racial ambiguity is often imbued with sexual meaning (Root, 1994). That Michael's body is visibly identified by others as Black, perceptions of him as a Black male will, at times, be made into an obstacle or be a source of others' justification for worry or paranoia. The stereotypes teachers hold about race will impact these children to greater or lesser degrees depending on their sensitivity, coping skills, and social support at home and in the community. More likely than not, the stereotypes will derive from seeing these children in monoracial terms, applying rules of hypodescent, and seeing them as only children of color. If they hold the prevailing perception of mixed heritage children, they may assume the children are confused, possibly unwanted, or alternately very special. Any of these assumptions place pressure on children to have a repertoire of coping skills that is extensive.

Traits

Of course, inherited influences also interact with traits. Whereas there may be some biological base to temperament and genetic influence on talents, and parents will attest to this, all four of the traits listed—temperament, social skills, talents, and coping skills—are subject to environmental influence and learning. Together, this grouping of traits is often construed as personality. Individual responses and personalities may be situation specific. In a different example, and in an attempt to control for some variance due to heritability, consider the following two siblings from racially mixed backgrounds.

At 23 years old, Teresa is 3 years older than Rod. Born to a Mexican American mother in Albuquerque, New Mexico, and a White father with some remote Native American ancestry, these two siblings often remark how similar yet how different they are. Teresa is very quiet, although articulate. She prefers to be in the background. She is very organized and holds a job that recognizes her organizational skills and level of responsibility. With an exceptionally beautiful voice, she solos with the church choir. When she sings, people remark that she's a different person. She jokes about being obsessive as she may stress over big decisions and mull over a problem or situation from many different angles. Although she may call on friends for help, she tends to try to first sort things out herself.

In contrast, Rod is the life of the party and a gregarious person; he observes that he does not particularly like being alone. Also very organized and responsible, he is different in that he reaches decisions quickly, but not so quickly that he appears impulsive. He seems to be fairly unaffected by stress. His motto is, "Make a decision and learn from it." Although admittedly tone deaf, he insists on singing duets with Teresa at family gatherings. He is particularly insightful as to how relationships among and between people work.

Both Teresa and Rod remember that they have had vestiges of these similarities and differences as far back as they can remember. Teresa was a loner; Rod was always with friends. Teresa was more pensive; Rod more spontaneous. One must also consider their sex-role socialization in the family. Rod has been rewarded for his outgoingness; this behavior has been equated with maleness on both sides of their family. On their maternal side, although the women are strong-willed and outgoing, they have been socialized to let the men take the center stage. On their paternal side, where the women and men are quiet, Teresa is reinforced for being ladylike. However, given that people give her feedback and she concurs that she is a different person when she sings, it remains a question as to how much is learned behaviorally and how much is biologically versus environmentally determined disposition for brother and sister.

Social Interactions With the Community

Last, all this interaction takes place in social contexts. From pilot interviews, five contexts seem to encompass most of our social interactions: home, school and/or work, community groups, socializing with friends, and outside your community. All of these environments provide reflections of how we are perceived. Insider and outsider rules are generated within these different environments. The degree to which they converge or are discrepant has bearing on identity. The degree to which one is experienced congruently with how one experiences oneself also influences the tensions that drive the identity resolution process (Root, 1990, 1994). With the exception of communities other than one's own, a process of negotiation—whether overt or covert—occurs over time so that individuals know what they can expect of others and how they are likely to be perceived. However, for a multiracial person, an excursion into a community that is unfamiliar or quite discrepant from one's own may result in reflections that are discordant with one's own sense of self. For example, children of multiracial heritage who grow up in communities where they have other multiracial cohorts have reflections of their phenotype. In a study that involved preteen public school children in Seattle, Washington, 20% of the African American heritage children and 20% of the Asian American heritage children came from interracial families (Cauce et al., 1992). They are exposed on a daily basis to other children and families with similar racial backgrounds. If a child from this community moves to a small midwest community, the regional history of race relations and the racial demographics may make them the other or make it difficult for them to identify as multiracial children. It is not uncommon for multiracial young adults who identify racially as people of color to be assailed by the loss of being recognized by others as belonging. This social location was possibly prenegotiated by parents, family members, elders, siblings, and friends. Subsequently, more than ever, young adults may become acutely aware that the company they keep may be used as a racial marker for interpretation of their phenotype or judging their racial authenticity (Twine, 1996).

Social interactions in the community and interaction with racial and ethnic identity also occur within the framework of generations. The construction of race is dynamic over time and in different communities.

This ecological model posits that the three groups of lenses, Inherited Influences, Traits and Social Contexts exist within the experience, socialization, and meaning of gender, regional history of race and ethnic relations, and class. Furthermore, all of these lenses interact with one another and influence racial and ethnic identity. For example, Theo, a third grader in an inner-city Missouri public elementary school, is named after his African American father. With brown curly hair, he has his mother's hazel eyes, set above his father's cheekbones, on a canvas of deep golden brown. His mother, White of Jewish ancestry, is the main caregiver, but Theo is picked up by his paternal grandmother everyday after school and stays with her for 3 hours until one of his parents can pick him up. In this part of the country, where hypodescent reigns, Theo is Black. His paternal side of the family imbues him with pride in his ethnic identity as an African American and emphasizes that he is their "little man."

Jewish tradition transmits this ethnic identity through his mother. His mother, although now a thousand miles from her nearest relative, is an active member of the synagogue and is teaching Theo to understand the meaning of the Jewish holy days. Theo is being brought up to be a Black man with an African American and Jewish sense of ethnic pride and identity. However, because almost all of these lenses assume some malleability with experience over time, it is possible that racial identity or ethnic identity can change over a lifetime and for different reasons (Root, 1990).

We have observed such changes on a large scale with the changes in self-identification, for example, from Oriental to Asian American or Negro to Black or African American. At this time, we are witnessing a similar change with multiracial persons who wish to have options to racially identify as mixed without necessarily specifying racial labels or to specifically identity with all the racial categories that apply. Consider the experience of Maria, 17 years old. Maria was born in Los Angeles to parents who are both of mixed heritages, a Chicana mother and Jamaican father. Her mother's ethnic identity is Chicana and her racial identity is White. Her father's racial heritage is African, Asian (Chinese), and White (Dutch). Living in the United States for the last 25 years, he has adopted a racial identity as Black, but ethnically his life is informed by a Jamaican tradition, although he acknowledges he was also much more ethnically African American on a daily basis due to the access to this culture and its traditions. Both parents wanted Maria to have appreciation for all her ethnic heritage. She has been raised to think of herself as racially mixed for several generations, not just Black and White. When she was in grade school, she told people she was Jamaican Chinese. However, by the beginning of high school in Los Angeles, Maria continued to identity herself as racially mixed, but began to assert an African American ethnic identity. Three years later, at 17 years old, she was taking Spanish and starting to explore a Chicano ethnic and political identity, but held onto an African American identity. It is left to be seen how her identity might continue to transform itself. Will she possibly explore her Jamaican roots as a source of ethnic pride? Will she continue to identity herself as mixed racially? Will she eventually say she is Black? Given the region of the country in which she lives, where other racially mixed people are prominent, she has many options.

Racial identification does not necessarily convey ethnic group member-ship (Hall, 1980, 1992; Stephan, 1992; Thornton, 1996). Both racial and ethnic identity interact with each other and with the other lenses. For ex-ample, a multiracial person of African, Filipino, and European heritage may identify with all of these heritages in a gathering of multiracial people, while at the same gathering being aware that the mixture, at times, takes background to the phenomenological experience generated by social inter-actions and historical depictions of a multiracial person. This same person may identify as African American in some social situations because that is what is salient to them in that moment; his or her Filipino and European heritage, although present, is a background lens. At a family gathering with predominantly Filipino family members, he or she may join through the shared experiences of this ethnic background. There will still be mo-ments when this person may acutely feel like an other. The racial and eth-nic composition of the school will make a difference in how a child identifies as well as the availability of options. If they are in a school in which there is a substantial portion of mixed children who identify as mixed, this racial identity becomes a possible option even in the face of op-position by others. If there are few other mixed children, or the only mixed children are Asian, White, or White–Black, this child may be identified by teachers as only Black. Obviously, discussions at home will also influence this child's racial and ethnic identity.

Being an other or even feeling marginal does not necessarily carry the negative connotations it has had in past literature (Stonequist, 1964). Weisman (1996) suggested that one can take the meaning of other and find connection, for there are many moments in our lives that everyone can be an other. To be marginal may also be an advantage in terms of how race is processed (Anzaldúa, 1990). This otherness allows a detachment from maintaining the racial system; this position also allows for constructive differentiation.

IMPLICATIONS FOR SCHOOL PRACTICES

Despite a movement to be more culturally sensitive in the classroom, some of the difficulty teachers may face is that culture serves as a euphemism for race. As such, multiculturalism in the classroom is still framed within a monoracial paradigm (Root, 1997a; Wardle, 1996). The different meanings among culture, ethnicity, nationality, and race are not well-understood by the nation; teachers, counselors, and school psychologists may not under-stand these concepts much better than the average person. To move educa-tional institutions to a broader understanding of race and ethnicity, Glass and Wallace (1996) suggested that, besides self-education, persons in the educational system may need to challenge institutions and their ideology. On a personal level, I suggest that all personnel responsible for preparing children for life in this world need to reconsider their paradigms of race and the rules that they implicitly or explicitly use to counsel or teach children. Listening and communicating will be imperative.

Consider what is set in motion when children register for school. The initial forms, in which the race or ethnicity of the child is listed, usually allow for only one designation. Those school districts that have made changes on these forms and allow for more than one designation demonstrate a willingness to consider that the child's experience may be more complex than has traditionally been recognized for children of mixed heritages. Having a registration form that allows a parent to accurately identify a child is a step toward a different racial dialogue on a microlevel and macrolevel. Something as minor as this form is a reminder to some teachers to try to think differently about race and ethnicity. Such a reminder may possibly set the stage for increased openness to in-service training on racial and identity development, even though some teachers may have had material on identity included in a class during their teacher preparation coursework.

In contrast to only a decade ago, there are resources and written materials for families and children that teachers can access (Wardle, 1996). Community support groups, as well as the umbrella organization—the Association for Multiethnic Americans—can be helpful resources (Brown and Douglass, 1996). Brown and Douglass (1996) provided information on forming multiracial family support groups. They and Wardle (1996) suggested ways in which to access literature.

School counselors and psychologists need to be aware of how the very tasks of childhood and adolescence for all children may interact with the ways in which people construct identity. Early interventions at the grade-school level into irrational constructions of race may have lifelong effects. Classroom discussions, with guidelines for discussing emotional issues, are suggested. Granted, the world outside of a child's family may not recognize race mixture and the contemporary meaning and challenge to our delusional racial system that mixed race children and their families pose. However, educators and counselors can instill some early experiences that may allow children to minimize some of the destructive differentiation that occurs around race and other differences surrounding core aspects of identity. For example, to celebrate ethnic groups, the teacher can use famous historical figures or current celebrities to teach children why people categorize people by race. For example, why are Frederick Douglass, Sojourner Truth, W. E. B. DuBois, and Langston Hughes only identified as Black? In literature courses, the ethnic and racial identity experiences of authors inform many of their works. Students can discuss how Ruth Ann Lum McGinn's novels on Chinese in America or Toni Morrison's work dealing with African American culture are informed by these issues. Furthermore, encouraging children to continue to engage in Absorption/Exposure, to guide them in constructive competitive strategies, and to provide a history of race relations may allow for more ethnical and responsible thinking and action in their reflective appraisals. Educators and counselors can make a difference in facilitating young people's tolerance and acceptance of ambiguity and difference.

Root (1997a) offered suggestions to educators. There are many individual interventions possible. For example, one can foster social and physical competencies that bolster a child's sense of self; help them to talk about the hurts they experience and anticipate the possible authenticity tests that they may encounter; provide the child with an understanding of the racism directed at them and the defenses to personally deal with personal assaults. Root (1998) provides an inventory of racial experiences that teachers can use for discussion to help children understand the racial brainwashing they may have received. In the classroom, the teacher can provide much needed educational information: cite multiracial role models; teach that race mixing is a natural consequence of people being friends; facilitate discussions about race and racial boundaries; and help students understand that race is a social and political construction. When civil rights are discussed in junior high or high school, teachers can facilitate discussions about how all the major civil rights legislation allowed people of different racial and ethnic backgrounds to have a chance for meaningful interactions with one another: the 1954 Brown v. the Board of Education decision; the Civil Rights Act of 1964; the Voting Rights Act of 1965; and the Fair Housing Laws of 1968. These meaningful interactions have led to some change, including many more interracial and interethnic relationships and many more children of mixed racial and mixed ethnic heritages. Help students to understand who the current racial system serves. Many resources exist to support educators and counselors. Community conferences, articles, support groups, and magazines for interracial living exist. (Root, 1996, provided a *Bill of Rights* that has been used to encourage and facilitate community and classroom discussion.)

Root (1994) suggested issues that may arise in counseling the mixed race person that may be subtle. Awareness of issues of power, belongingness, uniqueness, attractiveness, and worth are all core issues for all human beings. The persons who interact with children during the day have tremendous impact in all these areas.

REFERENCES

Allman, K. M. (1996). (Un)Natural boundaries: Mixed Race, gender, and sexuality. In M. P. P. Root (Ed.), *The multiracial experience: Racial borders as the new frontier* (pp. 277–290). Thousand Oaks, CA: Sage.

Allport, G. (1954). *The nature of prejudice.* New York: Addison-Wesley.

Anzaldúa, G. (1990). En rapport, in opposition: Cobrando cuentas a las nuestras. In G. Anzaldúa (Ed.), *Making face, making soul, haciendo caras: Creative and critical perspectives by feminist of color* (pp. 142–148). San Francisco: Aunt Lute Foundation.

Arce, C. H., Murguia, E., & Frisbie, W. P. (1987). Phenotype and the life chances among Chicanos. *Hispanic Journal of Behavioral Sciences, 9*(1), 19–32.

Atkinson, D. R., Morten, G., & Sue, D. W. (Eds.). (1979). *Counseling American minorities: A cross-cultural perspective.* Dubuque, IA: Brown.

Brown, N. G., & Douglass, R. E. (1996). Making the invisible visible: The growth of community network organizations. In M. P. P. Root (Ed.), *The multiracial experience: Racial borders as the new frontier* (pp. 323–340). Thousand Oaks, CA: Sage.

Cauce, A. M., Hiraga, Y., Mason, C., Aguilar, T., Ordonez, N., & Gonzales, N. (1992). Between a rock and a hard place: Social adjustment of biracial youth. In M. P. P. Root (Ed.), *Racially mixed people in America* (pp. 207–222). Thousand Oaks, CA: Sage.

Collins, P. H. (1991). *Black feminist thought: Knowledge, consciouness, and the politics of empowerment.* Boston: Routledge & Kegan Paul.

Cross, W. E., Jr. (1991). *Shades of Black: Diversity in African-American identity.* Philadelphia: Temple University Press.

Cross, W. E., Jr., & Fhagen-Smith, P. (1996). Nigrescence and ego identity development: Accounting for differential Black identity patterns. In P. B. Peterson, J. G. Draguns, W. J. Lonner, & J. E. Trimble (Eds.), *Counseling across cultures* (4th ed., pp. 108–123). Thousand Oaks, CA: Sage.

Daniel, G. R. (1992). Passers and pluralists: Subverting the racial divide. In M. P. P. Root (Ed.), *Racially mixed people in America* (pp. 91–107). Thousand Oaks, CA: Sage.

Erikson, E. (1968). *Identity: Youth and crisis.* New York: Norton.

Espin, O. M., & Gawelek, M. A. (1992). Women's diversity: Ethnicity, race, class, and gender in theories of feminist psychology. In. L. S. Brown & M. Ballou (Eds.), *Personality and psychopathology: Feminist reappraisals* (pp. 88–110). New York: Guilford.

Fernandez, C. A. (1992). La raza and the melting pot: A comparative look at multiethnicity. In M. P. P. Root (Ed.), *Racially mixed people in America* (pp. 126–143). Thousand Oaks, Ca: Sage.

Freire, P. (1970). *Pedagogy of the oppressed.* New York: Seabury Press.

Glass, R. D., & Wallace, K. R. (1996). Challenging race and racism: A framework for educators. In M. P. P. Root (Ed.), *The multiracial experience: Racial borders as the new frontier* (pp. 341–358). Thousand Oaks, CA: Sage.

Hall, C. C. I. (1980). *The ethnic identity of racially mixed people: A study of Black–Japanese.* Unpublished doctoral dissertation, University of California, Los Angeles.

Hall, C. C. I. (1992). Please choose one: Ethnic identity choices for biracial individuals. In M. P. P. Root (Ed.), *Racially mixed people in America* (pp. 250–264). Thousand Oaks, CA: Sage.

Helms, J. E. (Ed.). (1990). *Black and White racial identity: Theory, research, and practice.* New York: Greenwood.

hooks, b. (1984). *Feminist theory: From margins to center.* Boston: South End Press.

Jacobs, J. (1992). Identity development in biracial children. In M. P. P. Root (Ed.), *Racially mixed people in America* (pp. 190–206). Thousand Oaks, CA: Sage.

Johnson, D. J. (1992). Developmental pathways: Towards an ecological theoretical formulation of race identity in Black–White biracial children. In M. P. P. Root (Ed.), *Racially mixed people in America* (pp. 37–49). Thousand Oaks, CA: Sage.

Kich, G. K. (1996). In the margins of sex and race difference, marginality, and flexibility. In M. P. P. Root (Ed.), *The multiracial experience: Racial borders as the new frontier* (pp. 263–276). Thousand Oaks, CA: Sage.

Lerner, M. J. (1980). *The belief in a just world.* New York: Plenum.

Lovings v. Virginia, 388 U.S. 1 (1967).

Mahler, M. S. (1963). Thoughts about development and individuation. In M. Mahler (Ed.), *The selected papers of Margaret S. Mahler: Infantile psychosis and early contributions.* New York: Aronson.

Markus, H. R., & Kitayama S. (1991). Culture and the self: Implications for cognition, emotion, and motivation. *Psychological Review, 98*(2), 224–253.

McClintock, A. (1995). *Imperial leather: Race, gender, and sexuality in the colonial conquest.* Boston: Routledge & Kegan Paul.

Miller, J. B. (1986). *Towards a new psychology of women.* Boston: Beacon Press.

Miller, R. L. (1992). The human ecology of multiracial identity. In M. P. P. Root (Ed.), *Racially mixed people in America* (pp. 24–36). Thousand Oaks, CA: Sage.

Nash, G. B. (1995). The hidden history of mestizo America. *The Journal of American History,* December, 941–962.

Ossana, S. M., Helms, J. E., & Leonard, M. M. (1992). Do "womanist" identity attitudes influence college women's self-esteem and perceptions of environmental bias? *Journal of Counseling & Development, 70*(3), 402–408.

Padilla, A. M. (Ed.). (1995). *Hispanic psychology: Critical issue in theory and research.* Thousand Oaks, CA: Sage.

Parham, T. A. (1989). Cycles of psychological nigrescence. *The Counseling Psychologist, 17*(2), 187–226.

Perloff, L. S. (1983). Perceptions of vulnerability to victimization. *Journal of Social Issues, 39,* 41–62.

Phinney, J. (1990). Ethnic identity in adolescents and adults: A review of research. *Psychological Bulletin, 108*(3), 499–514.

Phinney, J. S., & Rotheram, M. J. (1987). *Children's ethnic socialization: Pluralism and development.* Thousand Oaks, CA: Sage.

Provine, W. B. (1973). Geneticist and the biology of race. *Science, 182,* 790–796.

Rogers, R., & Hammerstein, O. (1958). *South pacific* [Film]. (Available from CBS/Fox Video, Farmington Hills, MI).

Root, M. P. P. (1990). Resolving "other" status: Identity development of biracial individuals. In L. S. Brown & M. P. P. Root (Eds.), *Diversity and complexity in feminist therapy* (pp. 185–206). New York: Harrington Park Press.

Root, M. P. P. (Ed.). (1992a). *Racially mixed people in America.* Thousand Oaks, CA: Sage.

Root, M. P. P. (1992b). Reconstructing the impact of trauma on personality. In L. S. Brown & M. Ballou (Eds.), *Personality and psychopathology: Feminist reappraisals* (pp. 229–265). New York: Guilford.

Root, M. P. P. (1994). Mixed race women. In L. C. Diaz & B. Greene (Eds.), *Women of color and mental health: The healing tapestry* (pp. 455–478). New York: Guilford.

Root, M. P. P (1996). A bill of rights for racially mixed people. In M. P. P. Root (Ed.), *The multiracial experience: Racial borders as the new frontier* (pp. 3–14). Thousand Oaks, CA: Sage.

Root, M. P. P. (1997a). Biracial identity in school age children. In G. Bear, K. Minke, & A. Thomas (Eds.), *Children's needs II: Psychological perspectives* (pp. 751–759). Washington, DC: National Association of School Psychologists.

Root, M. P. P. (1997b). Contemporary mixed heritage Filipino Americans: Fighting colonized identities. In M. P. P. Root (Ed.), *Filipino Americans, transformation and identity* (pp. 80–94). Thousand Oaks, CA: Sage.

Root, M. P. P. (in press) Reconstructing race, rethinking ethnicity. In A. S. Bellack & M. Hersen (Eds.), *Comprehensive clinical psychology,* (pp. 141–160) London: Elsevier.

Russell, K., Wilson, M., & Hall, R. (1992). *The color complex: The politics of skin color among African Americans.* New York: Harcourt Brace.

Spickard, P. R. (1992). The illogic of American racial categories. In M. P. P. Root (Ed.), *Racially mixed people in American* (pp. 12–23). Thousand Oaks, CA: Sage.

Stephan, C. W. (1991). Ethnic identity among mixed-heritage people in Hawaii. *Symbolic Interaction, 14,* 261–277.

Stephan, C. W. (1992). Mixed-heritage individuals: Ethnic identity and trait characteristics. In M. P. P. Root (Ed.), *Racially mixed people in America* (pp. 50–63). Thousand Oaks, CA: Sage.

Stoler, A. L. (1995). *Race and the education of desire: Foucault's history of sexuality and the colonial order of things.* Durham, NC: Duke University Press.

Stonequist, E. V. (1964). The marginal man: A study in personality and culture conflict. In E. Burgess & D. J. Bogue (Eds.), *Contributions to urban sociology* (pp. 71–90). Chicago: University of Chicago Press.

Surrey, J. L. (1991). The self-in-relation: A theory of women's development. In J. V. Jordan, A. G. Kaplan, J. B. Miller, I. P. Stiver, & J. L. Surrey (Eds.), *Women's growth in connection: Writing from the stone center* (pp. 51–66). New York: Guilford.

Thornton, M. C. (1996). Hidden agendas, identity theories, and multiracial people. In M. P. P. Root (Ed.), *The multiracial experience: Racial borders as the new frontier* (pp. 101–120). Thousand Oaks, CA: Sage.

Twine, F. W. (1996). Heterosexual alliances: The romantic management of racial identity. In M. P. P. Root (Ed.), *The multiracial experience: Racial borders as the new frontier* (pp. 291–304). Thousand Oaks, CA: Sage.

Wardle, F. (1996). Multicultural education. In M. P. P. Root (Ed.), *The multiracial experience: Racial borders as the new frontier* (pp. 380–391). Thousand Oaks, CA: Sage.

Waters, M. S. (1990). *Ethnic options: Choosing identities in America.* Berkeley: University of California Press.

Weisman, J. R. (1996). An "other" way of life: The empowerment of alterity in the interracial individual. In M. P. P. Root (Ed.), *The multiracial experience: Racial borders as the new frontier* (pp. 152–164). Thousand Oaks, CA: Sage.

Wilson, T. P. (1992). Blood quantum: Native American mixed bloods. In M. P. P. Root (Ed.), *Racially mixed people in America* (pp. 108–125). Thousand Oaks, CA: Sage.

Young, R. (1995). *Colonial desire: Hybridity in theory, culture and race.* Boston: Routledge & Kegan Paul.

Zack, N. (Ed.). (1997). *Race/Sex: Their sameness, difference, and interplay.* Boston: Routledge & Kegan Paul.

5 Human Development and Ethnic Identity

Rosa Hernández Sheets
San Francisco State University

The purpose of this chapter is to conceptualize the construct of ethnic identity and begin the process of definition so that theoretical ideas from this area of study can be applied to school settings. The chapter is divided into four sections: a review of the literature in human development and ethnic identity; the development of an operational definition; the role of schooling in the formation and development of students' ethnic identity; and implications for school practices.

HUMAN DEVELOPMENT AND ETHNIC IDENTITY THEORY

In the United States, generally, four major human developmental theories—psychoanalytic (Erikson, 1950, 1968; Freud, 1940), behavioral (Skinner, 1957), humanistic (Maslow, 1968; Rogers, 1970), and cognitive (Bandura, 1977; Piaget, 1952)—guide and explain human development across the life span. The Eriksonian (1950, 1968) paradigm introduced the concepts of *life cycle, identity crisis,* and *identity* (Gleason, 1996; Turkle, 1987; Vander Zanden, 1995), which greatly influence how U.S. psychologists and educators view children's development (Branch, chap. 1, this volume; Gay, 1994; Greenfield & Cocking, 1994; Richardson & Silvestri, chap. 3, this volume; Sheets, 1997). This relatively new, monocultural perspective of development rooted in U.S. individualism suggests that the ways individuals resolve and cope with psychological crisis at particular stages in life influences the quality of life.

The constructs of ethnicity, ethnic groups, and ethnic identity differ conceptually when studied from different theoretical and disciplinary perspectives, such as phenomenology, sociology, anthropology, archaeology, education, and psychology. The conceputalization of these constructs is also influenced by factors such as, (1) the particular aspects being researched,(2) the area in the world where the research takes place, (3) the particular group under investigation, (4) the value orientation of the re-

91

searcher, and (5) the perceived sociopolitical, cultural position of the group under study (Jones, 1997; Sollors, 1996). Disagreement is further complicated by the fact that consistent definitions of terms, such as ethnicity, ethnic group, and ethnic identity, which affect research efforts, have not been established in the research literature. The lack of an operational definition is often reflected in language usage and methodological issues in the research on ethnic identity.

Language Usage

Two major areas of concern in language usage in ethnic identity research are language that blurs, or ignores, the conceptual boundaries that serve to establish distinct constructs and language that perpetuates feelings of superiority.

To some degree, examples of unclear language in the ethnic identity literature surfaces in almost every book, chapter, and journal article. Nonparallel language, generally without explanation, is used to describe participants and to establish conceptual frameworks. Frequently, Whites, excluded as an ethnic group in the theoretical framework, are included in the treatment, results, and discussion. Another example is the use of the word *American* to denote only individuals with U.S. citizenship. This practice interchanges continental, national, ethnic, and cultural identity. The inconsistent use of terminology in the literature may contribute to the confusion and lack of definition of the construct ethnic identity.

Language that perpetuates feelings of superiority are difficult to address because White superiority is typically viewed from two extremes: an irrational hatred that characterizes the behavior and attitudes of racial hate groups or a benevolent socially imposed privilege (McIntosh, 1989; Stanfield, 1985) that suggests that those endowed can address the problem by mere acknowledgment, awareness, and appreciation of their race and status. Instead, I believe that the use of a nice word, such as *privilege,* to describe racism can reinforce feelings of superiority and help construct personal and group identities based on the devaluation of others. When examined through other lenses, an attitude of privilege points to low levels of intellectual and emotional development (e.g., simplistic dualistic and linear thinking; Abell, in press; Root, chap. 4, this volume) and possible disorders, such as phobias, fears, and delusions (Hollins, personal conversation, May 8, 1996).

Methodological Issues in Research

The concept of *ethnicity* is narrower than the concept of *culture,* and although they are related, it is not a one-to-one relationship. Ethnic identity formation and development is influenced by membership in an ethnic group identified as a distinctive social group living under the shaping influence of a common culture. Therefore, knowledge of culture is critical to the study of ethnic identity. Research and scholarship, void of critical cultural dimensions, such as the sociopolitical and psychological context in which cultural groups operate, the behavioral patterns that help individuals maintain their ethnic identity as well as survive in hostile environments, and the attention to distinctive, particular worldviews found in various cultural groups is problematic (Branch, 1994, chap. 1, this volume; Hollins, 1997, chap. 10, this volume; Shade, Kelly, & Oberg, 1997). Perhaps overlooking the role that culture plays in ethnic identity development prompts scholars who focus on ethnic identity to rely on past theories of human development, to appropriate racial identity theories, and to describe and categorize dimensions of ethnic identity rather than examine the process of formation and development throughout the life span.

DEFINITION OF ETHNIC IDENTITY

Schermerhorn, cited in Sollors (1996), described an *ethnic group* as follows:

> A collectivity within a larger society having real or putative common ancestry, memories of a shared historical past, and a cultural focus on one of more symbolic elements defined as the epitome of their peoplehood. Examples of such symbolic element are: kinship patterns, physical contiguity (as in localism or sectionalism), religious affiliation, language or dialect forms, tribal affiliation, nationality, phenotypal features, or any combination of these. A necessary accompaniment is some consciousness of kind among members of the group. (Sollors, 1996, p. xii)

Jones (1997) defined *ethnic group* as "any group of people who set themselves apart and/or are set apart by others with whom they interact or co-exist on the basis of their perceptions of cultural differentiation and/or common descent" (p. 1). According to Jones, *ethnicity* includes

> all of those social and psychological phenomena associated with a culturally defined group identity as defined above. Ethnicity focuses on the ways in which social and cultural practices intersect with one another in the identification of, and interaction between ethnic groups (p. 1).

The formation and development of ethnic identity that takes place when an individual identifies and affiliates with a particular ethnic group is complex. This important personal and group identification has critical emotional, behavioral, and cognitive significance that affects all aspects of development. I theorize that ethnic identity forms and develops within at least four essential dimensions that by nature, integrate, intersect, and overlap: Content Components, Categorical Ascription, Situational and Environmental Context, and Processual Continuum. These dimensions begin at birth and continue throughout the life span. They are interwoven and embedded into the ways individuals process information cognitively, interact socially, and display behavior, and as such are consequential to all aspects of human development. Therefore, it is important to fully understand the process of ethnic identity formation and development, to discern how it affects social, cognitive, and behavioral development, and how to apply this knowledge to schooling.

Content Components

Phinney (1989, 1990) and others described *ethnic identity* through components—awareness, self-labeling, attitudes, behaviors—that result in the individual's identification with a particular group and with the acquisition of group patterns through membership. Similarly, Bernal and Knight (1993) viewed *ethnic identity* as a psychological construct that includes "a set of ideas about one's own ethnic group membership" (p. 7). These definitions address the descriptive content and apparent characteristics of ethnic identity. Of importance to note is that these components operate at two levels—individual and group (Branch, 1994)—and within two domains—self-given and other-ascribed. Although components are a critical part of the definition, components in and of themselves do not have explanatory capabilities: why and how identity forms and develops.

Categorical Ascription

Because ethnic groups in the United States are perceived as occupying sociopolitical, cultural positions within a hierarchical system, the adoption, demonstration, or privatization of ethnic practices are influenced by factors such as physical, cultural and ethnic markers, competition, emulation, social reproduction, power, situational events, and scales of inclusion and participation (Hollins, 1996, chap. 10, this volume; Jones, 1997). These factors influence the degree to which ethnic identity ascription, or *self-labeling,* is internally driven, externally imposed, or both. Some scholars believe that consistency in self-labeling and the recognition and performance of accepted modes of behavior in social spheres in which ethnic identity is reconfirmed and validated (Barth, 1969) begins around 8 years old (Aboud, 1984, 1987).

However, Spencer (1985) pointed out that identity is a developmental process in constant transformation. Developmentally, the ways young children accept, display, and incorporate ethnic identity content into their personal and group identity differs from the ways they are exhibited and given importance at other life ages. We know that young children (birth to 3 and 4 years old acquire ethnic values, customs, language styles, and behavioral codes long before they are able to label and know them as ethnic

(Sheets, 1997; Spencer, 1985). Scholars who study ethnic identity development in young children from a socialization perspective believe that the ethnic identity process for children of color begins at birth, at the earliest interactions between the child, family, and community (Cross, Strauss, & Fhagen-Smith, chap. 2, this volume; Cross & Fhagen-Smith, 1996; McAdoo, 1993; Sheets, 1997; Spencer, 1985). Sheets (1997) maintained that the continual presence of personal and societal markers such as skin color, language, food choices, values, and membership in a dominant or nondominant group instills in children ethnic roles and behaviors that prepare them for eventual self-labeling.

Likewise, Alba (1990) referring to White ethnics, maintained that this early home-life framework of acceptable alternatives creates a unique identity. He argued that this personality, informed by ethnicity, exists at deep levels, present even when individuals reject their ethnicity. This concurs with identity theory in social psychology, which theorizes that the multi-identities within an individual operate at different levels of importance. Stryker (1968) identified this degree of acknowledgment and commitment as *salience.* This element of choice in identity labeling for White ethnics appears to be less problematic for White ethnics than for ethnics phenotypically or culturally marked (Lee, chap. 6, this volume). Nonetheless, for a developing ethnic identity, feelings of solidarity with a particular ethnic group implies definite movement toward a conscious recognition of and commitment with the group (Alba, 1990; Gay, chap. 11, this volume; Yancey, Ericksen, & Juliani, 1976), resulting in self-identification with various degrees of salience. Thus, consciously or unconsciously, cognitively or behaviorally, individuals use ethnic identities to categorize themselves and others for the purpose of social interactions in diverse settings.

Situational and Environmental Context

The context and situations (e.g., locations, sociopolitical racialized ramifications, economic conditions, and time) in which ethnic identity unfolds is another dimension of ethnic identity (Branch, 1994; Root, chap. 4, this volume). This is an area in need of research. Family socialization patterns that instill values and social and behavioral codes in their offspring vary within same groups and are dependent in part on particular circumstances such as socioeconomic status, generational influences, and geographic location (Hollins, 1996; McAdoo, 1993; Root, chap. 4, this volume). If home-rearing practices determine how people use their cultural resources to adapt to new and distinct environments (Mintz & Price, 1992; Root, chap. 4, this volume), this indicates that the components of ethnic identity not only operate differently at different developmental ages, but also may be expressed differently in different contextual settings.

For example, acquisition of values and behavioral and social patterns are components in the ethnic identity development of young children that can precede self-labeling and recognition. Also, self-labeling informed by context is not as simple as suggested. It may or may not indicate recognition, commitment, and salience; the ability to self-label does not mean that contextually the same criteria is used to determine the labeling of others. Sheets (1998) found that 5-year-old children from African, Mexican, Minh, Loatian American, and Black/White racially mixed groups were able to classify themselves ethnically. These children readily provided distinguishing physical markers (eye shape, skin tone, and hair texture) and cultural elements (native language, food preferences, and ways of eating) as proof to distinguish themselves from others. However, they used authoritative or socially accepted reasons to classify others. For example, they say an individual is "Loas" because "My daddy said so" or someone is "Mexican" because "He was born in the hospital." The self-labeling at this age was also separate from attitudes of affiliation, commitment, and salience, but not from identifiable cultural behaviors associated with group patterns.

Research that examines how environmental context affects children's ethnic identity development—and its effect on present and subsequent development—or what types of sociopsychological events affect change in the development of individual and group ethnic membership were not available. However, there are bodies of literature that show that relentless, systematic, and consistent assault on a child's identity in school places students at risk (e.g., dropout, disciplinary issues and low attendance; Natriello, McGill, & Pallas, 1990; Sheets, 1996). Research data of how school-created trauma affects ethnic identity development were not available.

The components and process of ethnic identity appear to be highly responsive to changing contextual social, political, and economic conditions. Ethnic identity cannot be adequately examined as isolated elements, rather it should be examined as suggested by Mintz and Price (1992), as systems or patterns in their social context. Jones (1997) argued that ethnic identity is "based on shifting, situational, subjective identification of self and others, which are rooted in ongoing daily practices and historical experience" (p. 13).

Processual Continuum

A continual socialization process shapes the self to include recognition, significance, and importance of ethnic identity, which in turn enhances a sense of self and peoplehood. An ongoing, identity process that intersects with the individual's cognitive, social, and behavioral development appears to be the dimension of ethnic identity that involves the active maintenance of cultural boundaries in the process of social interactions with others. This developmental process influences degrees of recognition, salience, and commitment that a person ascribes to their personal and group identification in ethnic groups. Sodowsky, Kwan, and Pannu (1995) viewed the ethnic identity process as a social psychological phenomenon. Isajiw (1990) defined this process "as a manner in which persons account for their ethnic origin, locate themselves psychologically in relation to one or more social systems, and in which they perceive others as locating them" (p. 35).

Ethnic identity, examined as a social process in conjuction with other psychological developmental processes, can help make applications to practice, especially for children in school settings. Understanding the process of ethnic identity formation and development can provide teachers, counselors, and school psychologists with important knowledge needed to create environments, design curriculum and instructional strategies, and provide support services to facilitate positive ethnic identity development.

THE ROLE OF SCHOOLING
IN ETHNIC IDENTITY DEVELOPMENT

A factor contributing to the dominant status of the European American ethnic group has been the institutionalization of their culture and their ability to display their ethnic identity as the norm in school settings. Conversely, students from ethnic groups of color have had to construct, maintain, and develop their ethnic identities in situational contexts that often require them to restrict or suppress the natural display of internal ethnic behaviors. Negotiating aspects of their ethnic identity or neglecting the cultural dimensions of ethnic identity can be problematic. For example, privatizing ethnic behaviors (e.g., social discourse and cognitive preferences), given the elevated status of White ethnic groups, has real implications for students' construction of identity and development of attendant psychological processes.

Scholars point out that the psychological dimensions of ethnicity, if compromised, can create conflict for individuals whose social relationships and cultural practices become removed from their sense of identity (Bentley, 1987; de Vos, 1982). In classrooms, teachers may not be aware of the emotional and cognitive stress caused by this psychological dissonance. They may not be able to recognize ethnic signifiers embodied in children's cognitive and motivating structures. Students from some ethnic groups may be required to engage unfamiliar habits of mind from another culture without the benefit of assistance or acknowledgment of the arduous task (Hollins, 1996). Some of these students learn to engage unfamiliar habits of mind and succeed academically. Others do not overcome this barrier and are not successful in school. Students who fail under these conditions can be identified by race and ethnicity. Frequently, this adds to the description and expectations for this particular racial and ethnic group, reinforcing stereotypes and from some perspectives, justifying unlimited access to school resources for European Americans (Sheets, chap. 5, this volume).

Thus, when students compete for the same resources, such as teacher time, friendship connections, and mutuality of expectations, hierarchical ethnic relationships develop. Students from groups of color, located in an ethnic category with varied degrees of inequality are limited to the number of options available and forced to accommodate to an unfamiliar context by repressing their ethnic behaviors. Eriksen (1992) pointed out that cultural differences in and of themselves are unimportant, however, their importance is in the creation of options in social domains. The institutionalization of a dominant ethnicity in U.S. schools that demands either reproduction or resistance results in incongruities and contradictions for equitable access to educational opportunities.

IMPLICATIONS FOR SCHOOL PRACTICES

Ethnic identity may originate, form, and develop in private homes, however, it unfolds and is displayed in the immediate community sector and in institutional settings, such as school. Theoretical frameworks to guide research of identity formation and development must be developed to examine the construction of ethnic identity and its development in the context of social interactions with and without relational aspects to other groups. Jones (1997) pointed out that we lack adequate theoretical frameworks that "address the relationship between peoples' perceptions of ethnic identity (their own and others), and the cultural practices and social relations in which they are engaged" (p. 65). For example, what happens to social and cognitive development of children when they choose to maintain ethnic boundaries or when they are forced to privatize ethnic behavioral displays?

If ethnic identity informs social interactions and behaviors, we must explore the effects on children's cognitive and social development when their performance is reconfirmed and validated as accepted modes of behavior in schools. However, scholars must take care not to elevate observed regularities in ethnic behavior to the level of causal principles in the conceptualization and explanation of ethnic identity (Branch, 1994, chap. 1, this volume).

Changing teacher, administrator, counseling, and school psychologists preparation to include understanding and knowledge of ethnic identity formation and development (self and others) is central to changing classroom and school practices. University programs that fail to address ethnic identity development generally produce practitioners who are unable to work effectively with students from diverse ethnic groups. The impact on European American children, although less obvious, is nonetheless equally harmful because it perpetuates the development of a distorted European American ethnic identity (Sheets, chap. 9, this volume).

To improve practice, teachers, counselors, and psychologists must examine their own ethnic identity development as well as understand the ethnic identity development of their particular students. They must honor and validate differences without the need to oppress, idealize, or denigrate children and families who may not share the same ethnic group, life experiences, and value orientations. Students are able to achieve socially and academically at high levels of competency without sacrificing their ethnic identity. Opportunity to develop a comfortable, healthy, multifaceted identity through ethnic affirmation, day-to-day achievement, and validation of experiential background is at the essence of the learning–teaching–counseling process; preparation programs must provide ways to accomplish this end.

REFERENCES

Abell, P. K. (in press). Recognizing and valuing differences: Process considerations for preservice teachers. In E. R. Hollins & E. I. Oliver (Ed.), *Finding pathways to success: Teaching culturally diverse populations.* Mahwah, NJ: Lawrence Erlbaum Associates.

Aboud, F. E. (1984). Social and cognitive bases of ethnic identity constancy. *Journal of Genetic Psychology, 145,* 227–229.

Aboud, F. E. (1987). The development of ethnic self-identification and attitudes. In J. S. Phinney & M. J. Rotheram (Eds.), *Children's ethnic socialization: Pluralism and development* (pp. 32–55). Newbury Park, CA: Sage.

Alba, R. D. (1990). *Ethnic identity: The transformation of White America.* New Haven, CT: Yale University Press.

Bandura, A. (1977). *Social learning theory.* Englewood Cliffs, NJ: Prentice Hall.

Barth, F. (Ed.). (1969). *Ethnic groups and boundaries.* Boston: Little Brown.

Bentley, G. C.(1987). Ethnicity and practice. *Comparative Studies in Society and History, 29,* 24–55.

Bernal, M. E., & Knight, G. P. (Eds.). (1993). *Ethnic identity: Formation and transmission among Hispanics and other minorities.* Albany: State University of New York Press.

Branch, C. W. (1994). Ethnic identity as a variable in the learning equation. In E. R. Hollins, J. E. King, & W. G. Hayman (Eds.), *Teaching diverse populations: Formulating a knowledge base* (pp. 207–224). Albany: State University of New York Press.

Cross, W. E., Jr., & Fhagen-Smith, P. (1996). Nigrescence and ego identity development: Accounting for differential Black identity patterns. In P. B. Peterson, J. G. Draguns, W. J. Lonner, & J. E. Trimble (Eds.), *Counseling across cultures* (4th ed., pp. 108–123). Thousand Oaks, CA: Sage.

de Vos, G. (1982). Ethnic pluralism: Conflict and accommodation. In G. de Vos & L. Romanucci-Ross (Eds.), *Ethnic identity: Cultural continuities and change* (pp. 5–41). Chicago: University of Chicago Press.

Eriksen, T. H. (1992). *Us and them in modern societies: Ethnicity and nationalism in Mauritius, Trinidad and beyond.* London: Scandinavian University Press.

Erikson, E. H. (1950). *Childhood and society.* New York: Norton.

Erikson, E. H. (1968). *Identity: Youth and crisis.* New York: Norton.

Freud, S. (1940). An outline of psychoanalysis. In J. Strachey (Ed. and Trans.), *The standard edition of the complete psychological works of Sigmund Freud.* London: Hogarth.

Gay, G. (1994). *At the essence of learning: Multicultural education.* West Lafayette, IN: Kappa Delta Pi.

Gleason, P. (1996). Identifying identity: A Semitic history (1983). In W. Sollors (Ed.), *A classical reader* (pp. 460–487). New York: New York University Press.

Greenfield, P. A., & Cocking, R. R. (Eds.). (1994). *Cross-cultural roots of minority child development.* Hillsdale, NJ: Lawrence Erlbaum Associates.

Hollins, E. R. (1996). *Culture in school learning: Revealing the deep meaning.* Mahwah, NJ: Lawrence Erlbaum Associates.

Hollins, E. R. (1997). Culture. In C. A. Grant & G. Ladson-Billings (Eds.), *Dictionary of multicultural education* (pp. 72–74). Phoenix: Oryx Press.

Isajiw, W. W. (1990). Ethnic-identity retention. In R. Breton, W. W. Isajiw, W. E. Kalbach, & J. G. Reitz (Eds.), *Ethnic identity and equality* (pp. 34–91). Toronto: University of Toronto Press.

Jones, S. (1997). *The archaeology of ethnicity: Constructing identities in the past and present.* Boston: Routledge & Kegan Paul.

Maslow, A. H. (1968). *Toward a psychology of being* (2nd ed.). New York: Van Nostrand.

McAdoo, H. P. (Ed.). (1993). *Family ethnicity: Strength in diversity.* Newbury Park, CA: Sage.

McIntosh, P. (1989). White privilege: Unpacking the invisible knapsack. *Peace and Freedom,* July/August, 10–12.

Mintz, S. W., & Price, R. (1992). *The birth of African-American culture: An anthropological perspective.* Boston: Beacon Press.

Natriello, G., McDill, E. L., & Pallas, A. M. (1990). *Schooling disadvantaged children: Racing against catastrophe.* New York: Teachers College Press.

Phinney, J. S. (1989). Stages of ethnic identity development in minority group adolescents. *Journal of Early Adolescence, 9*(1–2), 34–39.

Phinney, J. S. (1990). Ethnic identity in adolescents and adults: Review of research. *Psychological Bulletin, 108,* 499–514.

Piaget, J. (1952). *The origins of intelligence in children* (M. Cook, Trans.). New York: International Universities Press.

Rogers, C. R. (1970). *On becoming a person: A therapist's view of psychotherapy.* Boston: Houghton Mifflin.

Shade, B., Kelly, C., & Oberg, M. (1997). *Creating culturally responsive classrooms.* Washington, DC: American Psychological Association.

Sheets, R. H. (1996). Urban classroom conflict: Student-teacher perception: Ethnic integrity, solidarity, and resistance. *The Urban Review, 28*(2), 165–183.

Sheets, R. H. (1997). Reflection 1: Racial and ethnic awareness. In J. Carnes & R. H. Sheets (Eds.), *Starting small: Teaching tolerance in preschool and the early grades* (pp. 16–21). Montgomery, AL: Southern Poverty Law Center.

Sheets, R. H. (1998). *Ethnic identity behavioral displays in an urban Kindergarten classroom: Implications for practice.* Unpublished manuscript.

Skinner, B. F. (1957). *Verbal behavior.* New York: Appleton- Century-Crofts.

Sodowsky, G. R., Kwan, K. K., & Pannu R. (1995). Ethnic identity of Asians in the United States. In J. G. Ponterotto, J. M. Casas, L. A. Suzuki, & C. M. Alexander (Eds.), *Handbook of multicultural counseling* (pp. 123–154). Thousand Oaks, CA: Sage.

Sollors, W. (Ed.). (1996). *Theories of ethnicity: A classical reader.* New York: New York University Press.

Spencer, M. B. (1985). Cultural cognition and social cognition as identity factors in Black children's personal growth. In M. Spencer, G. Brookins, & W. Allen (Eds.), *Beginnings: The social and affective development of Black children* (pp. 215–230). Hillsdale, NJ: Lawrence Erlbaum Associates.

Stanfield, J. H., II. (1985). The ethnocentric basis of social science knowledge production. *Review of Research in Education, 12,* 387–415.

Stryker, S. (1968). Identity salience and role performance: The relevance of symbolic interaction theory for family research. *Journal of Marriage and the Family, 30,* 558–564.

Turkle, S. (1987, April 5). Hero of the life cycle. *New York Times Book Review,* pp. 36–37.

Vander Zanden, J. W. (1995). *Human development* (5th ed.). New York: McGraw-Hill.

Yancey, W., Ericksen, E., & Juliani, R. (1976). Emergent ethnicity: A review and a reformulation. *American Sociological Review, 41* (June): 391–403.

II Research on Racial and Ethnic Identity Theory and Human Development

Because human development is a major component of educational foundations, educators and others who serve children—psychologists and counselors—may assume that mainstream developmental theories are applicable to all children without reframing in any way. This section provides research on ethnic identity development, in particular ethnic groups in the United States.

In chapter 6, Lee examines ethnic identity among Asian Americans, concentrating on how Asian American youth come to understand their ethnicities. She draws from the literature in psychology, sociology, and anthropology to arrive at a meaning of ethnicity. She determines that the psychological literature equates ethnicity to culture through linear (acculturation as a threat to ethnicity) and bidimensional (acculturation as a form of biculturalism) models, whereas the sociological and anthropological literature views ethnicity as primordial (emotional attachment) or instrumental (symbolic markers of ethnic group boundaries). Although some scholars view ethnicity as a personal choice, Lee maintains that it is not a choice for visible racial and ethnic groups because ethnicity is imposed on these individuals when dominant group members categorize them as ethnic minorities. An example of this categorization is *panethnicity,* the lumping together of various ethnic groups into one group.

When examining the relation of culture and ethnicity among Asian Americans, Lee discusses the potential cultural clash between Asians and the mainstream dominant culture, especially in the areas of family orientation and gender roles. She uses ethnographic research to describe how stereotypic images and racism directed toward Asian adolescents often results in the development of a panethnic Asian American identity as a means of group support to help cope with incessant discrimination. She concludes that although culture may be an aspect of ethnic identity, educators must consider the role of racism in the formation of racial and ethnic identity among Asian Americans.

Deyhle and LeCompte (chap. 7) examine the differences in the perspectives found among Navajo students, parents, and middle school policies

103

and practices concerning the stages of human development and parenting and how these differences may produce misunderstandings. The Eurocentric conception of child developmental stages, especially during the preteen stage, and the ways in which middle schools deliver services to this age group, differ and often run counter to Navajo cultural practices. These authors use two examples—control versus noninterference and shame versus acceptance—to document cultural differences and adult–child expectations in home and school environments.

Dehyle and LeCompe further describe the mismatch between middle schools and Navajo culture. They allege that "well-meaning attempts to improve education for Navajo children were impeded by normal institutional resistance" and by educational innovations that were not culturally relevant. According to these authors, inappropriate practices result from teacher preparation programs that assume monocultural child developmental principles are generalizable to all cultures. They conclude that teachers need to learn from parents and the community what is appropriate for their children and schools of education "should be held accountable for changing teacher training to eliminate biases introduced by ignoring cultural differences."

The authors in chapter 8 discuss the results of Rodriguez, Ramirez III, Korman's study examining cultural differences in family values and how these value differences affect the mental health of adolescent children. These authors explore the problems in past cross-cultural research that reflect a European worldview and in the investigations that fail to control for socioeconomic status.

In their study, the authors found that Anglo American adolescents had a higher modern family value orientation, whereas Mexican American adolescents had a bicultural value orientation and a less traditional family orientation than did the adolescents from Mexican families. Anglo and Mexican American adolescents reported experiencing a higher level of mental health symptoms than did Mexican adolescents. The authors determined that cultural elements (e.g., family values) contribute to differences among cultural and ethnic groups. In conclusion, the authors encourage educators to implement programs with a family values-based approach and to replace programs with assimilationist perspectives with bicultural and multicultural positions.

Sheets presents a qualitative research case study of an urban ninth grade Social Studies/Language Arts classroom in chapter 9. She describes the pedagogical behaviors and the classroom climate that facilitated ethnic identity development and competence. The findings indicated that when classroom instruction and climate were modified to affirm and accommodate students' ethnic identity and cultural knowledge, learning and positive ethnic identity development occurred. Students' attitudes and behaviors did not fit into the linear stages described by theoretical stage theory, rather, attitudes and behaviors depended on the individuals involved, the content of the social interaction, the actual situation, and the overall context in which events take place.

In this study, ethnic identity affiliation influenced student appraisal of events perceived as stressful, the use of available resources, and the types of coping strategies applied in adapting to stressful situations. The responses of students revealed that explanations, causes, and feelings inherent in their overt actions in most classrooms were experiences without teachers' awareness and acknowledgment of ethnic differences. European American students in this study, despite 8 years in desegregated classrooms, appeared to be unaware of how students from groups of color felt about them and about racialized issues and experiences.

6 "Are You Chinese or What?" Ethnic Identity Among Asian Americans

Stacey J. Lee
University of Wisconsin, Madison

As Chinese Americans growing up in a predominately White neighborhood, my sister and I socialized primarily with White children. In fact, the only Chinese Americans we knew were either relatives or old family friends who were like family. Although we often ate Chinese food and occasionally even spoke Chinese at home, our family rarely talked about being Chinese. One day when my sister, Leslie, was in kindergarten, she came home from school and asked our mother about her ethnicity. I will never forget that day. Our mother was cooking, and I was setting the table when Leslie came into the kitchen and asked our mother, "What am I?" Because our mother seemed a bit confused, my sister then said, "You know, what am I? Am I Mexican or what?" Suddenly, comprehending the nature of Leslie's question, our mother answered by saying, "Oh honey, you are Chinese. Mommy is Chinese. Daddy is Chinese. Stacey is Chinese. ..." After our mother rattled out a series of examples that included most of our living relatives, she asked my sister why she had asked her question. I could tell by our mother's expression that she was afraid that one of the White children was picking on her youngest child, but Leslie quickly explained that a "Chinese boy named Larry asked." Apparently, Larry was aware that he was different from the White kids at school. Furthermore, he recognized my sister as being like him and wanted to confirm his hunch. The next day when Leslie informed Larry that she was Chinese, he quickly asked her to be his girlfriend. He also told her that he was not surprised to find out that she was Chinese because she "looked Chinese." A few months after this incident, our family learned from Larry's mother that she encouraged Larry to play with Chinese children.

At the time of my sister's now famous question, I was 12 years old, I found her question naive, silly, and unsophisticated. I assumed the answer

107

to her question was obvious. Over the years, however, I have come to realize that my sister's question was actually filled with complicated meaning. In this chapter, I examine ethnic identity among Asian Americans. Specifically, I consider how Asian American youth come to understand their ethnicities. The following questions are addressed: How do relationships with individuals who are not Asian affect the way that Asian Americans feel about their ethnicities? How do Asian Americans define their ethnic identities? I draw from the literature in education, anthropology, sociology, and psychology. In an attempt to bring forward the voices of Asian Americans, I use examples from my qualitative research on Asian American high school and college students (Lee, 1996a, 1996b, 1997).

WHAT IS ETHNICITY—CULTURE OR WHAT?

Within much of the psychological literature, ethnicity is equated with culture. Sodowsky, Kwan, and Pannu (1995) wrote, "sharing of a cultural heritage, a sense of social relatedness, and symbolic cultural ties define ethnic identity" (p. 132). Ethnicity is a birthright. Individuals are born into a particular ethnic group whose members share a culture and history. People learn the norms and values of their ethnic group as they mature. Ethnicity is perceived as central to what an individual believes and how an individual acts. Rotheram and Phinney (1987), for example, asserted that ethnicity "patterns our thinking, feelings, and behavior in both obvious and subtle ways" (p. 11).

The assumption that ethnic groups are cultural groups has led researchers to focus on how contact between groups affects group culture. Two schools of thought dominate this acculturation literature: the linear model and the bidimensional model (Nagata, 1994; Phinney, 1990). The *linear model* assumes that individuals either maintain strong connections to their native cultures or develop strong ties to the dominant culture. Advocates of this perspective view the changes in culture that occur as the result of contact between cultural groups (e.g., acculturation) as a threat to ethnicity (Rogler, Cortes, & Malgady, 1991). On the other hand, the *bidimensional* or *bidirectional conceptualization of acculturation* assumes that an individual's relationship to that person's own culture is distinct from that person's relationship to the dominant culture (Berry, Trimble, & Olmedo, 1986). This perspective assumes that individuals can be bicultural. Despite differences between the linear and the bidimensional models, both assume a one-to-one relationship between culture and ethnicity.

Primordialists Versus Instrumentalists

Within the sociological and anthropological literatures, two theories of ethnicity compete for dominance: the primordialists and the instrumentalists (Espiritu, 1992). *Primordialists* maintain that ethnic groups are essentially cultural groups. According to this perspective, people within an ethnic group share a common tradition and history. Like Sodowsky et al. (1995) and others who wrote from a psychological perspective, primordialists see members of ethnic groups as being bound together by birth and they assume that the loss of culture signals the loss of ethnicity. Whereas primordialists believe that ethnic identity is an emotional attachment to one's cultural heritage, *instrumentalists* argue that ethnic groups are interest groups. That is, instrumentalists maintain that people remain ethnic when they believe that it is in their political or social interest. Although instrumentalists do not equate ethnicity with culture, they do not totally dismiss the significance of culture. Barth (1969), for example, asserted that culture is symbolically used to mark ethnic group boundaries. From this perspective, the actual content of culture can and will shift and change according to the ethnic group's perceptions of their interests. Cultural practices of a particular ethnic group will be transformed over time according to the group's needs. Fugita and O'Brien (1991) wrote:

> A central theme of the emergent ethnicity perspective, then, is to turn away from the process of assimilation and focus on evolving adaptive responses and ethnic identifications whose specific cultural content will change as the ethnic group faces different structural exigencies. (p. 21)

The common assumption made by instrumentalists is that individuals have a choice as to whether or not they identify themselves as members of their ethnic group. Similarly, from the psychological perspective, Rotheram and Phinney (1987) wrote "children initially learn from others what group they belong to, however, as they get older, they become aware of options in the extent to which they behave as and consider themselves to be members of an ethnic group" (p. 16). As Espiritu (1992) pointed out, however, the assumption regarding choice denies the fact that ethnicity is often imposed on people. Espiritu argued, "to conceptualize ethnicity as a matter of choice is to ignore 'categorization,' the process whereby one group ascriptively classifies another. Categorization is intimately bound up with power relations" (p. 6). For example, although Asian Americans may prefer to identify ethnically (e.g., Chinese, Vietnamese, and Thai), they cannot escape the dominant society's use of race rather than ethnicity as a marker (Cook & Helms, 1988; Root, chap. 4, this volume). Thus, they are often categorized as Asian regardless of how they act, how they may perceive themselves, or how they affiliate ethnically (Espiritu, 1992; Lee, 1996b; Waters, 1990). This homogeneous categorization has significant implications for how Asian Americans come to understand their ethnic identities.

Panethnicity—the lumping together of various ethnic groups into one group—is an example of an imposed category (Espiritu, 1992). The term *Asian American,* a panethnic label, was originally imposed on people from diverse Asian ethnic groups. Immigrants and refugees from various Asian countries often express frustration and confusion over being lumped into a panethnic group with people they feel they have little in common (Lee, 1996b). Thus, the imposed nature of ethnicity is particularly important to consider when attempting to understand the formation of ethnic identity among Asian Americans.

ETHNIC AWARENESS AND ETHNIC IDENTITY

In an ethnically and racially diverse country, such as the United States, individuals are more likely to be aware of ethnicity than in monoethnic societies. According to Phinney (1990):

> Ethnic identity is meaningful only in situations in which two or more ethnic groups are in contact over a period of time. In an ethnically or racially homogeneous society, ethnic identity is a virtually meaningless concept. (p. 501)

Differences in physical appearance and culture mark ethnic and racial boundaries. Rotheram and Phinney (1987) asserted that "initial awareness is likely to be based largely on obvious perceptual cues (especially skin color), language, or customs (distinctive food, holidays)" (p. 17). Like other groups, Asian Americans may first learn about ethnic and racial differences by observing visual cues and language differences. Asian American immigrants and refugees have reported that differences in physical appearance (e.g., skin color, hair color, and height) and language were the first things to make them aware of ethnic and racial groups in the United States (Lee, 1996b). Hmong college women told me that when they entered schools in the United States as children, they quickly learned that they were different from "Americans" because they did not speak the same language.

Some psychological researchers assert that the ability to recognize and distinguish ethnic differences must occur before people can develop a sense of their own ethnic identity (Aboud 1988; Rotheram & Phinney 1987). Thus, ethnic awareness is understood to be a precursor to ethnic identity and self-identification. It should be noted, however, that children may participate in their ethnic cultures before acquiring a sense of their own ethnic identities. For example, Sheets (1997) maintained that children as young as 3 and 4 years old "acquire ethnic values, customs, language styles, and behavioral codes long before they are able to label and know them as ethnic" (p. 17). Because of the often more visual nature of racial differences, it may be easier for children to recognize racial differences before they recognize ethnic differences. Young children between 3 and 5 years old are able to "perceive and describe physical differences associated with race before they are able to understand that these attributes can categorize people as members of specific racial groups" (p. 17).

Returning to the example of my sister and her friend Larry provides an illustration of the link between ethnic awareness and identity. Remember that Larry first approached my sister because he thought that she "looked" Chinese. Larry distinguished my sister from the White children at their school based on her physical appearance. Larry was not only aware of ethnic differences, but he was also able to accurately identify his own ethnicity as a Chinese American. Furthermore, he was able to recognize similarities between himself and my sister. Although my sister was generally aware of the existence of ethnic differences—remember that she asked our mother whether or not she was Mexican—she could not accurately label herself before the kitchen scene with our mother. Because Leslie understood the basic idea that ethnic differences exist, she was able to accurately self-identify her ethnicity once our mother told her. Finally, I would suggest that Larry's ability to ethnically identify himself was likely due to the fact that his parents often spoke about being Chinese. By contrast, in our family, ethnicity was rarely explicitly discussed while my sister was in grade school.

CULTURE AND ETHNIC IDENTITY AMONG ASIAN AMERICANS

As previously noted, much of the research on ethnic identity focuses on the issue of culture. The specific research on ethnic identity among Asian Americans focuses specifically on the central role of the family in Asian cultures. In contrast to White Americans who are described as being individualistic, Asian Americans are described as having a collective, family-oriented identity. In describing the role of the family in Asian American ethnic identity development, Sodowsky et al. (1995) explained that "for many U.S. Asians, the sense of self ... is strongly tied to the family" (p. 147). Similarly, D. W. Sue and D. Sue (1990) wrote:

Although the Asian immigrants and refugees form very diverse groups, there are certain areas of commonality such as deference to authority, emotional restraint, specified roles and hierarchical family structure and family and extended family orientation. (p. 197)

Although D. W. Sue and D. Sue (1990) recognized the diversity within Asian American communities, they concluded that Asians share certain key cultural characteristics, including a strong family orientation.

Some researchers have suggested that the significant differences between Asian cultures and mainstream American culture may make it difficult for Asian Americans to preserve their ethnic identities (Sodowsky, Maguire, Johnson, Ngumba, & Kohles, 1994; D. W. Sue & D. Sue, 1990). D. W. Sue and D. Sue (1990) wrote, "As Asians become progressively exposed to the standards, norms, and values of the wider society, increasing assimilation and acculturation are frequently the result" (p. 201). The assumptions here are that social contact between groups lead to assimilation of one group, and that culture is equal to ethnicity.

In examining the differences between mainstream American and Asian cultures, some educational researchers have suggested that Asian American children may experience trauma and confusion in their attempts to reconcile the two cultures. In her research on Chinese immigrants in New York City, Sung (1987) argued that Chinese children who become involved in gangs do so in response to the pressure created by cultural conflict. Studies on the intergenerational conflict between Asian immigrant parents and their children point to the problems that can occur when children begin to embrace dominant cultural values (Lee, 1996a; Smith-Hefner, 1993; Sung, 1987; Wakil, Siddique, & Wakil, 1981). Ethnographic research on Cambodian immigrants/refugees in the United States suggests that many parents perceive American cultural values as being a threat to their native cultures. Cambodian parents have been found to be particularly threatened by American gender norms because they believe that preservation of their ethnic identities depends specifically on the maintenance of traditional gender roles for women (Ledgerwood, 1990; Smith-Hefner, 1993). By contrast, school-aged Cambodian girls have been found to embrace what they see as the freedom offered by American society (Lee 1996a; Smith-Hefner 1993). Smith-Hefner (1993) found that the intergenerational differences regarding beliefs about gender led to family tension and conflict and in extreme cases, the differences escalated into violence. In my research on Cambodian adolescent girls, I spoke with several girls who said that they had contemplated running away from home in order to escape parental authority and expectations regarding appropriate gender behavior (Lee, 1996a).

D. W. Sue and D. Sue (1990) suggested that U.S.-born Asian Americans may find it particularly difficult to negotiate the differences between mainstream American culture and Asian culture. In addressing the counseling needs of U.S.-born Asians, they point to the framework presented by D. W. Sue and D. Sue (1971). D. W. Sue and D. Sue (1971) identified three types of Asian Americans, each characterized by the way they see themselves in relationship to other Asians and to others who are not Asian. The first type, the *traditionalist,* socializes primarily with ethnic group members and adheres strictly to the values of the native culture. The second type, the *marginal man,* seeks to conform to the dominant culture and rejects the native culture. The third type, the *Asian American,* actively resists the racism of the dominant society and attempts to reconcile viable aspects of his/her heritage with the present situation (D. W. Sue & D. Sue, 1990). The significance of S. Sue and D. W. Sue's (1971) framework was that it attempted to address the way in which racism and the conflict created by the differences between Asian cultures and the dominant culture affect the identity of Asian Americans.

Researchers who equate culture with ethnicity overlook the possibility that individuals can desire to transform their cultures and still have pride in their ethnicities. Researchers must consider whether members of ethnic groups really become less ethnic when they change their cultures. Are individuals less ethnic if they reject their cultures? In an attempt to answer this question, consider the case of Hmong refugees in the United States.

First Generation Hmong College Women

Ethnographic studies on Hmong refugees in the United States suggest that Hmong elders believe that the preservation of their ethnic identities depends specifically on the preservation of strict cultural norms regarding gender (Donnelly, 1994). Within Hmong culture, there exists a strict hierarchical relationship between men and women, in which women submit to the authority of men. Hmong women marry during adolescence and gain status on having children (Donnelly, 1994; Goldstein, 1985; Walker-Moffat, 1995).

My current research examines the life experiences of first generation Hmong college women between the ages of 18 and 32 (Lee, 1997). One goal of the study has been to understand the process of cultural transformation. Hmong college women recognize that Hmong culture is in the process of significant change, and they describe themselves as central agents of this change. All the women express the desire for increased gender equality within the Hmong community. Women believe that if they complete a college education, they will gain greater independence and greater gender equality. Many women are delaying marriage until after they get their college degrees, thereby altering the structure of the Hmong family. In reflecting on her role in the transformation of Hmong culture, Joua, a 31-year-old Hmong woman, says:

> Culture changes everyday, and I look at myself as changing the culture in my family and in my community. When you decide to stick with education and realize that education is important and really decide to go forward that's when you change it.

Although Joua recognizes that her actions are changing Hmong culture, she does not believe that she is any "less Hmong" than the more traditional elders. Joua is proud of her Hmong ethnicity and works to promote greater equality for Hmong in the United States. She participates in the Hmong American community at the local and national level and attended the 1996 International Women's Conference in Beijing as part of the Hmong women's delegation. While in China, Joua traveled to Hmong ethnic enclaves in order to learn more about the diversity of the Hmong experience. In short, although women like Joua are recreating and transforming the role of Hmong women within their culture, they continue to assert a distinct ethnic identity as Hmong people.

Interestingly, several Hmong women reported that their mothers and/or older sisters encouraged them to pursue higher education and to transform gender roles. For example, Lia, a 21-year-old undergraduate at a large midwestern university, stated that her mother always encouraged her to go to school in order to ensure her independence.

> My mother has always told me she says it's hard being a Hmong wife because you always have to feel like … you always depend on someone else and you don't have your own identity. She would never want us to feel that way. She wants us to be our own individual. The only way to do that is that you go to college, you get a good job. She has always said to me to go.

The fact that some mothers are encouraging their daughters to go to college in order to change the nature of gender relations within families suggests that cultural transformation is not solely the purview of the younger generation. Although the mothers are encouraging their daughters to change gender roles, they insist that their daughters remember that they are Hmong.

RACISM AND ETHNIC IDENTITY AMONG ASIAN AMERICANS

Although culture is undeniably an important aspect of one's ethnic identity, the equating of ethnicity with culture underestimates the social, political, and utilitarian nature of ethnic groups (Barth, 1969; Fugita & O'Brien, 1991). In this section, I examine how relationships with non-Asians affect the formation of ethnic identity of Asian American students. Specifically, I look at how interracial relationships affect the way that Asian Americans come to understand their ethnic and racial identities.

Like other minority groups in the United States, Asian Americans have been stereotyped by the dominant group. Images of Asian Americans range from the stereotype that all Asians are high achieving, model minorities to the stereotype that Asian Americans are unassimilable foreigners (Lee, 1996b; Okihiro, 1994; Osajima, 1988). In addition to being stereotyped, Asian Americans are the victims of verbal and physical violence. Experiences with racism serve to remind Asian American students that they are different from other racial minorities and that they are not seen as equal to White Americans. In short, Asian Americans are told implicitly and explicitly that they are not welcome in the United States.

Whereas some Asian Americans respond to racism and discrimination by asserting ethnic and racial pride, others respond to racism by hating their ethnicity and race. In my ethnographic research on Asian American high school students (Lee, 1996b), I encountered several Asian American adolescents who internalized the racism they faced. These Asian Americans attempted to emulate the behavior of White students. They socialized with White students and idolized the physical appearance of White people. They rejected their ethnic and racial identities and made fun of themselves and other Asians. Several of these students referred to all Asian Americans as *chinks,* and all Asian American activities as *chink activities.* In short, these students were very much like the marginal Asians described by S. Sue and D. W. Sue (1971).

Similarly, in my study of Hmong college women, I met some women who had internalized the stereotypes that Hmong are stupid, backward, and foreign (Lee, 1997). These women explained that they have been made to feel unwelcome in the United States by others who tell Hmong people to "go back to where you came from." These women question their own self-worth and worry about what non-Asians think about them. In school, their self-doubt leads them to withdraw. Blia, a 21-year-old college student, explains that she is afraid to speak in her college classes because she fears that all the non-Asian classmates are judging her. In her words, "College is really intimidating. I think that I'm inferior. I don't know as much. I don't have the cultural background. I don't have the economic upbringing to perhaps know something."

Interestingly, I found that the internalization was more common among women under the age of 24 years. These women came to the United States as very young children and have few memories of life before coming to the United States. Furthermore, these women report that they have learned little or nothing about the history of Hmong Americans or other Asian Americans while in school. Many of these women assert that they are confused about the details of the Hmong war involvement and the reasons that the Hmong came to the United States.

By contrast, Hmong women over the age of 24 are clearer about the circumstances surrounding the Hmong refugee status, and they are better able to resist the racism they face. For example, Mao, a 24-year-old Hmong woman, maintains that she is proud of being Hmong. Although she has experienced discrimination in the United States, she asserts that "racist people are ignorant." In the following quote, Mao recalls an incident that occurred when she was a teenager. This incident helped to shape her identity as Hmong American:

This lady [said], "Why the Hmong, like why they on welfare? Oh those Hmong just have a lot of kids, just stay home, you know, they have a lot of—just keep having children, and just stay home, receiving aid, receiving all those benefits, just stay home, just keep on having kids. Why don't they—don't they just move back to their country?"

Mao maintains that Hmong people should work hard in order to disprove the welfare stereotype. Experiences with racism have not motivated Mao to reject her identity. She concentrates her efforts on trying to positively impress the dominant group rather than directly challenging their racism.

ASIAN AMERICAN PANETHNICITY

As noted earlier in this chapter, the dominant group originally imposed the panethnic Asian American category on people of Asian descent because they assumed that all Asians were the same. Espiritu (1992) noted that although Asian Americans originally rejected the panethnic category, they embraced an Asian American identity in the 1960s for political reasons. In describing the development of Asian American panethnicity, Espiritu (1992) wrote:

> at least in its origin, pan-Asian ethnicity was the product of material, political, and social processes rather than cultural bonds. Asian Americans came together because they recognized that pan-Asian alliance was important, even essential, for the protection and advancement of their interests. (p. 164)

Chinese and Korean Adolescents

In my ethnographic study on Asian American high school students, I discovered that the majority of Asian American students embraced some form of a panethnic identity in response to racism (Lee, 1996b). Students who embraced a panethnic identity as Asians or Asian Americans did so because they believed that Asians shared a similar experience in the United States. Asian American students from various Asian ethnic groups asserted that by joining together with other Asian Americans, they received emotional and social support. In the following quote, a Vietnamese student describes her attitude toward Asian American panethnicity:

> It's like this when you come to America, people don't know the difference between a 1975 refugee and like a third-generation Japanese American. So, whatever you do, they'll look at you the same. So, in my feeling, it's like we all share the same history because we're all Asian. (p. 45)

Similarly, Teddy Lee, a Chinese immigrant from Hong Kong, asserts that he has embraced panethnicity because of experiences with racism:

> First of all, if you talk about people from Laos, Cambodia or Vietnam most of them [have] been through war and a lot of them came as refugees. So there is a similarity; they are all refugees. And for certain Chinese, like for lucky people like me, we never been through any war, we don't have any similarity between us. But, there's only one thing we have in common—that [of] being Asian—a lot of us have been picked on by other kind of race.

Teddy defines himself as both Chinese and Asian. Thus, his panethnic identity as an Asian is an additional identity.

Another student in my study, Young, a Korean American high school student who identifies herself as both Korean and Asian American, embraced panethnicity after a personal encounter with racism. Her story illustrates the way racism can motivate an identity transformation.

> I used to think I was White. I wanted to be White. This was when I lived in a small town. No one discriminated against me there—not in an overt way. I had White friends. Then in fourth grade, I moved here. I saw that Asians were treated like the scum of the earth. I thought that wasn't going to happen to me. I don't have an accent. I have White friends. But I walked around and people called me chink. They called me chink to my face. (Lee, 1996b, p. 110)

Initially, Young attempted to reject her ethnic identity. In fact, she asserts that she wanted to be White. She assumed that other Asian Americans were discriminated against because they were culturally different (e.g., spoke with an accent). After her own experiences with racism, however, Young began to believe that, regardless of how she acted, non-Asians would always see her as Asian. Her personal experiences led her to embrace her Korean identity and to embrace a panethnic identity as an Asian American. For Young, cultural aspects of her ethnic identity were secondary to the social and political aspects of her identity.

The expression of panethnicity among Asian American high school students demonstrates the way in which contact with outsiders influences ethnic group identity. Asian Americans from various Asian ethnic groups formed a panethnic social group based on their experiences with racism. Students embraced Asian American panethnicity because they believed that it was in their self- and group-interest. The experience of these students suggested that we cannot separate the issue of minority status from ethnicity when considering ethnic identity among Asian Americans and other racial minorities in the United States. Issues of race and power are central to the ethnic and racial identities of Asian American students.

The differences between their home culture and mainstream culture can create internal conflict for some Asian American students. For Asian American youth, struggling to reconcile two cultures, the way in which individuals who are not Asian respond to Asian culture affect the way they see themselves. Furthermore, the process of cultural transformation can create intergenerational conflict within families.

Despite the significance of culture in an individual's life or an ethnic group, I would argue that culture is not the defining element of ethnic identity. My research on Asian American high school and college students suggests that a sense of ethnic identity is not dependent on an individual's connection to the individual's native culture. People can have strong ties to their ethnicities without expressing cultural behavior or beliefs associated with their group. Furthermore, as the case of Hmong college women suggests, individuals can transform significant aspects of their culture (e.g., gender roles) and maintain a strong sense of their ethnic identities.

In short, the formation of ethnic and racial identity among Asian Americans (e.g., how Asian Americans define themselves in relation to others and their attitudes toward their ethnicity) is largely influenced by interracial relationships. Although culture is an aspect of ethnic identity, educators must consider the impact of racism on the formation of ethnic and racial identity among Asian Americans. Interracial relationships influence the way Asian American students perceive themselves, members of their ethnic group, and others who are not Asian.

IMPLICATIONS FOR SCHOOL PRACTICES

As social institutions, schools play a significant role in shaping the formation of ethnic and racial identity among Asian American children. Schools can either foster positive ethnic identities or they can contribute to the formation of negative (e.g., self-hating) ethnic identities among Asian American students. Educators who work with Asian American youth need to respect Asian American cultures and recognize the impact of racism on Asian Americans.

Educators who work with Asian American immigrants and refugees need to be especially aware of the possible differences between home and school culture and the intergenerational tension that can exist in homes in which cultural transformation may be occurring. Schools need to reach out to Asian American families and bring them into the schools. As Walker-Moffat (1995) noted, the use of bilingual and bicultural counselors in elementary and secondary schools can help build the connections between home and school. Bicultural and bilingual counselors can serve as resources for teachers who are learning about their Asian American students and they can help Asian American immigrant students and parents negotiate the school system.

Although schools should recognize and respect the cultures Asian Americans children bring to school, educators should avoid equating culture with ethnicity. Multicultural curricula that define Asian Americans by their cultural practices run the risk of stereotyping. Similarly, preservice and in-service training programs that focus on specific cultural attributes can lead to practice that is simple-minded and stereotypic. In her research on Southeast Asian students, Walker-Moffat (1995) discovered that in the early 1980s, many school districts responded to the large influx of Southeast Asian students by developing in-service programs that were "broadly descriptive and tended to emphasize the exotic or unusual aspects of these cultures. For example, lists of cultural behaviors were sometimes distributed that included warnings against such actions as touching a Buddhist child's head" (p. 150). As Walker-Moffat (1995) argued, these training programs failed to recognize the diversity of Southeast Asians cultures. When we equate culture with ethnicity, we ignore the fact that cultures are constantly in the process of being transformed and we deny the reality of cultural diversity within ethnic and racial groups. As Banks (1997) noted, "the characteristics of ethnic groups and socioeconomic classes can help us understand groups but not individual students" (p. 62).

Multicultural curricula must include discussions of power and inequality that are central to the experiences of Asian Americans and other racial minorities. Rather than focusing solely on Asian cultures, multicultural curricula should focus on the experiences, struggles, and achievements of Asian Americans. Multiculural curricula should teach Asian American and other students about the nature and history of anti-Asian racism. By teaching about the history of Asian Americans, schools can help Asian American youth construct an image of themselves within a broader framework (Grant & Sleeter, 1989; Ladson-Billings, 1995; Sleeter & Grant, 1993). I suggest, for example, that students like Blia might experience less confusion about their identities if Hmong students were taught about the role of the Hmong in the war. Although the teaching of Asian American history cannot alone combat the impact of racism, knowledge of Asian American histories can help Asian Americans resist racism. In short, schools can help foster the formation of a positive ethnic and racial identity among Asian American students by providing them with the opportunity to learn about Asian American experiences and histories.

REFERENCES

Aboud, F. (1988). *Children and prejudice.* New York: Basil Blackwell.

Banks, J. A. (1997). *Educating citizens in a multicultural society.* New York: Teachers College Press.

Barth, F. (Ed.). (1969). *Ethnic groups and boundaries.* Boston: Little, Brown.

Berry, J., Trimble, J., & Olmedo, E. (1986). Assessment of acculturation. In W. Lonner & J. Berry (Eds.), *Field methods in cross-cultural research* (pp. 292–324). Newbury Park, CA: Sage.

Cook, D., & Helms, J. E. (1988). Visible racial/ethnic group supervisees' satisfaction with cross cultural supervision as predicted by relationship characteristics. *Journal of Counseling Psychology, 35*(3), 268–274.

Donnelly, N. (1994). *Changing lives of refugee Hmong women.* Seattle, WA: University of Washington Press.

Espiritu, Y. L. (1992). *Asian American panethnicity: Bridging institutions and identities.* Philadelphia: Temple University Press.

Fugita, S. S., & O'Brien, D. J. (1991). *Japanese American ethnicity: The persistence of community.* Seattle: University of Washington Press.

Goldstein, B. (1985). *Schooling for cultural transitions: Hmong girls and boys in American high schools.* Unpublished doctoral dissertation, University of Wisconsin, Madison.

Grant, C. A., & Sleeter, C. (1989). *Turning on learning: Five approaches for multicultural teaching plans.* Columbus, OH: Merrill.

Ladson-Billings, G. (1995). Toward a theory of culturally relevant pedagogy. *American Educational Research Journal, 32*(3), 465–491.

Ledgerwood, J. (1990). *Changing Khmer conceptions of gender: Women stories and the social order.* Unpublished doctoral dissertation, Cornell University, Ithaca, NY.

Lee, S. J. (1996a, November). *Changing notions of gender: Understanding intergenerational conflict between Cambodian parents and children.* Paper presented at the National Association of Multicultural Education, Annual Conference, Minneapolis, MN.

Lee, S. J. (1996b). *Unraveling the model-minority stereotype: Listening to Asian American youth.* New York: Teachers College Press.

Lee, S. J. (1997). The road to college: Hmong women's pursuit of higher education. *Harvard Educational Review, 67*(4), 803–827.

Nagata, D. (1994). Assessing Asian American acculturation and ethnic identity: The need for a multidimensional framework. *Asian American and Pacific Islander Journal of Health, 2*(2), 108–124.

Okihiro, G. (1994). *Margins and mainstreams: Asians in American history and culture.* Seattle: University of Washington Press.

Osajima, K. (1988). Asian Americans as the model minority: An analysis of the popular press image in the 1960's and 1980's. In G. Y. Okihiro, S. Hune, A. A. Hansen, & J. M. Liu (Eds.), *Reflections on shattered windows: Promises and prospects for Asian American studies* (pp. 165–174). Pullman: Washington State Press.

Phinney, J. S. (1990). Ethnic identity in adolescents and adults: Review of research. *Psychological Bulletin, 108*(3), 499–514.

Rogler, L. H., Cortes, D. E., & Malgady, R. G. (1991). Acculturation and mental health status among Hispanics: Convergence and new directions for research. *American Psychologist, 46*(6), 585–597.

Rotheram, J., & Phinney, J. (1987). Introduction: Definitions and perspectives in the study of children's ethnic socialization. In J. S. Phinney & M. J. Rotheram (Eds.), *Children's ethnic socialization pluralism and development* (pp. 10–28). Newbury Park, CA: Sage.

Sheets, R. H. (1997). Reflection 1: Racial and ethnic awareness. In J. Carnes & R. H. Sheets (Eds.), *Starting small: Teaching tolerance in preschool and the early grades* (pp. 16–21). Montgomery, AL: Teaching Tolerance Project.

Sleeter, C. E., & Grant, C. A. (1993). *Making choices for multicultural education: Five approaches to race, class, and gender* (2nd ed.). Englewood Cliffs, NJ: Merrill/Prentice-Hall.

Smith-Hefner, N. (1993). Education, gender and generational conflict among Khmer refugees. *Anthropology & Education Quarterly, 24*(2), 135–158.

Sodowsky, G., Kwan, K. L., & Pannu, R. (1995). Ethnic identity of Asians in the United States. In J. Ponterotto, J. M. Casas, L. Suzuki, & C. Alexander (Eds.), *Handbook of multicultural counseling* (pp. 123–154). Thousand Oaks, CA: Sage.

Sodowsky, G. R., Maguire, K., Johnson, P., Ngumba, W., & Kohles, R. (1994). World views of White American, Mainland Chinese, Taiwanese, and African students; An investigation into between-group differences. *Journal of Cross-Cultural Psychology, 25*(3), 309–324.

Sue, D. W., & Sue, D. (1990). *Counseling the culturally different: Theory and practice.* New York: Wiley.

Sue, S., & Sue, D. W. (1971). Chinese American personality and mental health. *Amerasia, 1,* 36–44.

Sung, B. L. (1987). *The adjustment experience of Chinese immigrant children in New York.* New York: Center for Migration Studies.

Wakil, S. P., Siddique, C. M., & Wakil, F. A. (1981). Between two cultures: A study in socialization of children of immigrants. *Journal of Marriage and the Family, 43*(4), 929–940.

Walker-Moffat, W. (1995). *The other side of the Asian American success story.* San Francisco: Jossey-Bass.

Waters, M. (1990). *Ethnic options: Choosing identities in America.* Berkeley: University of California Press.

7 Cultural Differences in Child Development: Navajo Adolescents in Middle Schools*

Donna Deyhle
University of Utah

Margaret LeCompte
University of Colorado–Boulder

Many years ago, Margaret Mead went to Samoa at the urging of her professor, Franz Boas, to test the universality of a widely held belief about human development: that sexual maturation in adolescence produced a period of *sturm und drang*, of stress, anxiety, and emotional upheaval. Her analysis of the lives of teenagers in Samoa and other Pacific Island societies (Mead, 1928, 1930) indicated that, at least in some cultures, coming of age is not fraught with sexual tension and ambivalence. She suggested that while the process of biological maturation is unmistakably regular among human beings, how human beings react to that process varies according to each society.

The theory Mead was testing had been developed in and fitted people in Western Europe. It did not, however, describe the behavior of the adolescents Mead studied. Mead and others came to feel that adolescence as westerners know it may be culturally produced, and the rules that develop for appropriate ways to cope with physical maturation may be guided more by social norms than by biological dictates.

As social scientists, our own research has also confirmed the importance of a culturally-based framework that views adolescence as a socially constructed phenomenon. We are aware that these same social constructions of adolescents and their development are used as the conceptual framework underlying programs such as middle schools. To the extent that they represent the constructions of one culture only, such frameworks may put adolescents from other cultures at risk.

In this article, we examine how the design of middle schools is informed by cultural differences in the ways Anglos[1] and Navajos view the stages of human development—especially adolescence—and interpretations of child development and their concomitant requisites for appropriate parenting. We look at the differences between how Anglos and Navajos view child development and parenting, and how these differences help to create misunderstanding in the middle school. Although there is wide variability in lifestyles among both Anglo and Navajo people, members of each group share underlying cultural patterns that influence their behavior and beliefs. These patterns generally legitimate different ways of growing up and of raising children, which constitute "cultural boundaries" (Erickson, 1987) or behavioral evidence of different cultural standards of appropriateness.

The presence of cultural boundaries, by themselves, is a politically neutral phenomenon. However, cultural boundaries can become politically charged when the ideas of one group are granted more legitimacy than those of another group, or are imposed on others. Under these circumstances, cultural boundaries become cultural borders and serve as the genesis of misunderstanding, abuse of power, and oppression. In the two communities we studied, Navajo culture often is used as a border to deny equality by privileging the cultural practices of Anglos over those of Navajos. In particular, educational institutions deny equality by ignoring or denying the existence of the culture of their Navajo students.

CONCEPTIONS OF CHILD DEVELOPMENT

In the public schools, cultural beliefs about the stages of child development and behaviors appropriate for raising children are embedded in western science and counterpoised to Navajo ways of viewing the same biological stages and of rearing children who are at various stages of development. Navajo children face conflict not only because their parents' conceptions of proper ways to raise children are different from those of Anglos, but also because of a related set of differences in attitudes and beliefs about stages in child development.

These include ideas about the age at which a child is responsible for or capable of adult behavior, the degree to which the behavior of children should be controlled by adults, and acceptance of sexual maturity. Where Anglo notions are institutionally reinforced, as they are in schools, they act to disadvantage Navajo children and to further derogate practices that Navajo families believe are appropriate for their children.

While western science treats cognition, moral development, and social development separately, Navajo culture integrates all aspects of development into a unified approach to life experiences and learning. Navajos are concerned far earlier than Anglos with gender role differentiation and have formal ways to recognize life stages, many of which are still practiced.

They also stress the reciprocal nature of relationships among people in the family and community, while western science, or Anglo culture, focuses on individual—rather than collective—cognitive, social, and moral issues.

Avoidance of sexuality in Anglo theories of development reflects western ambivalence about sex in general. Reproduction is relegated to biology—a subject few preteens study in detail—while the bodily changes accompanying physical maturation are treated either as inconvenient and embarrassing or as obstacles to clear intellectual or moral endeavor. Anglos separate biological from social maturity and believe early adolescence is a period of dependence in which parents and teachers are required to provide strong guidance and to protect children from unwise decisions.

Navajo culture begins to emphasize gender role differentiation and acquisition of gender appropriate adult behavior much earlier than does Anglo culture. Navajo culture provides little or no time "in-between" when the individual is neither a child nor an adult. Social and physical maturity occur simultaneously. Within Navajo traditional stages of child development, *Nitsidzikees Dzizlii* ["one begins to think and do things on one's own"] occurs between the ages of 6 and 9. The stage *Hanitsekees Niliinii Hazlii* [one's thoughts begin existing] occupies ages 10 to 15, followed by *Ada Nitsidzikees Dzizlii* [one begins to think for oneself].[2] By age 15, girls and boys are socially and sexually mature; Navajos expect that their physically mature children will begin to exercise socially mature behavior and assume its consequences. These cultural differences mandate different adult–child and parent–child relationships, as illustrated by Table 7.1.

In general, a preteen Navajo child is considered to be nearing adulthood, while an Anglo child of the same age is still considered to be both physically and socially immature. While Table 7.1 greatly over-simplifies cultural differences and certainly does not display all the possible difficulties these differences create in schools, it points out the source of considerable conflict. We have limited discussion in this article to several of these differences that prove particularly troublesome in middle schools: control over versus noninterference in children's affairs, and shame versus acceptance of sexual maturity. The examples that follow come from our own fieldwork on the Navajo Nation.[3]

A DEFINITION OF THE MIDDLE SCHOOL

Middle school children have constituted a problematic age group for public schools. Many states do not certify teachers specifically to teach this age group. The process of rapid physical, intellectual, and social maturation that children ages 11–15 undergo make them difficult for teachers to handle. One remedy for the troublesome characteristics of early adolescence has been the institution of middle schools, which are limited to grades 6–8 and designed to meet the special needs of the 11–15-year-old child.

TABLE 7.1
Some Cultural Differences in Adult/Child Role Expectations

Anglo	Navajo
9–15 year olds:	9–15 year olds:
• are still children; they do not become adults until at least 18	• are becoming adults; they become adults after puberty
• are too immature to make their own decisions	• must learn to make their own decisions and assume the consequences
• do not know what is best for them	• are acquiring understanding of what is in their best interest
• should do what adults tell them to do	• should not be forced to do something they are unwilling to do
Adults:	Adults:
• are responsible for their children's behavior	• do not control their children's behavior
• must make wise decisions on behalf of their children	• Should not interfere in the behavior decisions of others, even their own children
• must make their children obey their directions	• can only provide suggestions and guidance for behavior
• must prevent sexual activity among their children	• Should discourage sexual activity among their children
• should permit gender undifferentiated work/social activities, roles, and expectations among their children	• Should encourage gender segregated work/social activities, roles, and expectations among their children
• show they care for their children by controlling them	• show they care about their children by respecting their independence

While they differ somewhat from expert to expert, middle schools are characterized by:

- integrated interdisciplinary instruction.
- organization of children into cohorts instructed by a group of teachers who work, often for several years, with the same group of students.
- increased attention to psycho-social needs of children.
- reconceptualization of the teacher role to include counseling and mentorship so that each child has a special adult role model.

- reduction of competition among students, especially by eliminating tracking and ability grouping and by emphasizing cooperative, rather than competitive, academic and athletic activities.
- flexible scheduling and grouping.
- increased parent involvement in school activities (Carnegie Council on Adolescence, 1989; Connors & Irvin, 1989; Jones, 1990; Wiles & Bondi, 1981).

Middle schools are to deliver the kind of integrated, cross-disciplinary, and challenging instruction needed to keep preteens interested in school. Critical to the success of the middle school is an increase in the intimacy of peer group and adult–child relationships, hence the creation of student cohorts that limit the number of students each teacher interacts with, and the shift in teacher role from mere instructor to adult role model and mentor. Implicitly, they also provide shelter for girls from the sexual predations of high school males, while giving boys respite from competition with the same high school boys, whose athletic prowess might damage the self-esteem of preteen boys. As will be illustrated in the following sections, several aspects of this definition of a middle school run counter to Navajo cultural practices.

CONTROL VERSUS NONINTERFERENCE

Jack[4] had been absent from school all week His English teacher responded with frustration: "That seventh grader was away from home for 5 days, and his parents don't care!" He pointed to the week's absentee list. "Almost one-third of my Navajo students were absent this week. Their parents just don't support their education. How can I teach when they are not in my classes? And Jack, he is a good student when he comes to class, a real nice kid."

Deyhle had known Jack for 8 years and agreed with his teacher—he was a pleasant young man. She also had grown to understand that Jack was being raised in a Navajo family, with culturally distinct values and behaviors. He lived on the reservation in a mobile home with his parents, brother, two sisters and their husbands and five children, and traveled almost 100 miles each day to attend school. He enjoyed school and he enjoyed life in the Navajo community. Both worlds required different kinds of responsibilities—responsibilities that sometimes conflicted.

Several days later Deyhle heard a Navajo explanation for Jack's absence from school. At the laundry Jack's sister explained why her parents went to the nearby town. "They went to look for Jack. He went to see Rambo II with friends and never came home. If he was in trouble we would know. But now the family needs him to herd sheep tomorrow." Because Jack's family, like most reservation-dwelling families, had no telephone, they could not call to locate him. She explained that their crops were ready to be planted, sheep needed to be sheared, and a Native American Church[5] meeting needed to be planned. The whole family was needed at home to help.

That evening Jack and his parents stopped by Deyhle's home on their way home from town. Their Pathfinder was crammed with groceries, a new generator, parts for a water pump, and water barrels. With proper Navajo courtesy they waited in their car until Deyhle acknowledged their presence and invited them inside. As they unfolded from the car, Jack's dad said, "We found him. And now he gets to work on the water pump in the garden." His mother turned in his direction and said teasingly, "Now maybe school will look easy!" Jack stayed at home for several days, helping with the irrigation of the corn field, before he decided to return to school.

Jack's story illuminates many issues. One is the difference between Anglo and Navajo philosophies of parenting. Specifically, Navajo conceptions of early adulthood and the value of noninterference guide and frame patterns of youthful social interactions both in and outside of school. Navajo parents are not likely to assume the roles Anglo teachers and schools might expect of them because they have different views of childrearing. In turn, Navajo youth do not act the way Anglo teachers and schools expect them to act because they are presented with an alternative and viable set of values from their parents (Deyhle, 1991).

The integrity of Navajo culture can be seen clearly in the relationships between parents and their children. Two apparently opposing concepts function within Navajo culture. The autonomy of the individual regarding possessions and actions is strongly maintained, while at the same time the consensus and cooperation of the group is desired (Kluckhohn & Leighton, 1962; Lamphere, 1977; Leighton & Kluckhohn, 1948). Appropriate cooperative behavior is encouraged, but individualistic behavior is respected without overt punishment. As Lamphere (1977) points out, "the phrase t'a'a'bee bo'holni'i ['it's up to him or her to decide,' 'it's his or her business,' or 'it's his or her area of concern'] combines Navajo emphasis on autonomy and consensus, and it implies egalitarian rather than hierarchical authority relations" (p. 41).

Authority relations between parent and child are egalitarian among Navajos, in contrast to the hierarchical relationships found among Anglos. Anglos expect, at some level, to "rule" their children; Navajos do not believe such a degree of control is possible or appropriate. This means that many Navajo parents, as with Jack's parents, are unwilling to make decisions for their children, even it if means poor school attendance. By contrast, school personnel, who view this culturally specific behavior as "permissive," are critical of Navajo parents' "lack of control" over their children.

Concurrent with the Navajo behavioral ideal of egalitarian authority relations is the ethic of noninterference. Although any relationship involves a measure of influence or control, among Navajos direct interference, either verbal or physical, is regarded as inappropriate behavior. Childrearing patterns teach Navajo youth that noninterference in any social interaction is decent and normal. Children are reluctant to interrupt adult activities and adults respect children's play activities and do not interfere in them. Thus, Navajo youth grow up understanding how to act "successfully" without coercion and learn to mistrust even gentle attempts to manipulate or control them. In short, it is not appropriate to control others, regardless of one's individual desires. It is not polite or decent to tell people what they should do; adults, including young teenagers, are considered capable of making their own decisions.

A subtle example of this principle can be seen in proper "visiting" etiquette when approaching a home on or off the reservation. When interviewing families Deyhle was instructed in this ethic by Jan, her 13-year-old Navajo translator. As they approached the home of Jan's aunt the first house on her list, and uncle, she said, "Sit here and wait. That way if they don't have time for us, or it is bad, it doesn't hurt them." They sat for 5 minutes in silence. The front door of the mobile home opened and her uncle smiled and waved. She turned and said, "See, now we can go in 'cause we are wanted."

It would have been considered rude to get out of the car before someone in the house had acknowledged the visit—as Jack and his parents had done when they waited outside Deyhle's house. The visit can be either ignored or accepted, without causing any face-to-face embarrassment between the guest and visitor. Neither party is "imposed on" or rejected by the event; the ethic of noninterference allows for the freedom, privacy, and dignity of both parties. It also can lead to confusion and frustration in interactions between Navajos and Anglos, who are accustomed to "friendly" directives.

The ethic of noninterference contrasts sharply with the Anglo value of being one's "brother's keeper," which can be manifested in giving advice, directions, or verbal coercion to "help" others do what is viewed as in their best interest (Wax & Thomas, 1961). Anglo children learn, from their elders, peers, mass media, and in school to manipulate others to achieve personal gains. They are taught via games and stories that great leaders were ones who managed to get others to follow—the theme underlying the game, "Follow the Leader." They learn that to be "successful" one must be an expert manipulator of people or events. These "human relations skills" are highly valued in Anglo society and their nonexistence among Navajos leads to both miscommunication and negative stereotyping in schools.

An ethic of noninterference does not mean that Navajo parents do not provide guidance in their children's lives and schooling. Parents make their desires known, often through "teasing" rather than admonishments and commands. Teasing among Navajos is a traditional form of social control, a subtle means of reinforcing the solidarity of the Navajo community and culture. It is also used as a means of "nudging" one to act appropriately without directly demanding a change of behavior (Kluckhohn & Leighton, 1962).

Jack's mother and father teased him by suggesting that work at home was going to be harder than classwork and that he might want to consider returning to school. They believed he should be in school, but they left the ultimate decision for him to make. From the Navajo parents' perspective, it is inappropriate to make decisions for their middle- and high- school-aged children, whom they consider to be nearing adulthood and capable of making their own decisions. They guide their children and make their opinions known, but the cultural values of individual autonomy for and noninterference in the affairs of youth are still practiced. Anglo parents and school officials, who classified these parents as both "uneducated" and "uncaring," interpret this to mean that Navajo parents do not "take care" of their teenaged children.

SHAME VERSUS ACCEPTANCE

In the mid-1980s, the general failure of middle grade schooling was attributed to discontinuities between elementary and secondary schooling. Mainstream educators came to believe that the poor academic performance of preteens could be attributed to the social–emotional demands associated with rapid sexual maturation. Preadolescents simply were too preoccupied with growing up to excel in school. Their raging hormones and uneven physical development interfered with logical thought processes. Preteens were defined as people in need of special guidance from adult role models until body, intellect, and soul could catch up with one another. Of particular concern was the uneven maturation of boys and girls; girls often achieve their full stature and reproductive capabilities more quickly than boys, who often continue to resemble their elementary school peers for a few more years.

These differences were viewed by educators as potential sources of low self-esteem, poor social adjustment, and subsequent academic failure (Wiles & Bondi, 1981). They also correspond to the Anglo version of child development and the patterns of adult–child relations deemed appropriate by Anglos (see Table 7.1). They do not, however, coincide with Navajo beliefs about social and biological maturation or the way Navajos believe children should be prepared for life.

The fact of sexual maturity is accepted at an earlier age among Navajos than it is among Anglos. For females, this maturity is celebrated and affirmed with *Kinaalda,* a Navajo puberty ceremony that marks the beginning of Navajo womanhood.[6] Birth and the security and power of women in the Navajo matriarchy give pregnancy, even at an early age, a different meaning.

Deyhle's Navajo friend, Sue Jones, stopped by to visit with her 6-year-old daughter. Deyhle asked how her other daughters, both in high school, were doing in school. With an embarrassed smile she said, "I'm going to be a grandmother. I'm too young to be a grandmother! It's Jan, she's going to have a baby."

Jan was 14 and had just started eighth grade. She had her *Kinaalda* the previous year. "It was that guy we took in. He had no parents. But we didn't expect he would do this to our daughter. I always told my daughters that they were like flowers. They were beautiful roses that opened up. And not to let that be spoiled. But what can you do? I can't tell them important for them to what to do. They are responsible for what they do."

Over the next 8 months, Jones prepared for the birth of her first grandchild. She helped her daughter with her diet, advice, support, and gathering baby blankets and clothes. The excitement of the entire family was evident in endless talk about names for the baby. The family encouraged Jan to remain in school, and Jones prepared to assume childcare responsibilities for the baby while her daughter finished school. Shortly after Jan finished eighth grade, her baby was born. With the support of her family, Jan returned to school in the fall.

Her mother explained. "Some parents discourage their daughter to return to school. They say, 'Daughter, you need to grow up now. You have a baby.' They said that about Jan. But we want her to finish school. It is important for her to finish." Jan left school in the middle of the year. She said, "The teachers, you know, they look at you differently. They know you have had a baby and they stay away from you. I didn't like the way they looked at me." Holding her baby she smiled, "I really wanted a baby of my own. I would be really happy, then, at home with my baby. That's what us Navajos do."

Since Jan was Navajo, she was not punished, not forced to leave home or get married, and not pressured to give her baby up for adoption. Had Jan been Anglo, she may have been forced to accept one of these options. Certainly the fact of her pregnancy would have been hushed up to avoid shame and embarrassment to her family. By contrast, while Jones would have preferred for her daughter to postpone childbirth until she had finished school and found a man with whom she wanted to share her life, Jan's success in creating new life and her new social position in Navajo culture overshadowed other considerations. Although Jan's family, like most Navajo families, feel temporary embarrassment and regret when a young girl becomes pregnant, has a baby, and leaves school, there still was joy and support for the young mother and acceptance of the new baby (Deyhle, 1992).

Teachers in Jan's school, however, view pregnancy either as a biological imperative or a mistake. A science teacher explained, "The girls turn 14 and all they can think of is [being] 'boy crazy.' The Navajo race is a pure one and survival is important. I'm a biologist and I speak from this angle. [They get pregnant because] it is reproduce." This teacher's pseudo-scientific explanation for teenaged pregnancy may be a bit extreme. However, Anglo theories of development that guide the professional training of teachers generally do not place the maturation process within a cultural frame work. They provide no way to treat adolescent sexual maturity or behavior as normal or to legitimate it with culturally sanctioned forms of social interactions, as the Navajo do with *Kinaalda*. As a consequence, Anglo educators and the schools in which they work render the inevitable process of physical growth and development embarrassing and unattractive to students, and slightly indecent and academically troublesome to their teachers.

MISMATCH BETWEEN
MIDDLE SCHOOLS AND NAVAJO CULTURE

In the following sections, LeCompte describes the events surrounding the establishment of a middle school in Castle Rock District, which serves an overwhelmingly Navajo population. Critical to our discussion is that issues of cultural difference in the ways developing children are viewed and treated never entered into the middle school planning process. This is not surprising because teacher training generally does not prepare teachers to consider cultural issues to be critical and integral factors in the teaching and learning process. The consequence was that although Castle Rock educators were genuinely interested in good teaching, the fact that cultural differences other than language were ignored, rendered invisible, or considered to be irrelevant meant that any changes in educational structure or institutional delivery that might have been beneficial to Navajo children were accidental. Table 7.2 presents a comparison between the objectives of

TABLE 7.2
Comparison of Middle School Goals with Navajo
Cultural Goals for Children Ages 9–15

Middle School Goals	*Navajo Cultural Goals*
• Increased adult guidance and parental involvement	• Attenuation of adult guidance and involvement
• Protection from premature adulthood and sexuality	• Practice in and mastery of gender appropriate skills
• Avoidance or minimization of gender differences	• Formal recognition of gender differences
• Blurring of gender differences in work roles	• Acquisition of gender appropriate work skills/roles
• Reduction of competition and public comparisons	• Avoidance of competition and public comparisons
• Integrating instruction across disciplines and content areas	• Learning the interdependence of all human beings and animals with the physical and social environment

the middle school and the expectations Navajo parents have for their 9–15-year-old children.

While some features of middle school philosophy, such as reduction in competitive activities and integrated curricula, are congruent with Navajo culture, others are not. A critical area of conflict is that the pattern of adult–child guidance mandated in middle schools acts to infantilize 11–15-year-old Navajos who, as Table 7.1 indicates, already are becoming adults in their own culture. A second area of concern is that, following mainstream Anglo theories of child development, the middle school model fails to confront directly the reality of sexual maturation processes, perhaps the most salient factor in the lives of 11–15 year olds.

In Castle Rock, well-meaning attempts to improve education for Navajo children were impeded not only by normal institutional resistance but by uncritical acceptance of educational innovations that were not entirely appropriate for the culture of the children served and by misinformation about or ignorance of Navajo culture. Compounding these issues was the bias in teacher training institutions toward treating multicultural issues as an add-on or elective, rather than as a conceptual frame that should underpin the practice of any human institution. Such bias permits prospective teachers to believe that the principles of child development they learned in educational psychology classes are generalizable to all cultures.

PLANNING A MIDDLE SCHOOL IN CASTLE ROCK

The new principal at Castle Rock, Frank Lewis, began the planning process for the middle school by setting up committees, one of which was to design a middle school philosophy for Castle Rock. He began discussions with the philosophy committee by asking members to define the differences between middle school children and high school or elementary school children, as a way to decide what unique needs their special age group had. The most frequent topic of conversation was what teachers felt to be the ludicrous mismatch in body size and physical development between middle-school-aged girls and boys. "Some of our boys are just like the intermediate kids, while the girls are already women, with breasts and developing and all that. They just look so funny together!"

The mismatch in physical development was aggravated by the high proportion of overaged students, a consequence of Castle Rock District's practice of retaining many children because of poor academic performance. According to teachers, some of the sixth graders were "so big that they were sprouting beards!" The teachers worried that sexually mature or precocious students were a bad influence on the other children. They believed that the older, physically more mature students bullied the younger ones and caused discipline problems.

Much discussion also was devoted to issues of protection: Middle school children needed to be protected from older children, from predatory adults, and from each other until they were mature enough to handle adult emotions and interactions. These discussions contrasted sharply with Navajo practices displayed in Table 7.1, which, while not leaving children unprotected, help children learn at an early age to assume adult responsibilities—and to take the consequences of their actions.

Another factor was general teacher resistance to the concept of middle schools. A majority of the Castle Rock faculty consisted of former high school or junior high school teachers who had moved to the middle school when the junior high school (grades 7–9) was eliminated. They felt the physical maturation process of preteen students interfered with academic work. Subject matter specialists found the behavior of preadolescents particularly exasperating; they felt such children were not ready yet for serious study. "I don't even like to teach ninth graders," said one former high school teacher. "By the time kids get to tenth grade, their hormones have settled down a little and they can begin to think again."

These teachers also resisted the change in teacher roles mandated by the middle school (see discussion at beginning of article), especially the interdisciplinary and integrated approach to instruction; increased emphasis on psycho-social needs, counseling, and mentoring; and cooperative grouping. These approaches, they said, babied children, were inappropriate requirements for teachers, and took too much time from an already crowded school day.

Notable at planning meetings and during many meetings with the principal alone was the absence of any discussion of how cultural differences might affect the organization of middle schools on the Navajo Nation. LeCompte suggested that Navajos might have different ways of interpreting and addressing biological stages, and that the interpretations Navajos had might differ from those Anglos learned in their child development courses. As evidence, she mentioned *Kinaalda,* and in particular, how Linda Thomas, a sixth grade teacher, believed that the matter-of-fact way Navajos treated biological maturity among females seemed to help her students deal more responsibly with their physical adulthood.

In an interview with LeCompte earlier in the year, Thomas said that, in her opinion, though Navajo culture might be changing. It still was a powerful force in the lives of her students. She wanted to form a study group among the teachers to learn more about Navajo notions of development. Sitting in her classroom after school, she said: "We just don't Know much about what our Navajo parents think. And I think it would really help us if we did. [For example] girls in my class are starting to have their periods. And I know that almost all of them have a *Kinaalda,* that ceremony girls have to celebrate it. It's supposed to be 4 days or something like that, and some of them have shorter ones because it interferes with school, or they postpone it till their next period if there is a big exam or a basketball game they have to play, but they still have it." Her voice became incredulous. "You know, most of the teachers don't even know that. It isn't even that the traditional ceremonies interfere with school. If the kids care about school, they'll figure out a way to do both—have the ceremony and still make it to school. It really helps them." She paused. "I think that the girls who have had the *Kinaalda* and the boys who saw the ceremony are a lot more mature. They are the only ones who don't giggle and get all silly when we talk about reproduction in biology. They seem to have a grown up sense about it all, to sort of take it for granted."

That the information Thomas possessed about her Navajo students was not shared by her colleagues became clear in a meeting of the philosophy group. The teachers were stymied. "What's *Kinaalda?*" they asked. "Oh, it's just an old ritual," said Lewis. "Hardly anybody does it anymore. And besides, biology is biology. What's important is to make sure that these kids feel good about themselves." He stopped to refer to his notes. "Now, let's work on designing athletic activities so that those little boys don't feel stupid. And if we can make [the mentorship program] work, and I know some people here don't really believe in it, but if we can just stick to our guns I think we can make these kids feel more like school is a place that cares about them."

AVOIDING THE CULTURE CONCEPT

Castle Rock's transformation to a middle school also was impeded by both administrative and teacher resistance to the concept of cultural differences. Lewis had been hired with the specific expectation that he would bring the philosophy of the school into accord with its new grade-level reorganization. He had spent all his professional career teaching on the Navajo Nation, and although he was Anglo, he was viewed by the administration as very knowledgeable about Navajo children. However, even Anglos such as Lewis, who have worked with Navajos for years, often have acquired a store of distorted, incomplete, or biased knowledge about Navajo culture (Breningstall & LeCompte, 1992; LeCompte, 1993). As we indicate in the following pages, Lewis was no exception. His reliance on Bob George, the primary school principal, for the theoretical underpinnings of his middle school also led to avoidance of cultural issues. In an interview regarding the relevance of culture to stages of child development, George told LeCompte:

> I don't think culture has much to do with it. Child development, you know, Piaget and all that, those ideas are just generalizable for all cultures. I didn't think much of the courses I had in the school of education, but I think that what we learned in those ed psych courses is pretty much true for all kids. All kids really grow up in the same way.

Lewis echoed George's assertion: Biology was biology, and culture didn't have anything to do with it. It was true that Lewis cared deeply about the feelings of children and worked hard to implement a number of innovations that benefited the school, especially its special education program. However, the solutions he sought came from the United States educational mainstream and, like his reaction to *Kinaalda,* rendered cultural considerations more or less irrelevant.

Teacher resistance to cultural differences was fueled by their belief that Navajo culture was disintegrating. With the exception of a few "traditionals who demonstrated visible signs of commitment to cultural practices, such as the long bun into which traditional men bound their hair, they believed few people in their district practiced traditional rituals. Interviews over a 2-year period (1991–1992) with all the middle school teachers indicated-that most believed cultural differences were irrelevant to their teaching. Only 3 percent said they made any alteration in how they taught to accommodate their predominantly Navajo student population. For the most part, the alterations involved speaking more slowly for students who spoke English poorly and avoiding forcing students into public recitations (Breningstall & LeCompte, 1992; LeCompte & Wiertelak, 1991, 1992). In fact, except for murals of southwestern life and landscapes lining the hallways, the school and its classrooms were practically devoid of material evidence demonstrating its location in the heart of the Navajo Nation.

CONCLUSION

We have tried not to hold teachers and administrators in the districts we studied accountable for training they had not received or for ideas not contained in the training they did receive. However, we have used their stories to make clear the consequences that accompany failure to consider cultural issues in schooling. As the mainstream of American education becomes increasingly non-White and non-European in origin, the importance of these issues will become more and more apparent, and marked by increasing conflict between school and community—as has been the case in the communities we studied. Some conflict will arise over taken-for-granted assumptions embedded in culture, such as the different stance Navajos and Anglos take toward sexual maturation and adulthood. Since biological maturation occurs while a child is in middle school, differences in cultural practices surrounding puberty can be expected to be a source of conflict in these institutions.

Since middle school children are beginning to test and shed their dependence upon adults, another source of potential conflict is the differing amount of legitimate authority over children cultures accord to parents and teachers. Like many Anglo educators, including those who criticized Jack's parents, Lewis defined "caring for" children in terms of control over their behavior. Teachers—and parents—who did interfere in the lives of their students—or children—not when they were making unwise choices were teachers and parents who role teachers in the middle school were to assume did not was, in Lewis's eyes, a way to show students that care. The mentoring "school is a place that cares about them."

Navajo students and their parents, however, often see this kind of caring as culturally inappropriate and unwarranted interference. They also find it devoid of the kind of caring and attention they feel they really need: tutoring with homework, more explanation of difficult assignments, and help in making up work when transportation or family problems cause them to be absent (LeCompte, Wiertelak, & Murphy, 1993).

These differences in the definition of "parent involvement" were not known or considered by the Castle Rock planning committees, which spent considerable time on ways to increase parent involvement. Their focus was on inducing more parents to come to school so they could reinforce school expectations for school work and attendance, rather than on learning from the parents what they and the community thought appropriate for their children.

In our work, we have noticed how Anglo notions of appropriate ways of growing up are institutionalized in educational systems. At the same time, Navajo notions of appropriate ways to raise children are derogated by teachers who are ignorant or disrespectful or native culture. Much research has asserted the importance of multicultural education and the need for educators to develop sensitivity to the culture of the students they teach. However, our own research in two Navajo communities indicates that multicultural education has done little to overcome deeply rooted patterns of ignorance and bigotry that Anglos hold regarding children of color, especially in the middle and upper grades. We believe educators should be held accountable for recognizing and eliminating these patterns of prejudice. We also believe schools of education should be held accountable for changing teacher training to eliminate biases introduced by ignoring cultural differences.

NOTES

*This chapter is reprinted with permission from: Deyhle, Donna, & LeCompte, Margaret. (1994). Cultural Differences in Child Development: Navajo Adolescents in Middle Schools. *Theory Into Practice, 33*, 156–166. (Theme issue on "Rethinking Middle Grades"). Copyright 1994, College of Education, The Ohio State University.

Both authors contributed equally in the conception and writing of this article. The authors are grateful to Mary Ellen Wiertelak and Dana Murphy for assistance in preparing graphics for this article, to the Metropolitan Life Foundation which has provided support for LeCompte's research in "Castle Rock," and to the Spence Foundation for its support of Deyhle's research on the Navajo Nation. Although they must remain unnamed, the authors would like to thank the hundreds of Anglo and Navajo people who made their research possible.

1. Although somewhat contested as a term that attempts to represent all majority people, we use the term "Anglo" as a cultural descriptor, rather than "White" which can be more narrowly interpreted as a racial descriptor. Navajos in both communities also used the term "Anglo."

2. See Begay and Begay (1982) for a detailed chart comparing the developmental stages of Piaget, Kohlberg, Erickson, Havighurst, and traditional Navajo stages.

3. As an ethnographer, Deyhle has conducted research over the past 10 years in a border reservation community. Her research has focused on Navajo youth, their families, the schools they attend, and their economic and social lives in the Navajo community. LeCompte was a consultant and researcher for a school district on the Navajo Nation undergoing restructuring. Over the past 4 years she worked with the administration and teachers to implement a culturally compatible curriculum. From these two vantage points we tie together the issues of culturally constructed knowledge and school restructuring.

4. All names appearing in this article are pseudonyms.

5. The Native American Church, commonly referred to as the Peyote religion, is a pan-Indian, semi-Christian, nativistic religious movement in the course of whose ritual believers eat the Peyote cactus, a substance containing more than 10 alkaloids, the best known of which is mescaline. It is pan-Indian in the sense that its origins are traced to the Plains Indian nativistic religious movements at the turn of the century. It was introduced to the Navajo from the Ute, their neighbors to the north of their reservation. See Aberle (1982).

6. With a Navajo girl's first menses, she becomes a young woman and has a "coming of age" ceremony to usher her into adult society. The chief aim of the 4-day ceremony is to impart the physical, moral, and intellectual strength she will need to carry out the duties of a Navajo woman, following the example set by Changing Woman in the creation story. Details of the ceremony are reported by Begay (1983) and Frisbe (1964).

REFERENCES

Aberle, D. P. (1982). *The Peyote religion among the Navajo.* Chicago: University of Chicago Press.

Begay, S. M. (1983). *Kinaalda. A Navajo puberty ceremony.* Rough Rock, AZ: Rough Rock Demonstration School, Navajo Curriculum Center.

Begay, S. M., & Begay, W. (1982). *Comparisons of Navajo and western scientific theories of cognitive and personality development, birth through adolescence.* Rough Rock, AZ: Rough Rock Demonstration School.

Breningstall, O., & LeCompte, M. D. (1992, December 2–6). *Constructing success, constructing failure: Culture, achievement and identity among Navajo adolescents.* Paper presented at the meeting of the American Anthropological Association, San Francisco.

Carnegie Council on Adolescent Development. (1989). *Turning points: Preparing American youth for the 21st century.* Washington, DC: Carnegie Corporation of New York.

Connors, N. A., & Irvin, J. L. (1989). Is "middle-school-ness" an indicator of excellence? *Middle School Journal, 21,* 12–14.

Deyhle, D. (1991). Empowerment and cultural conflict: Navajo parents and the schooling of their children. *Qualitative Studies in Education, 4,* 277–297.

Deyhle, D. (1992, January). Constructing failure and maintaining cultural identity: Navajo and Ute school leavers. *Journal of American Indian Education,* 24–47.

Erickson, F. (1987). Transformation and school success: The politics and culture of educational achievement. *Anthropology and Education Quarterly, 18,* 262–275.

Frisbe, C. J. (1964). *Kinaalda: A study of the Navajo girl's puberty ceremony.* Middletown, CT: Wesleyan University Press.

Jones, M. G. (1990). Cooperative learning: Developmentally appropriate for middle level students. *Middle School Journal, 22,* 12–16.

Kluckhohn, C., & Leighton, D. (1962). *The Navajo.* New York: American Museum of Natural History.

Lamphere, L. (1977). *To run after them. Cultural and social bases of cooperation in a Navajo community.* Tucson: University of Arizona Press.

LeCompte, M. D. (1993, April 12–16). *Controlling the discourse of culture: School reform as an obstacle to reform in an American Indian public school district.* Paper presented at the annual meeting of the American Educational Research Association, Atlanta, GA.

LeCompte, M. D., & Wiertelak, M. E. (1991, November 24–27). *The multiple voices of empowerment: How one school defined restructuring.* Paper presented at the meeting of the American Anthropological Association, Chicago.

LeCompte, M. D., & Wiertelak, M. E. (1992, December 2–6). *Constructing the appearance of reform: Restructuring, site-based management and shared decision-making in a Navajo school district.* Paper presented at the meeting of the American Anthropological Association, San Francisco.

LeCompte, M. D., Wiertelak, M. E., & Murphy. D. (1993, February 1). *Report of a survey of high school teachers and seniors: Opinions on the 90-minute period* (Evaluation report submitted to "Castle Rock" high school teachers and administrators).

Leighton. D., & Kluckhohn, C. (1948). *Children of the people.* Cambridge, MA: Harvard University Press.

Mead, M. (1928). *Coming of age in Samoa: A psychological study of primitive youth for Western civilization.* New York: Murrow.

Mead, M. (1930). *Growing up in New Guinea: A comparative study of primitive education.* New York: Murrow.

Wax, R. H., & Thomas, R. K. (1961). American Indians and White people. *Phylon, 22,* 305–317.

Wiles, J., & Bondi, J. (1981). *The essential middle school.* Columbus, OH: Merrill.

8

The Transmission of Family Values Across Generations of Mexican, Mexican American, and Anglo American Families: Implications for Mental Health

Norma Rodriguez
Pitzer College

Manuel Ramirez III
University of Texas, Austin

Maurice Korman
University of Texas Southwestern Medical Center, Dallas

It has been observed (Ardila, 1993; Betancourt & Lopez, 1993; Ramirez, 1983) that a North American–Western European ideology is dominant in cross-cultural psychology. The North American and Western European perspectives, based on notions of cultural and racial superiority, conceive of the cultures and families of people of color as interfering with the cognitive and emotional development of children and adolescents. Ramirez and Castaneda (1974) identified the exclusivist and superiority perspectives of the North American and Western European paradigms as a damaging culture view in developmental psychology. This perspective, prominent in research on Mexican Americans, served as the basis for enacting educational policies and practices congruent with mainstream, middle-class American values. These strategies suggest that Mexican Americans and other ethnic and cultural groups of color must assimilate if they hope to achieve and adapt to American society (Buriel, 1984). However, most of the research supporting the damaging culture hypothesis (Diaz-Guerrero, 1955; Heller,

1966, 1971; Holtzman, Diaz-Guerrero, & Swartz, 1975) has been fraught with conceptual and methodological difficulties (Ramirez, 1983; Ramirez, in press). This study addresses some of these shortcomings by employing a cultural values approach in examining the family values and mental health of Mexican, Mexican American, and Anglo American adolescents.

Heller's (1966, 1971) conclusions evidenced the European worldview in research focusing on Mexican Americans. According to Heller, Mexican Americans fail to achieve in American society because they have a language problem with a foreign accent often persisting into the third generation, are trained for dependent behavior, and seldom show initiative or freely express their own ideas. Large families retard the progress of adolescents, Heller concluded, by failing to socialize children in the habits of self-discipline and independent behavior necessary for school achievement. Heller also implied that Mexican American children are products of a culture dominated by values that make it difficult for them to succeed in American educational settings.

The European worldview appears in research on Mexican children, adolescents, and young adults. Diaz-Guerrero (1955) concluded that the dynamics in Mexican families and the corresponding separation of sex roles in the culture contribute to a disproportionately high incidence of neuroses among Mexicans. Furthermore, the Mexican family encourages the development of a passive orientation to life, and provides almost every aspect of the ideal setting for the development of the Oedipus Complex in males and females.

Additional evidence of this worldview can be found in research by Holtzman et al. (1975). These researchers compared Anglo American children in Austin, Texas with Mexican children in Mexico City and found that the Mexican children had scored lower than the Anglo American children on several of the intellectual and cognitive measures and tests used. They used this research evidence to suggest that mainstream, middle-class American culture, in comparison to Mexican culture, promotes the development of a dynamic, complex, and sophisticated level of psychological functioning by emphasizing autonomy in childrearing, an active style of coping with life's problems and challenges, and by providing greater opportunity for cognitive development. However, they failed to note that most of the instruments used had been developed with Anglo Americans in the United States and thus, are of questionable validity for use with Mexican children.

The North American and European worldviews, however, are still very much in evidence in a recent paper by one of the authors of the previous study. Diaz-Loving, Reyes-Lagunes, and Diaz-Guerrero (1995) concluded that the problems with graduate education in psychology in Mexico can be attributed to the strong hierarchical structure of Latin American affiliative, obedient, sociocentric societies—the damaging culture view.

What is particularly problematic with studies supporting the damaging culture view is that the supposed underlying cultural differences have sel-

dom been examined. Instead, researchers erroneously equate cultural or ethnic group membership with culture and make attributions about a culture solely on the basis of group membership (Buriel, 1984). This approach, however, tells us little about the components of culture thought to influence behavior (Betancourt & Lopez, 1993; Phinney, 1996) and makes the assumption that cultural and ethnic groups are homogeneous (Buriel, 1984). According to Betancourt and Lopez (1993), both mainstream and cross-cultural psychologists have failed to address the study of culture adequately. Although mainstream psychologists usually do not include the study of culture, cross-cultural psychologists tend to focus on differences between or among cultural groups without identifying the specific elements of culture that are thought to influence behavior. Betancourt and Lopez (1993) stated:

> As a general approach, we propose that both mainstream and cross-cultural investigators identify and measure directly what about the group variable (for example, what cultural element) of interest to their research influences behavior. Then, hypothesized relationships between such variables and the psychological phenomenon of interest could be examined and such research could be incorporated within a theoretical framework. We believe that an adherence to this approach will serve to enhance our understanding of both group-specific and group-general (universal) processes as well as contribute to the integration of culture in theory development and the practice of psychology. (p. 630)

Another problem with studies supporting the damaging culture view and other studies on culture in general, is the confounding of socioeconomic status (SES) with culture. This complex issue has no easy solutions. On the one hand, there are studies that attribute differences to culture despite failing to control for SES when comparing two or more economically dissimilar cultural groups (Buriel, 1984). This approach may be misattributing the effects of SES to culture. On the other hand, researchers who are cognizant of the potential impact of SES on a given psychological phenomenon often follow up significant group differences with an analysis to statistically remove the effects of SES. Betancourt and Lopez (1993) noted:

> Although this approach has the advantaged of reducing the likelihood of misattributing to culture the influence of SES, the possibility of confusion still exists. It is possible, for instance, that cultural influences are not identified and are wrongly attributed to SES. (p. 632)

Also, given that the effects of SES and culture are so intertwined for certain groups of people, how is it possible to statistically remove the effects of SES? Although there are no easy solutions to this complex issue, perhaps a more effective research approach would be to examine cultural groups from the same SES background and then identify the underlying cultural variables thought to influence particular behaviors.

Still another problem with research in this area is reflective of the *etic–emic controversy*. This distinction was first applied in anthropology by Pike (1954) who made an analogy with the terms used in linguistics—phon*etic*s involves the use of a universal coding system for sounds employed in any language, whereas phon*emic*s involves the use of meaning-bearing units in a particular language. Pike argued in favor of using the emic approach to enter a culture and see it from the perspective of its own members. However, most mainstream and cross-cultural psychologists have been reluctant to reject universalistic principles (Ramirez, 1983; Ramirez, in press). Instead, researchers continue to use etic approaches, and at times, disguise them as emic approaches. For instance, researchers sometimes translate an instrument into another language, failing to recognize that the cultural content of the instrument remains the same (Matsumoto, 1994). This is evident in the study by Holtzman et al. (1975), in which they tested Mexican children with the Spanish version of instruments originally developed for Anglo Americans.

Given the limitations of approaches that cross-cultural and mainstream psychologists typically employ when purportedly examining the influence of culture, we decided to take a cultural values approach to examining the transmission of family attitudes across generations and to determine whether these attitudes are having an impact on the mental health status of Mexican, Mexican American, and Anglo American adolescents. The approach focuses on family. Previous research has shown that Latinos, in contrast to Anglo Americans, hold strong family values (Ramirez & Castaneda, 1974), that the internal family structure of Latinos remains relatively unchanged during the acculturation process (Rueschenberg & Buriel, 1989), and that even the most highly acculturated Latinos embrace stronger values in the area of perceived family support than Anglo Americans (Sabogal, Marin, Otero-Sabogal, Marin, & Perez-Stable, 1987).

Consistent with research by Ramirez and Castaneda (1974) and Castaneda (1984), we distinguished two opposing sets of family values and corresponding socialization practices—traditional and modern. Traditional family values and socialization goals emphasize the role of a supernatural force in explaining the purpose and meaning of existence (manifested in religious values and practices); identification with and loyalty to the family and community; cooperative interpersonal relationships and achievement; and respect for authority, which is viewed as a source of wisdom and guidance. Modern family values and socialization goals emphasize the role of science in explaining the origins of life; development of an individualistic identity; competitive interpersonal relationships and achievement; and an egalitarian social organization. Although there is evidence of intragroup variability in family values, Mexican culture has been found to be most reflective of traditional family values, whereas Anglo American culture has been found to be most reflective of modern family values (Ramirez & Castaneda, 1974). Mexican American culture, on the other hand, reflects an amalgamation of traditional and modern family values, or a bicultural value orientation.

PURPOSE OF THE STUDY

The purpose of this study was to examine whether cultural differences in family values exist among Mexican, Mexican American, and Anglo American families and if so, to determine whether parents' family values are related to the family values and mental health of their adolescent children. As previously mentioned, we attempted to deal with some of the criticisms concerning research on culture by: employing a cultural values approach, minimizing the confounding of SES (and family structure) with culture by only soliciting participation from middle-class, intact families, and combining etic and emic approaches to instrument development and data gathering.

Hypotheses

The hypotheses of this study were as follows:

1. There will be significant differences in family values among groups of adolescents and parents of three cultural groups—Mexican, Mexican American, and Anglo American. These differences will be attributable to cultural differences among the three groups and not to SES or family structure because all families will be middle-class and intact. Anglo Americans will be more modern in their family values and attitudes, Mexicans more traditional, and Mexican Americans will be a combination of modern and traditional (bicultural).

2. There will be significant positive relationships between family values of parents and adolescents in the modern (Anglo) and traditional (Mexican) groups, but not in the bicultural (Mexican American) group because the parents and adolescents of this group are likely to be in different stages of forging a new cultural identity that will reflect an amalgamation of traditional and modern values (Ramirez, 1967; Ramirez & Castaneda, 1974).

3. There will be significant differences in the frequency of mental health symptoms reported by Mexican, Mexican American, and Anglo American adolescents. Among the adolescents, the modern (Anglo) and bicultural (Mexican American) groups, in contrast to the traditional group (Mexican), will report experiencing a higher frequency of mental health symptoms because

of the emphasis on individual achievement and the hypercompetitiveness of mainstream, middle-class American society (Ramirez & Price-Williams, 1974; Sampson, 1988; Spence, 1985).

4. There will be significant positive relationships between parental family values and adolescents' mental health symptoms in all three cultural groups. Among each of the cultural groups, parents who endorse more modern family values (e.g., individualistic identity and competitive orientation) will have children who report a higher frequency of mental health symptoms; their children will feel more individual pressure to excel and will have a difficult time dealing with failure (Horney, 1937).

METHOD

Participants

Participants were two-parent families with an adolescent child. The adolescents consisted of 45 Mexicans (18 girls, 27 boys), 39 Mexican Americans (12 girls, 27 boys), and 43 Anglo Americans (27 girls, 16 boys). The adolescents' ages ranged from 12 to 14 years, with 96% of them being 12 or 13 years of age. Mean ages were 12.57, 12.73, and 12.75 years for the Mexican, Mexican American, and White adolescents, respectively. All the families were intact and determined to be of middle-class standing on the basis of three measures of SES—income, education, and employment of parents. Participants were treated in accordance with the American Psychological Association (APA; 1992) ethical principles.

Instruments

The Family Attitude Scale (FAS; Ramirez, 1967; Ramirez & Carrasco, in press) is a 30-item scale developed specifically to assess traditional and modern family values among Mexicans, Mexican Americans, and Anglo Americans. The FAS consists of eight factorially derived clusters: Loyalty to the Family, Strictness in Childrearing, Respect for Adults, Separation of Sex Roles, Male/Age Superiority, Time Orientation, Religious Ideology, and Cooperation Versus Competition. A sample item reads, "Uncles, aunts, cousins, and other relatives should always be considered to be more important than friends." Respondents use a 4-point Likert scale ranging from 1, *Strongly Agree,* to 4, *Strongly Disagree,* to rate each item. After the required reverse coding of 9 of the items, lower scores correspond to a more traditional value orientation, whereas higher scores correspond to a more modern value orientation. The internal consistency for this scale was .74 for Mexicans and Mexican Americans and .77 for Anglo Americans.

The *Mental Health Symptoms Checklist* (MHSC; Diaz-Guerrero, Ramirez, & Iscoe, 1983) is a 19-item self-report measure that asks respondents to rate on a 4-point scale the frequency with which a list of mental health symptoms are experienced. The MHSC was developed specifically to be used with Mexicans, Mexican Americans, and Anglo Americans, and consists of four clusters: Depression, Anxiety, Hypochondriasis, and Paranoia. A sample item reads, "How often do you worry about unimportant matters?" Higher scores correspond to a higher self-reported frequency of mental health symptoms. The internal consistency for this scale was 0.86 for Mexicans, 0.89 for Mexican Americans, and 0.90 for Anglo Americans.

Items of the FAS and MHSC, which were originally developed in Spanish, were translated to English, whereas items originally developed in English were translated to Spanish. All items were then backtranslated until all discrepancies between the original and backtranslated versions were corrected.

Procedure

Participants in this study were recruited from Austin, Texas (an urban center in Central Texas), the Rio Grande Valley (a rural, semiurban community of the South Texas–Mexico border region), and Monterey, Nuevo Leon, Mexico (an urban center in Northern Mexico and the second largest city in that nation). The families in this study participated in other observations as part of a larger study.

In Austin, a school roster obtained from the Austin Independent School District was used to generate the participant pool. Mexican American and Anglo American seventh grade students who were not on the Reduced/Free School Lunch Program were randomly selected to participate. In the Rio Grande Valley, Mexican American and Anglo American, middle-class, seventh grade students were identified by school personnel (e.g., principals and teachers) and invited to participate. A letter explaining the purpose of the study and soliciting participation was sent to the parents of these students. Parents who expressed interest in participating in the study (via a returned postcard) were contacted by a researcher to determine the family's eligibility for the study. Only intact, middle-class (as further determined by parents' income, education, and occupation) families where both parents were of the same ethnicity and who had a child in the seventh grade were invited to come to the research setting to participate in the study. Mexican American and Anglo American families were offered $50 as compensation for their time.

In Mexico, an initial pool of participants who were in the first year of a private secondary school (the equivalent of seventh grade in the United States) were identified by school personnel. Subsequent participants were recruited using the snowball effect; names and telephone numbers of other

potential participants were obtained from families who initially participated in the project. As with the U.S. sample, letters explaining the purpose of the study were sent to parents, and parents who expressed interest
were contacted by phone to determine eligibility. The research team in
Mexico advised us that the parents would be offended by the offer of
money in return for their participation, so instead, pocket calculators were
presented to the Mexican children who participated.

Families who agreed to participate were invited to a building on a university campus in Austin, a church activity center in the Rio Grande Valley,
and the private office of a well-respected psychiatrist in Monterey. The
families completed the FAS and MHSC in the respective locations.

RESULTS

All of the following significance tests were performed with an a priori al-
pha level of .05.

Statistical Test of Hypothesis 1

To test for significant cultural and gender differences on the total score of
the FAS, a 2 (gender) × 3 (culture) ANOVA was performed separately for
adolescents and parents.

Adolescents.   Results of the ANOVA for adolescents yielded a significant main effect for culture (F [2, 126] = 23.92, p < .01). To determine
which cultural groups differed on the FAS, a Tukey's Honestly Significant
Difference (THSD) test was performed. Results of the THSD test showed
that Mexicans reported a significantly more traditional family value orientation (M = 2.18, SD = 0.21) than Mexican Americans (M = 2.39, SD =
0.25), and Anglo Americans reported the most modern family-value orientation (M = 2.62, SD = 0.35). No significant differences were found by
gender or for the interaction between gender and culture.

Parents.   Results of the ANOVA for parents yielded a significant main
effect for culture (F [2, 253] = 21.63, p < .01). Results of the subsequent
THSD test showed that Anglo Americans reported a significantly more
modern family-value orientation (M = 2.73, SD = 0.25) than Mexican
Americans (M = 2.55, SD = 0.38) and Mexicans (M = 2.45, SD = 0.19). As
with the adolescents, no significant differences were found by gender or
for the interaction between gender and culture for the parents.

Statistical Test of Hypothesis 2

The next set of analyses consisted of stepwise multiple regression analyses
that were run to predict the adolescents' FAS total scores. These analyses

were run separately for each cultural group and the predictors consisted of mothers' and fathers' FAS total scores.

Mexicans. For Mexicans, mothers' FAS total scores were positively related to their children's FAS total scores (F [1, 43] = 6.04, p < .05). Mothers' FAS scores accounted for 10% of the variance in their children's FAS scores. Mexican fathers' FAS total scores were not significant in predicting their children's FAS total scores.

Mexican Americans. For Mexican Americans, neither the mothers' nor the fathers' FAS total scores entered into the regression equation.

Anglo Americans. For Anglo Americans, mothers' FAS scores were positively related to their children's FAS scores (F (1,41) = 9.04, p < .01). Mothers' FAS scores accounted for 16% of the variance in their children's FAS scores. Anglo American fathers' FAS total scores were not significant in predicting their children's FAS total scores.

Statistical Test of Hypothesis 3

To test for significant cultural differences in the MHSC, a one-way ANOVA was performed on the adolescent data. Results of the ANOVA yielded a significant cultural effect (F [2, 126] = 5.58, p < .01). A THSD test revealed that Anglo American (M = 1.88, SD = 0.49) and Mexican American (M = 1.82, SD = 0.45) adolescents reported significantly greater mental health symptoms than Mexican adolescents (M = 1.58, SD = 0.39).

Statistical Test of Hypothesis 4

The last set of analyses consisted of stepwise multiple regression analyses that were run to predict the adolescents' mental health symptoms. These analyses were run separately for each cultural group, and the predictors consisted of mothers' and fathers' FAS total scores.

For Mexican Americans, mothers' FAS scores were positively related to their children's mental health symptoms (F [1, 37] = 6.61, p < .05), indicating that mothers who adhered to more modern family values had children who reported experiencing a higher frequency of mental health symptoms, whereas mothers who adhered to more traditional family values had children who reported experiencing a lower frequency of mental health symptoms. Mothers' FAS scores accounted for 13% of the variance in their children's mental health symptoms. Mexican American fathers' FAS total scores were not significant in predicting their children's mental health symptoms. In addition, for Mexicans and Anglo Americans, neither mothers' nor fathers' FAS total scores were predictive of their children's mental health symptoms.

DISCUSSION

As expected, the study found significant cultural differences in family values among the adolescents, with Mexican adolescents the most traditional, Mexican American adolescents the most bicultural, and Anglo American adolescents the most modern. Among the parents, Anglo Americans reported a significantly greater modern family-value orientation than Mexican Americans and Mexicans. Thus, these findings provide support for a bicultural value orientation of Mexican American adolescents relative to their more traditional Mexican and their more modern Anglo American counterparts. However, the study did not find a parallel bicultural value orientation among Mexican American parents. Although contrary to the researchers' expectations, this can be understood in terms of the more diverse cultural exposure that Mexican American adolescents experience in comparison to their parents. That is, these adolescents spend several hours a day in academic environments predominantly reflective of modern value orientations, whereas their family environments reflect a combination of modern and traditional value orientations. Thus, these adolescents learn to balance differing value orientations. The Mexican American parents, on the other hand, may have greater opportunities to interact with others and engage in situations predominantly reflective of traditional value orientations. Thus, their values are more aligned with their traditional Mexican heritage.

The researchers hypothesized that positive relationships would exist between Mexican and Anglo American parents' FAS scores and their children's FAS scores and that no relationship would exist between Mexican American parents' and children's FAS scores. The results showed that Mexican and Anglo American mothers' and not fathers' FAS scores were positively related to their children's FAS scores; no relation was found between Mexican American parents' and children's FAS scores. This indicates that Mexican mothers transmit their traditional family values to their children and Anglo American mothers are transmitting their modern family values to their children. Although researchers expected that Mexican and Anglo American mothers' and fathers' FAS scores would be related to their children's FAS scores, the nonsignificant contribution of fathers' FAS scores to the prediction of their children's FAS scores may be due to the more active role that the mothers play in the transmission of cultural values. That is, the Mexican and Anglo American children may have greater opportunities for interaction with and socialization by their mothers, thus allowing for greater exchange of ideas and beliefs regarding family values.

The researchers also correctly hypothesized that Anglo American and Mexican American adolescents would report experiencing a higher frequency of mental health symptoms than their Mexican counterparts. As expected, Anglo American and Mexican American adolescents exhibit a higher frequency of mental health symptoms due to the continual emphasis on individual achievement and competition with others evident in mainstream, middle-class American society (Ramirez & Price-Williams, 1974; Sampson, 1988; Spence, 1985).

Finally, the results of the test of our fourth hypothesis were only partially supported. Although we expected to find a positive relationship between parental family values and adolescents' mental health symptoms for all three cultural groups, this was only observed for Mexican Americans. Among Mexican American families, mothers who hold more modern family values tend to have children who report experiencing a higher frequency of mental health symptoms, whereas mothers who hold more traditional family values tend to have children who report experiencing a lower frequency of mental health symptoms. It is likely that Mexican American adolescents who are exposed to modern values in the school setting, as well as in the home by their mothers, are responding to the need for individual achievement and fear of failure with greater mental health difficulties. This finding is consistent with studies reviewed by Buriel (1984) that showed that Mexican Americans who embrace traditional values are psychologically healthier and are able to adjust more effectively in American society than Mexican Americans who reject these values. This suggests that *assimilation,* or adoption of modern values entirely, is not conducive to the psychological well-being of Mexican Americans.

Overall, the results of this study did not support the North American and Western European paradigms nor the damaging culture perspectives. The findings indicated the usefulness of a cultural values theoretical framework in understanding the components of culture thought to influence behavior. Family values can be used effectively to distinguish between Mexican culture, which is more reflective of traditional family values, and Anglo American culture, which is more reflective of modern family values. Family values also aid in distinguishing between Mexican American culture (bicultural) and Anglo American culture in adults and among Mexican, Mexican American, and Anglo American culture in adolescents. Thus, these findings demonstrate differences in family values among these three groups, attributed to cultural differences among the three groups and not to SES or family structure. This theoretical framework also helps illustrate that cultural values are transmitted from one generation to the next. Specifically, our findings showed that Mexican and Anglo American mothers transmit family attitudes to their adolescent children. Furthermore, this theoretical framework helped identify a cultural element—family values—related to a psychological phenomenon of interest—adolescent mental health.

We agree with the recommendations made by others (Betancourt & Lopez, 1993; Buriel, 1984; Phinney, 1996); it is time for researchers to begin to directly measure the cultural elements thought to contribute to differences between cultural–ethnic groups. In this study, we have chosen to measure family values as the underlying cultural element that distinguishes Mexicans, Mexican Americans, and Anglo Americans. In addition to values, Phinney (1996) suggested that researchers consider the role that two other key aspects of ethnicity—ethnic identity and minority status—play in explaining psychological functioning. As Betancourt and Lopez (1993) noted, we can enrich our understanding of culture in psychology by employing theoretical frameworks that incorporate underlying cultural elements that influence behavior.

IMPLICATIONS FOR SCHOOL PRACTICES

Years ago, Ramirez and Castaneda (1974) proposed a philosophy of cultural democracy for educational intervention with people of color in the United States. This philosophy entailed providing an opportunity for children and families to make an informed choice with respect to ethnic identity, promoting respect for values and learning styles of cultures different from that of mainstream American middle-class culture and encouraging the development of bicultural and multicultural identities and orientations to life. Based on the philosophy of cultural democracy, a multidisciplinary, multicultural, and bilingual educational program—*Nuevas Fronteras de Aprendizaje* (New Frontiers of Learning)—was developed and implemented in several communities in Texas and California (Cox, Macaualy, & Ramirez, 1982). *Nuevas Fronteras de Aprendizaje* is a preschool and early elementary educational program based on the concepts of traditional and modern values and bicultural and multicultural development. Individualized instruction matches the teaching styles of teachers and the content of the curriculum to the preferred cultural learning styles of the children. Program goals include encouraging children and parents to develop cognitive flexibility and multicultural orientations to life.

More recently, Darder (1991) recommended a bicultural pedagogy that combines the principles of liberation theology with those of cultural democracy. Darder described a program implemented at Pacific Oaks College that reflects this new philosophy. Another program being implemented in California, *Challenging Latinos to Access Resource Opportunities* (CLARO; Flores, personal communication, April 10, 1996), also uses the bicultural and multicultural perspective in intervention work with Latino adolescents at risk for dropping out of school, for participating in gang violence, and for using and abusing alcohol and drugs. This program uses supportive, culturally based groups and activities to assist Latino adolescents in defining their identities and in learning alternative solutions to the problems they face in an urban multicultural environment. The program enables participants to develop strategies to cope more effectively with feelings of alienation, lack of information, poor living conditions, language barriers, racial discrimination, unemployment, and poverty. Trained facilitators lead support group discussions that focus on identity, definition of male roles, gang violence, drugs, and alcohol, nonviolence, the mestizo heritage, bilingualism, cultural differences and similarities, and spiritual preparation.

We encourage the development and implementation of the types of programs just described. The study we reported argues for a family-values-based approach, particularly in working with Mexican American adolescents. Our research findings suggest that family values differ across cultural groups and that adherence to traditional values by Mexican American mothers is related to positive mental health adjustment in their children. Thus, we must develop educational interventions with Mexican American adolescents with the family in mind. Furthermore, assimilationist perspectives must be challenged and replaced with bicultural and multicultural perspectives.

In a study on the relationship between acculturation and family functioning in Latino families in California, Rueschenberg and Buriel (1989) concluded:

> Public policies based upon assimilationist perspectives continue to operate and there is little information to help determine what the relative merits or harmful effects of such policies are for these families. For example, among various groups of human service providers there is the commonly held view that total assimilation into mainstream U.S. society is a necessary prerequisite for successful adaptation into adjustment for life in the United States. For families of Mexican descent, this assimilation entails rejection of intrafamilial patterns which are closely associated with cultural heritage. The evidence from this study suggests that assimilation does not occur and is not necessary. (p. 242)

The findings of this study support the conclusions summarized above and argue for a cultural values theoretical framework for doing research and interventions with Latinos and other ethnic and cultural groups of color.

ACKNOWLEDGMENTS

This research was funded by the Hogg Foundation for Mental Health, Austin, TX and The University of Texas Southwestern Medical Center, Dallas, TX. We wish to express our gratitude to Nicolas Carrasco, Ph.D., Susanne Doell, Ph.D., and Fidel de la Garza Gutierrez, M.D. for their assistance in data collection, Lisa Talavera Garza for entering the data reported in this study, and Steven R. Lopez, Ph.D. for his helpful suggestions and comments.

REFERENCES

American Psychological Association. (1992). Ethical principles of psychologists and code of conduct. *American Psychologist, 47,* 1597–1611.

Ardila, R. (1993). Latin American psychology and world psychology: Is integration possible? In U. Kim & J. W. Berry (Eds.), *Indigenous psychology* (pp. 170–176). Newbury Park, CA: Sage.

Betancourt, H., & Lopez, S. R. (1993). The study of culture, ethnicity, and race in American psychology. *American Psychologist, 28,* 629–637.

Buriel, R. (1984). Integration with traditional Mexican American culture and sociocultural adjustment. In J. J. Martinez, Jr., & R. H. Mendoza (Eds.), *Chicano psychology* (2nd ed.). New York: Academic Press.

Castaneda, A. (1984). Traditionalism, modernism, and ethnicity. In J. L. Martinez & R. H. Mendoza (Eds.), *Chicano psychology* (pp. 35–40). San Diego, CA: Academic Press.

Cox, B., Macauly, J., & Ramirez, M. (1982). *New frontiers: A bilingual early learning program.* New York: Pergamon.

Darder, A. (1991). *Culture and power in the classroom: A critical foundation for bicultural education.* New York: Bergin & Garvey.

Diaz-Guerrero, R. (1955). Neurosis and the Mexican family structure. *American Journal of Psychiatry, 112,* 411–417.

Diaz-Guerrero, R., Ramirez, M., & Iscoe, I. (1983). *The impact of culture change and economic stress on the physical and mental health of Mexican, Mexican American, and Anglo families.* Austin, TX: Hogg Foundation for Mental Health.

Diaz-Loving, R., Reyes-Lagunes, I., & Diaz-Guerrero, R. (1995). Some cultural facilitators and deterrents for the development of psychology: The role of graduate research training. *International Journal of Psychology, 30*(6), 681–692.

Heller, C. S. (1966). *Mexican American youth: Forgotten youth at the crossroads.* New York: Random House.

Heller, C. S. (1971). *New converts to the American dream?* New Haven, CT: College & University Press.

Holtzman, W. H., Diaz-Guerrero, R., & Swartz, J. D. (1975). *Personality development in two cultures.* Austin: University of Texas Press.

Horney, K. (1937). *The neurotic personality of our time.* New York: Norton.

Matsumoto, D. (1994). *Cultural influences on research methods and statistics.* Monterey, CA: Brooks/Cole.

Phinney, J. S. (1996). When we talk about American ethnic groups, what do we mean? *American Psychologist, 51,* 918–927.

Pike, K. (1954). *Language in relation to a unified theory of structure of human behavior (Part 1).* Glendale, CA: Summer Institute of Linguistics.

Ramirez, M. (1967). Identification with Mexican Family Values and Authoritarianism in Mexican Americans. *The Journal of Social Psychology, 73,* 3–11.

Ramirez, M. (1983). *Psychology of the Americas: Mestizo perspectives on personality and mental health.* New York: Pergamon.

Ramirez, M. (in press). *Multicultural/ multiracial psychology: Mestizo perspectives in personality and mental health.* Northvale, NJ: Aronson.

Ramirez, M., & Carrasco, N. (in press). *Revision of the Family Attitude Scale.* University of Texas at Austin. Manuscript in preparation.

Ramirez, M., & Castaneda, A. (1974). *Cultural democracy, bicognitive development and education.* New York: Academic Press.

Ramirez, M., & Price-Williams, D. R. (1974). Achievement motivation in Mexican American children. *Journal of Cross-Cultural Psychology, 7,* 49–60.

Rueschenberg, E., & Buriel, R. (1989). Mexican American family functioning and acculturation: A family systems perspective. *Hispanic Journal of the Behavioral Sciences, 11*(3), 232–242.

Sabogal, F., Marin, G., Otero-Sabogal, R., Marin, B. V., & Perez-Stable, E. J. (1987). Hispanic familism and acculturation: What changes and what doesn't? *Hispanic Journal of Behavioral Sciences, 9,* 397–412.

Sampson, E. E. (1988). The debate on individualism. *American Psychologist, 43,* 15–22.

Spence, J. T. (1985). Achievement American style: The rewards and costs of individualism. *American Psychologist, 40,* 1285–1295.

9 Relating Competence in an Urban Classroom to Ethnic Identity Development

Rosa Hernández Sheets
San Francisco State University

Social interactions and relationships among and between individual students, groups of students, and teachers are lived through a multitude of identity dimensions, such as ethnicity, culture, race, class, socioeconomic status, gender, ability, nationality, sexual orientation, and age. In classrooms, these interactions shape and are shaped by the ways certain identities are given meaning. Thus, particular dimensions of students' identity can provide, enhance, or deny students access to resources present in classrooms. For example, students who can display rather than privatize aspects of their ethnic identity experience a harmonious cognitive–social developmental process or students who can use friendship connections have access to consensual validation, social support, and coping assistance to stressful events.

The assumption that competency in schooling for students is located in the facilitation and affirmation of ethnic identity development (Branch, 1994; Gay, 1987, 1994a, 1994b, chap. 11, this volume), in access to the significant contribution of friendship to coping behaviors (Azmitia & Montgomery, 1993; Hartup, 1996; Newcomb & Bagwell, 1995; Schunk, 1987; Seiffge-Krenke, 1995), and within the practice of *culturally mediated* learning and teaching (Hollins, 1996) is examined in this study. Therefore, theoretical ideas from scholarship on ethnic identity formation, the role of friendship in the sociocognitive development of adolescents, and the implementation of culturally mediated pedagogy guide this study. This research concentrates on how *student competence,* defined as positive ethnic identity development, accelerated achievement in school work, and social adjustment, unfolds when instruction and context are modified as described in the methodological section of this chapter.

157

METHODS

This study used a qualitative methodology to examine the relationship among ethnic identity, friendship, and competence under spontaneous conditions in an urban classroom (Agar, 1980; Fine & Sandstrom, 1988; Miles & Huberman, 1984). Interviews, classroom observations, questionnaires, student work, school records, and daily classroom observations over a 4-month period were used to examine the ways in which ethnic factors influence the social and academic competence of students. Interviews were used as the primary source of student perception of competence. Student interactions, relationships, expressions of and behaviors of identity, and use of cultural knowledge were examined through student documents and classroom observations. Classroom dialogue, student autobiographies, daily journals, and reflective essays provided student voice. School records disclosed specific labeling information, such as race, ethnicity, attendance patterns, disciplinary actions, and grade-point averages (GPA).

This study took place at Lincoln High (pseudonym), one of ten high schools in an urban school district in the Pacific Northwest. Located in a predominately White middle-class community, most of the ethnic students of color were bussed from the central, southern, and international sections of the city. In the 1995 to 1996 school records, the student enrollment (1,114 students) included 18.1% African Americans, 2.4% American Indians, 33.5% Asians, 8.7% Hispanic non-Whites, and 37.3% Whites.

The participants in this study were high-school freshmen—18 females and 9 males ($N = 27$)—enrolled in the language arts–social studies 2-hour block at Lincoln High in spring semester 1996. Students identified themselves in the following categories: 6 Asians (5 females: 1 Pilipina, 1 Vietnamese, 1 Thai, 1 Chinese, 1 Cham, and 1 male East Indian), 10 African Americans (6 females, 4 males), 6 first generation Biracial Americans (4 females: 2 White/Black, 1 Japanese/White, and 1 Vietnamese/White, and 2 males: both White/Black), and 5 European Americans (3 females: 1 Irish/Italian/English, 1 German/Irish/English, 1 French/Polish/Norwegian/Swedish, and 2 males: 1 Jewish, 1 German/English/Italian).

Throughout this chapter, the term *Asian American* is used when referring to the Pilipina, Vietnamese, Thai, Chinese, Cham, and East Indian students. *European American* describes the polyethnic Irish/Italian/English, French/Polish/Norwegian/Swedish, German/Irish/English, and German/English/Italian students; the Jewish male student is identified individually. For *Biracial students,* the first racial or ethnic designator indicates the mother, the second the father. School records classify White/Black Biracials as African American, and the Asian/White Biracials as Japanese and Vietnamese, respectively. *Block* refers to the 2-hour Language Arts/Social Studies classroom.

LIMITATIONS OF THE STUDY

The data generated from this study were provided by an intact classroom of ninth-grade students classified as at-risk by the freshman teachers and the curriculum administrator. Students selected for this classroom may not represent a typical ninth-grade student at Lincoln High. All data were collected and analyzed by the researcher. The researcher's employment in the school district in which the study took place may have influenced the findings. Efforts to control for limitations included the use of multiple data sources (*triangulation*) and data collection–analysis strategies recommended by Assor and Connell (1992), Miles and Huberman (1984), and Silverman (1993). Interviews were audiotaped, fieldnotes were recorded immediately after the contact, and consistency checks were used that included established coding schemes, data-display matrices, negative evidence, and testing findings for confirmability prior to coming to conclusions.

PROGRAM DESCRIPTION

The pedagogical behaviors in the classroom context and process of instruction promoted ethnic identity development, incorporated friendship connections, used student cultural knowledge, and made changes in student–teacher communication patterns, and attended to issues of racism, prejudice, and discrimination.

Context

The classroom climate was viewed as a fundamental resource to facilitate healthy ethnic identity development, to provide consistent access to supportive social interactions, and to model mutuality of high expectations. Racialized issues were directly confronted and examined in daily social interactions and organized discussions. Students chose research projects, used community resources (e.g., they conducted ERIC searches at university libraries and visited local professors and doctoral students of color for additional knowledge, skills, and mentoring), and experienced firsthand, real-life examples of individuals displaying positive ethnic identity.

The teacher's desk was located in a back corner and used as a table. Daily, fresh flowers sat on a high stool in the front center of the room. Students used the computer lab, generally monopolized by honor students, 2 hours per week. By choice, students worked independently or in self-selected groups, moving their desks to preferred spaces, except during whole group discussions when a circle format was used. They often listened to music softly and snacked.

Process

Ritual student–teacher classroom behaviors mired in procedural issues, such as rules and tardy procedures, teacher-dominated dialogue, competitive individual assignments, which in the past had generated failure for these students and were substituted with increased opportunities for talk, collaboration, and group products. Teacher focus was not on curricular content but rather on the instruction itself—the mediation between student–student and student–teacher. Communication patterns were reconstructed and communication practices were predominantly student to student in small and large groups. They were student-led and student-initiated based on student-selected needs and issues. If students felt that a prejudicial and/or racist statement or discriminatory act was witnessed in the classroom, hall, or school merited discussion or action, they called for a circle, and the ensuing discussion would be student-led. Whoever initiated the discussion began with an explanation. When another person was acknowledged, that person assumed control, and so forth. The teacher raised her hand as did the students. Interruptions and one-on-one dialogues evolved naturally, adding spontaneity and reality.

FINDINGS

The data analysis reveals that *student competence* as defined by the study—positive development of ethnic identity, achievement in school work, social adjustment—was demonstrated when classroom instruction and climate were modified to accommodate students' cultural knowledge (Hollins, 1996). The results suggest a cyclical and continual relationship among friendship, social–academic competence, and ethnic identity development. That is, the nurturing, supportive elements provided by the preferred same-race friendships reinforced competent behaviors that were demonstrated through traditional symbols of achievement (e.g., school products, grades, honors credit, and national recognition) and behavioral markers (e.g., improved attendance, lowered disciplinary actions and minimal student–student conflict). These resulting competent coping skills increased self-confidence and solidified friendships that in turn, enhanced learning and provided opportunity for ethnic identity to develop.

Ethnic Identity Development

Preethnic and postethnic identity attitude scales were not administered, therefore, conclusions cannot be made about whether students developed higher levels of identity in terms of theoretical stage theory; however, the data did suggest that in this classroom context, students had an opportunity to display attitudes and behaviors associated with a healthy ethnic identity (e.g., pride in self, allegiance to referent group, and acceptance of differences). Three trends emerged—self-labeling, stage theory, and ethnic identity as a socialization process.

Self-Labeling. The terms *race* and *ethnicity* were used interchangeably by these students. When asked to clarify African American, students used race as a category and ethnicity to mean either individual or group membership in a referent group. Asian students used *Asian* to mean membership in their referent group in this classroom and ethnicity for their personal referent group. European American students used the term *White* for both their race and ethnicity. Biracial American students talked about their races as separate entities and indicated personal membership in a mixed-race category and the right to belong in the ethnic group(s) of choice depending on the situation. Their group membership was generally in a group of color. White and Asian students placed self and others in one of three racial categories: *Black, Not White,* and *White.* European American students, at times, identified with their ancestors' country of origin, but this connection seemed to lack personal cultural experiences. One student, Stan, ethnically identified himself as Jewish. European American students began to acknowledge their ethnic heritage.

Stage Theory. The students' ethnic identity did not appear to fit into the linear stages described in the current ethnic developmental stage theory literature on adolescents. Description of typical behaviors and attitudes could not be used to place ethnic students of color in specific stages. Rather, particular situations, events, and written student documents could be used to place individual students and same-race and/or same-ethnic student groups in multiple stages within the theoretical racial and ethnic identity linear stages. Attitudes, perceptions, and behaviors represented in these data were neither consistent, stable, nor constant. The pattern that emerged suggested that attitudes, perceptions, and behaviors depended on (1) the individuals involved, (2) the content of the social interaction and/or relationship, (3) the actual situation, and (4) the general overall context in which the event took place. For example, all of the ethnic students of color, including the Biracial American students, made negative comments about White teachers in general, about particular White teachers, and about White peers that could be used to place them at the second stage of most ethnic identity stage theory levels (e.g., Awareness and Encounter Stage; Ponterotto & Pedersen, 1993; Search/Moratorium; Phinney, 1993; and Struggle for Acceptance; Kich, 1992). Yet, these same students (even on the same day) made or wrote comments and demonstrated behaviors suggesting placement in higher, or the highest, levels of ethnic identity stage theory, as well as all the stages in between. I was unable to find ethnic identity stage theory applicable to European American adolescents. However, as individuals and as a group, they were the most consistent and stable regarding racial stage theory placement. Their behaviors were generally similar to those described in the Disintegration stage (Helms, 1993). The students sought reassurance that racism is not the White person's fault, offered explanations for avoiding intimate contact with Biracial Americans, African Americans, and Asian Americans, and began to acknowledge the dilemma of being White.

Ethnic Identity as a Socialization Process.   Ethnic identity is an aspect of identity assumed to be a central task of adolescence (Erikson, 1968; Marcia, 1981; Phinney, 1993). This was not true for the African American students. Data from this study indicate that ethnic identity as a critical aspect of identity for these students was not "something" that began or was central only during adolescence, rather the dimensions of race and ethnicity began and were central early in their school life and continually affected their social and cognitive development. They reported that they were often forced to resolve issues about self, teachers, and school expectations that differed from their own worldview. For example:

> I never got along with my teachers. I always knew I was smart even when the teacher was mean. [another] teacher would talk to me about cooperation with other teachers and how Black people have a hard time. (Bernie, African American)

> I always wanted to go to school, but when I got there it wasn't what I expected. The teachers were White and mean. I never did like school but I learned to deal with it. (Teecia, African American)

Relationship Between Ethnic Identity and Competence

Ethnic Identity and Academic Competence

By choice, students formed four research groups: Gossip (6 African American females and 2 White/Black Biracial females), Interracial Relationships (4 African American males and 2 White/Black Biracial males), Peer Pressure (5 Asian females, 2 Asian/White Biracial females, and 1 East Indian male), and Truancy (3 European Americans females, 2 European American males, and 1 White/Black Biracial female).

Academic Content and Results.   In this classroom, there were no organized cultural celebrations, lessons, or activities, however, evidence of

ethnic affirmation was observed in the students' selection of research topics and in their classroom interactions. The research topics chosen by the
ethnic groups of color—African American and White/Black Biracial females (*None of Ya Business: African American Student Perception of Gossip*),
African American and White/Black Biracial males (*Student Perception of Interracial Relationships: Can Love Cross Colors*), and Asian American and
Asian/White Biracial students (*High-School Student Perception: The Impact
of Peer Pressure on Sex Life, Drug Use, and Conformity to Social Group Standards*)—made direct linkages to both their immediate social needs and cultural–experiential knowledge (Hollins, 1996). The European American
group, with one White/Black Biracial (Dee), chose a more general educational issue, *Student Perception of High-School Truancy.*
    Students felt comfortable working in self-selected, same-ethnic groups.
They generally completed assignments and demonstrated high levels of
academic achievement. The four research studies completed by these students were accepted by blind review for presentation at the 1996 National
Association of Multicultural Education National Conference (NAME).
Nine of 26 students (1 African American male and 2 African American, 3
Biracial, 1 European American, 1 Pilipina American, 1 Vietnamese American females) earned honors credit on their academic transcript as a result
of exemplary portfolios. Although most students in Block received As as final semester grades, academic success generally did not transfer to their
other four classes. In their other classes, most students showed high levels
of absenteeism, low grades, and a substantial number of disciplinary actions, indicating that students' lack of achievement in other classes may
have resulted from problems present in particular classroom situations,
rather than the generally perceived factors attributed to school failure
(e.g., low basic skills, home problems, and poverty).

Stress-Coping Strategies.   Racial categories and ethnic identity affiliations influenced student appraisal of events perceived as stressful, the
use of available resources, and the types of coping strategies applied in
adapting to stressful situations. Students reported differences between
their appraisal of and subsequent coping actions to stressful events in the
general school environment and in their responses in Block. As reported in
Seiffge-Krenke's (1995) research, these students also responded differently
to the same stressful event, used friends for social and academic support,
and selected from a choice of coping strategies influenced by access to different types of resources available in diverse classroom settings.
    The stress-coping strategies most often used in the Block classroom
generally united African American, Asian American, and Biracial American students. In Block, these students appraised and evaluated stress resulting from academic and racialized events as less threatening and less
harmful (Lazarus & Folkman, 1991), whereas the stress reported in their

other classes was characterized with a higher degree of harm, loss, and/or was seen as being threatening. For these students, the common strategies in Block included feelings of anger, joy, and empathy (*affect*). They were typically reflective when appraising the situation (*cognition*), followed by direct confrontation with the perpetuators of the stress event. They asked for help or found acceptable solutions from available resources that often included friends (*action*), for example, "We're having trouble organizing our data. It's good that we stuck through this madness and got things accomplished" (Gen, Pilipina).

The strategies observed and self-reported by ethnic students of color in the classroom differed from their self-reports of coping in other classrooms. African American and White/Black Biracial students reported that in other classes they most often ignored (affect), trivialized (cognitive), and resisted through avoidance and student–teacher confrontations (action).

> I try to avoid problems, especially with teachers. But if they keep it up I tell them off. I mostly cut class. They [classes] don't mean anything. (Dave, Biracial White/Black)

> I usually sleep, that is if I bother going [to class] at all. (Mia, African American)

Asian American and Asian/White Biracial students reported shame and anger (affect), self-criticism and optimism (cognitive), and passive resistance in the form of silent submission and passivity (action).

> I don't fight back, even when I know teachers and kids are wrong. I just stay there and get mad inside. I do nothing. It's just for a semester. (Michaela, Japanese/White Biracial)

> Sometimes I get depressed and cry at home but I hide it at school. I just do my work even if I'm mad. I don't show it even when I hear racist jokes and remarks. (Gen, Pilipina)

European American students exhibited similar behavior as African American, Asian American, and Biracial American students when encountering academic difficulties in Block. However, if the stress resulted from discussions on racial issues or involved stressful interactions with different-race students in the classroom, they worked through shame and guilt (affect), often brooded when they felt wronged or misunderstood (cognition), and withdrew and avoided stressful events (action). For example:

> I guess race goes both ways, but it can get you down. It's not easy being White in a minority school. (Sam)

> A lot of people think since you're White you don't experience racism and that you have no culture or history. Yes, I'm ashamed of some things my ancestors

were involved in, but I wasn't part of those things and it's time people, especially in this class, forgive those mistakes. (Sharon)

In their other classes, European American students reported that they
used disappointment, guilt, and joy (affect), optimism and self-criticism
(cognitive), and asked for help and found solutions (action).

I feel bad when I don't handle problems. I'm not proud of myself when I
don't do my best but teachers do mostly try to help you when you ask even
when you're out of line. (Sam)

When I feel guilty I find it hard to cope. I usually cry and vent to my listening
friends. I may ask the teacher for more time. (Rita)

Gender Differences. In Block, European American females asserted
and explored their gender identity. Females in the Truancy group were often aggressive toward the European American males, who were usually
tentative, conciliatory, or upset. This group's inability to work coopera-
tively and collaboratively resulted in two separate groups by gender. Gender interplay was not observable in the Peer Pressure group, with only one
East Indian male; however, as found by Filardo (1996), African American
(and White/Black Biracial) students showed greater equality and were
more verbally supportive of each other in mixed gender social interactions
than were their European American peers.

Collaboration Styles and Roles. The Gossip and Interracial Relationship groups positioned themselves side-by-side in the front of the
room and worked collaboratively and communally by mixing and sharing
tasks, satisfying group needs, and depending on individual skills and roles.
For example, Alex (African American) generated percentages for all the frequency counts, Dave (White/Black Biracial) made multiple copies of documents, Teecia (African American) mediated intergroup disagreements and
organized daily tasks for both groups, and Walter (African American) han-
dled all out-of-classroom errands. When physical separation between
these two groups occurred, it was short term and mutually accepted. The
threat of peer exclusion was a powerful tool used to maintain a work tone
deemed acceptable by the group.

The Gossip and Interpersonal Relationships groups worked collaboratively with the Peer Pressure group. They assigned and accepted tasks
based on ability and resources (e.g., students with computers typed; those
with neat handwriting rewrote fieldnotes; artistic students designed matrix charts and posters; and leaders ran focus groups). Students in these
three groups helped each other through cross-group assignments, for example, Maneet (East Indian), using his computer at home, typed the final

questionnaire form for all three groups; Walter (African American) obtained teacher permission to release students from other classes for all interviews and focus groups; Teecia (African American) was present during the first Peer Pressure group discussion and Michaela (Japanese/White Biracial) designed matrix charts for all three groups.

The Truancy group worked independently of the other three groups. At first, they cooperated as a group by dividing the tasks evenly and fairly, based on the amount of time they perceived each individual task would take. Although they sat together in a group, an individualistic goal structure prevailed with each member working independently to complete their assigned piece of the project. The girls were in control of assignments and the boys repeatedly complained that the girls bossed them around. The girls countered by explaining that the boys did not do their share and worried how this might affect their final grade. Eventually, this group disintegrated into separate groups by gender.

All four groups willingly shared knowledge (e.g., explaining how to fill out Request to Report Form and keep opinions and comments separate from fieldnotes; concepts such as triangulation, data reduction matrix, and frequency counts). The Gossip group was recognized as the high-status group. Academic help, social advice, and whole-group event approval (e.g., what movie to watch, the best day to schedule a trip to the university library, and when to plan videotaped focus groups) was solicited more often from this group than from other groups.

Classroom work styles also differed. The Gossip and Interpersonal Relationships groups used classroom time effectively. They stayed on task and students who wasted time were kept in check by group norms. The Peer Pressure group took the necessary time to report on the status of their project and to assign new homework; however, they spent most of the class time socializing. The Truancy group either socialized in dyads or worked independently. They monitored group work only when portfolios were due.

Perceived Difference in Classroom Climate. In general, students reported that this was their favorite class. They thought the class was stressful in terms of work load, however, it was also the class that gave them the most freedom, opportunities to voice feelings, opinions, choices, and knowledge about other races. Students commented, "Block is my favorite class because the students get to be in charge. The teacher doesn't act like a superior power" (Sue, Chinese American), "I love this class. Sometimes this class is so stress[ful]. There's too much work. It's confusing putting all that stuff together, the survey, the field notes and the incident reports" (Lan, Vietnamese/White Biracial), and "I can't believe all the freedom we have. In this class everybody has an opportunity to put in their input and feel comfortable about what they're saying. We're in control of our learning" (Michaela, Japanese/White Biracial).

Along with the similarities in the course evaluation, differences by ethnic groups emerged. African American students wanted the right to be themselves and felt that being a majority in number was important. Comments such as, "You don't have to kiss up in this class to get a good grade" (Tafani); "In this class I felt empowered to stand up and express what I believe" (Alex); and, "I feel more comfortable. I can be Black. Maybe [because] I have more of my kind in this class" (Walter). Asian American students enjoyed open discussions on racism and the teaching style of the teacher: "Before this class to tell you the truth I didn't like White people. I thought they were all racist air heads, but after this class I think differently about all the races" (Fatima, Cham American); "It's hard if you're not White. People team up and tease you everyday for being Asian. In this class I could be myself" (Sue, Chinese); and "I knew from the first day the way you teach is different. We could have strong feelings about our ethnicity and pride in our race, yet pretty much everybody got along" (Trinh, Vietnamese). Biracial students were able to self-label as biracial and were accepted in ethnic groups of choice.

Three of the five European American students described feelings similar to those expressed by ethnic students of color. However, although the European American group received the most teacher time in Block, two of the five European American students felt other groups were favored. They commented:

This class was very different from my other classes. We had a lot of fun. We learned a lot. We could say what we wanted. Rosa didn't hold it against you, but sometimes I think the Black kids were favored. (Rita)

I loved this class and I learned a lot. I looked forward to ending the day in Block. We could have a bad day and it was no big deal. But, I thought that the Asians were treated better just because they're Asians. (Stan, Jewish)

African American, Asian American, and Biracial American students did not think that any ethnic group was favored. When responding to allegations that Asian and Black students were favored, African American students made the following observations:

I think the White kids notice that this class is different. I've heard Rita complain that you favor Blacks. I know you like us and you think we're smart, but you get on our case when we mess up just the same. I don't think it's that you treat us better, it's that you treat us equal and they're not used to that. In most classes White kids get treated better, so they get used to that. (Tafani)

Bernie (African American) agreed and added,

I think they don't like that you don't trip when we say what we feel. White teachers don't let you to put White kids down. Like when we talk about

something racial ... [teachers] act like they're scared and they're always saying "Don't go there."

Asian American and Asian/White Biracial American students also felt
White teachers were more concerned with the feelings of White students.
Lan (Vietnamese/White Biracial) commented,

> Remember when Trinh [Vietnamese American] said "all our sophomore class
> officers are people of color." Well you couldn't say that in front of a White
> teacher cause they'd think you were saying that the White kids lost. But
> that's not what she meant. I think she was just surprised that we all won.

Perceptions of difference in school climate might have resulted from repeated race-related discourse, which often united ethnic students of color
who were a majority in number. Gen (Pilipina American) noted,

> Well this class is more racially balanced. But there's more minorities than
> Whites, so maybe they don't feel like they're in power like in other classes.
> Usually [in other classes] we're all separated. We never get to sit together. We
> do feel special in this class and maybe they can tell.

Although these open discussions led to expressions of freedom and equity and increased students' knowledge of diverse cultural values and experiences, it also led to feelings of discomfort for European American
students (Helms, 1993). Often European American students were accused
by ethnic students of color of not listening and wanting everything their
way. Walter (African American) exclaimed, "Why talk! All we're doing is
making noise. They just don't hear." Trinh (Vietnamese American) added,
"Whites think they're all that. When they don't win, like when they don't
get the best grade, they say, 'Oh! You don't have a life. All you do is study'
or 'You guys are rude. You need to speak English'."

European American students responded, "I have been in mixed classes
all my life. This is the first time I've heard how Blacks and Asians really feel
about me. Some of the things you're saying are not right. Don't blame all
White people." (Rita) And, "I think teachers treat all people the same"
(Stan).

As the conversation continued, ethnic students of color complained
that European American students could not listen to their perspective and
that reaching a common goal for Whites meant that they had to agree with
a White perspective. When they reached this point in the conversation, African American, Asian American, and Biracial American students would
routinely stop talking, commenting, "They can't understand that other
styles are as good as theirs" (Sue, Chinese American).

Rita's (European American) weekly reflection expressed discomfort and
dissonance:

Rosa, I know you're fair and don't take sides, but sometimes when we have discussions on racism it feels like the other students are blaming us for what happened in the past. My ancestors weren't there. I didn't do it and it didn't happen to them.

Yet, Gen's (Pilipina American) reflection that same week revealed a different perspective:

Yes we have a few arguments about race and we talk about the past. Whites act so surprised when they realize we have strong opinions about our ethnicity and we also have pride in our race. Just because we are treated fairly in this class some people get uncomfortable.

Ethnic Identity and Social Competence

Social, civic, and leadership skills practiced in Block extended beyond the classroom. Two students—Sophia (African American) and Fatima (Cham American)—won two of eight Student-of-the-Month second semester citizenship awards. Eleven of 12 candidates for sophomore class office were Block students. They were elected to three of four positions—sophomore President, Vice President, and Treasurer.

Racial concordance in the selection of friendship groups in the classroom, as reported by the research, prevailed (Ennett & Bauman, 1996; Hartup, 1993; Schofield, 1982). Students worked collaboratively in five self-selected groups and segregated themselves by ethnicity and gender. Biracial students, except for Dee (White/Black) who chose a European American group, were in African American or Asian American groups. Friendship connections reported by the literature as a resource for European American children in the United States (Azmitia & Montgomery, 1993; Hartup, 1996; Newcomb & Bagwell, 1995; Schunk, 1987) and for German adolescents in Germany (Seiffge-Krenke, 1995) also provided consensual validation, social support, and assistance with academic tasks for African American, Asian American, and Biracial American students. Same-ethnic friendships also afforded African American, Asian American, and Biracial American students opportunities to express and endorse awareness, self-identification, preference, attitudes, and behaviors associated with positive ethnic identity development (Brookins, 1996; Rotheram & Phinney, 1987). Social group differences surfaced.

African Americans as a Social Group.

African American students embraced their own group's values and attitudes and established community with other ethnic groups of color (Boykin, 1986). They began to accept European American peers in this classroom as individuals as well as members of a White group. They freely brought up issues of racism and often demonstrated a desire to eliminate other types of oppression, such as religious discrimination, sexual orientation, and sexism. For example, Alex (African American) initiated a circle discussion when he heard the comment "That's gay!" used in jest. He found it prejudicial and distasteful "especially in this class." He sought and obtained peer approval that it not be used.

African American students exhibited a high level of acceptance toward self and toward Asian American and Biracial American students, but in trying to both understand and judge accurately the differing actions and perceptions of European American students, they constantly vacillated between indifference, annoyance, and anger to sympathy, coolness, and harshness depending on the situation.

The following incident is an example of differences in perception among African American and European American students. The Interracial Relationship group asked for help when a particular finding indicated that most of the Asian Americans, Biracial Americans, and African Americans they surveyed at Lincoln High thought the White girls were the easiest—sexually. However, the data was inconclusive from the White sample. The White students surveyed insisted that it "depended on the girl" or "on the situation." Some even said that the question was "immature" and "stupid." Confused about the conceptual differences among a finding, an interpretation, and a conclusion, Alex (African American) called for a lesson. As the topic of the mini-lesson caught interest, the Interracial Relationship group was surrounded by the rest of the class. The group seemed annoyed that the European American students verbally joined and actively tried to control what they perceived to be a private lesson, but nonetheless, they carried on. Alex (African American) insisted that this was an example of a stereotype. Levi (African American) argued it was not a stereotype because it was a fact; he knew from personal experience. In addition, Levi added, "We have data, everybody said so except the Whites." Teecia (African American) advised that they record their comments as an opinion and use these ideas in either the interpretation or conclusion. The heated discussion continued for about 30 minutes, without teacher comment. European American students in the class agreed with the White student sample, whereas students of color felt that Whites were not honest and open when the focus was on them, but thought they knew everything about people of color. Finally, Walter turned to Alex and said very softly, "Ain't it just like White folks to know nothing when it's about them." This statement was followed by a series of intentional subvocalizations and directed eye signals from other ethnic students of color. When the European American students realized that no one was responding to their comments, the discussion stopped, the group dispersed, and the small group, along with the teacher, discussed the differences between a finding and an interpretation of a finding.

African American students expressed and demonstrated an ability to work with diverse groups, but reported a preference to work with their own kind. Working with each other was a significant resource that they claimed was often denied in other classrooms. They felt nurtured and comfortable in a communal environment and voiced displeasure and frustration when isolated in other classrooms.

> I can work in any group, but I feel more comfortable with my friends. I learn better. That's what I like about this class. In my other classes they always separate us and put us way in the back. (Mia)

> I can work with different people other than my close friends. I'm finally in a class where I'm not a minority. Everybody in our group is [cool]. We can be ourselves and concentrate on the work instead of dealing with mess all the time. (Tafani)

They stated that academic work in a same-ethnic group was easier, more meaningful, and race affected learning; "Maybe because we're by race is the reason I do twice the work" (Alex).

African American students formed close alliances with each other, expressed pride in their race and ethnicity, and heightened their sense of loyalty, allegiance, and affiliation. For example, African American students often reacted to statements and/or actions of European American students among themselves. They would use certain cultural codes and social cues (i.e., eye signals, intentional subvocalizations, and body language) to exclude others from their discussions and activities. Although they were generally friendly and tolerant of European American students, at times, African American students expressed frustration and disenchantment with European Americans. Berni captured this feeling in a weekly reflection essay:

> Sometimes I just give up trying to explain. I don't want to waste my time attacking or defending. When I notice that they [European Americans] want to win instead of understand, I just chill and let them talk all they want. They seem to always want to judge everything by their standards. It's not that I don't care, it's that I don't want to waste my time.

Asian Americans as a Social Group. Like African American students, friendships enhanced racial identification and affirmed ethnic affiliations and preferences. Being together, working together, and talking among themselves about what they perceived to be important was generally how they directed their efforts in the classroom. They often said that they were appreciative for the sense of security felt in this classroom. Comments such as Gen's (Pilipina American), "In this class, it's OK to be Asian" and Sue's (Chinese American), "We need more classes like this one, where we can be ourselves" were typical. Although courteous, comfortable, and helpful when interacting with European Americans, they often voiced distrust and at times avoided contact with them. They formed supportive alliances with biracial and African American students.

Asian American students embraced their individual ethnic identity and appeared to function most often at Kim's (1981) highest levels—Redirection and Incorporation. They also acknowledged and identified with a Panethnic Asian category (see Lee, chap. 6, this volume). However, at times, they isolated themselves from other groups (Stage 2, Awareness, Encounter, Search) and they often expressed a high level of prejudice toward Whites (Stage 3, Identification and Emersion; Ponterotto & Pedersen, 1993).

Asian American students also felt angry about perceived constant racial harassment by teachers and students (see Lee, chap. 6, this volume). They believed this racist treatment was a result of ignorant racist attitudes. Frustrated because they felt they had no control over this mistreatment, they believed it was exacerbated by their small stature and by the commonly held misconception of their unwillingness to fight. "You don't hear them calling you names!" exclaimed Sue (Chinese American), referring to her perception that European American students did not dare use racial epithets in front of African American students. Teecia (African American) quickly added, "They call us names behind our backs."

In the classroom, Asian Americans focused on the reciprocity, equality, trust, and loyalty dimensions provided by friendship (Doll, 1996; Hartup, 1996) and enumerated the advantages of working in their preferred group.

> We have all become good friends. It's easy to work with people that you trust and respect and with people you feel want to be around you. (Gen, Pilipina)

> We can relate better to each other in this group. Nobody has to prove anything to anybody cause even though we're not all the same, we're all Asians. I feel safe in this group. (Michaela, Biracial Japanese/White)

Once friendships were established, keeping and being a friend was a top priority:

> Everybody in this group are friends and that's important to us. We treat everybody equally. Everybody knows how we feel about stuff like pressures from friends and parents. (Fatima, Cham American)

Biracial Americans as a Social Group. Biracial students generally reflected similar attitudes and behaviors and felt more comfortable and accepted in the groups that represented their ethnic heritage of color, except for Dee (Biracial White/Black). She self-identified as Biracial and gave explicit reasons for her group choice. She focused on social skills, situational manipulation, and the right to interact with whomever she chose, regardless of other people's discomfort (Root, 1996).

> I'm Biracial, mom's White and dad is Black. I'm able to make friends in all the racial groups. I don't care what people think. In this class I chose this group

because of Rita. We've been best friends since first grade. If people don't like it, it's their problem.

Biracial students were able to express and exercise their right for simultaneous membership, multiple identities, and situational affiliations with different groups (Root, 1992). Lan (Vietnamese/White Biracial) and Dave (White/Black Biracial) explained the difference between individual self-labeling and categorization as a Biracial versus affiliation with a particular racial or ethnic group (Root, 1992, 1996; Sheets, 1997). They did not seem to think that one classification compromised the other.

> I know I mostly choose Asian friends, but I know I'm biracial, half French as a matter of fact. I like to be mostly around Asians and Vietnamese. (Lan)

> I hang with Blacks and Whites. Sometimes the Black guys get mad when I hang with Whites. The Whites don't care because they think I'm Black. I'm both Black and White. I'm Biracial, but I'm really Black. (Dave)

European Americans as a Social Group.   European American students, like African American students, indicated an ability to work with other groups. They were the only students that reported that they had friends in other racial and ethnic groups and explained that their group choice was based on a particular individual and not because of race or ethnicity. They did not acknowledge the benefits of being in a same-race or same-ethnic group and openly admonished African American, Asian American, and Biracial American students for what they perceived to be exclusionary tactics. They were uncomfortable with the close, loyal friendships that developed within and among the student groups of color. They commented:

> I can hang with all the groups. I chose my group to be with Sam. I have many Black friends. It really doesn't matter what group I'm in. (Stan)

> I'm able to work with everybody. Dee's my best friend so we chose the same group. I think that Black and Asian kids separate themselves all the time if the teacher lets them. It's so silly. I don't really know why they want to do it. We should find a way to change that. (Rita)

DISCUSSION

Several messages emerged from this investigation. Ethnicity, as a critical dimension of identity, emerged as a consequential factor in daily social and academic experiences in school. Students exhibited ethnic awareness, identification, attitudes, preferences, and behaviors and demonstrated higher levels of academic and social competence, all of which speak convincingly of the need to incorporate ethnic identity developmental theory in schooling.

The European American students in this study, despite spending 8 years in desegregated classrooms, appeared to be unaware of how students from groups of color felt about them, about racialized issues, and experiences. European American students succeeded academically and were socially competent; however, at times they were uncomfortable with the racial dialogue, same-race, same-ethnic friendship choices and found it difficult to share classroom resources. As they began the process of examining their ethnic identity, they questioned their social and cultural positions, reflected on new psychological states of being, and examined ethnic markers used to define self and others. Sharon explained, "It feels different. Hearing people's feelings on a different level, you know how they view me. Makes me see myself. I have to open up so I can explain who I am, since I'm not who they think I am. I have a culture too."

Students' responses revealed that explanations, causes, and feelings inherent in their overt actions in most classrooms were experienced without teachers' awareness and acknowledgment of ethnic differences. When students experienced a classroom climate that encouraged ethnic identity development, they were aware of differences between Block and other classrooms. Comments, such as; "Most teachers don't care if you're Biracial, they just assume you're just Asian or Black" (Michaela, Biracial Japanese/White); "I felt proud of those Black professors at the university and I know that I'm a scholar too even if teachers don't think Blacks are smart" (Alex, African American); and "I know I'm something other than just White. I want to find out about my heritage" (Sharon, European American), were common.

Students spoke candidly about their observations and feelings about ethnic differences and entitlements. They examined racism, prejudice, and discrimination from an adolescent's perspective of fairness. Students were respected and appreciated both as individuals and as members of ethnic and cultural groups.

When the teacher was removed as the dispenser of goods and entitlements, students were able to position themselves and use cultural–experiential knowledge to impose their own rules with specified consequences for their violation, which in most cases meant exclusion from the group. This developmental social growth was psychologically empowering and served to establish student standards and criteria for behavior. This clarity of values, self-governing, interest, care, and support of the needs of others are signs of clarified ethnic identities (see Gay, chap. 11, this volume).

During small and large group conversations, turntaking based on student-determined, culturally governed, changing criteria gave more students access to voice. Students told their stories from their vantagepoint and expected that their view would be heard. For example, Asian American students used voice as an opportunity to clarify their ethnic identity. African American students were able to use cultural communication styles, accelerated verbal skills, and ways of behaving, interacting, and emoting feelings and attitudes that embodied, rather than conflicted with, their ethnic and cultural values. They experienced being recognized as experts by their peers. Alex (African American) explained what collaboration and open communication meant to him, "I feel like a Black scholar when I discuss my data with my group or with the class. I can speak my mind and not get in trouble. We can laugh, be free, talk loud or soft, be Black and be smart."

Although the four classroom groups worked on separate research projects, movement and cordial cross-ethnic interactions among individuals and between groups occurred often and naturally. A strong feeling of community, characterized by cultural integrity and respect for each other, predominated even when there were strong differences of opinion. The intimate, valuable, loyal friendships that developed in same-race and same-ethnic relationships or in the biracial relationships with peers from their racial heritage of color did not appear to take place in the general cross-ethnic friendships (see Branch, chap. 1, this volume). However, bonds of solidarity, as a class, developed as they identified as one group.

The mutuality of student–teacher perception of competence affirmed, encouraged, and resulted in high levels of academic achievement. Although Block was labeled at-risk, these students perceived themselves as special and a waiting list to get into Block was kept by the school counselor, indicating that other freshmen also shared this view.

As in other research, the goal of this study was not to identify friendless students, to encourage cross-racial friendships, nor to teach social skills by intervening and forcing friendship patterns. Friendship was seen as a mutually constructed selection, framed in cultural values, practices, and perceptions. In this study, the purpose of friendship as a mutually supportive relationship among students of the same racial, ethnic, and cultural group was to provide an authentic social–academic context, whereby students could use this relationship to affirm and maintain ethnic identity through affiliation, community, responsibility, commitment, and loyalty. To have a friend and to be a friend were basic resources that helped students cope with stressful racialized events as well as contribute to their social, cognitive, and identity development.

Although the friendship connections united cross-ethnic and Biracial Asian American students by providing an outlet for examining peer pressures and social groupings operating in a high school structure, it solidified African American and White/Black Biracial students. A feeling of community was often expressed in their reflective essays. They were able to learn by identification, imitation, and forming emotionally binding commitments to their research project. African American students actualized and verbalized their new roles and status, assuming full ownership of their research product. Although all the student research studies were superior in terms of design, content, and presentation, only *None of Ya Business: Afri-*

can American Student Perception of Gossip and *Student Perception of Interracial Relationship: Can Love Cross Colors* contained, in my opinion, extraordinary elements that can only be described as scholarly passion.

Because the classroom resources were divided equitably, European American students, perhaps used to having exclusive access to most or all parts of the educational environment, struggled at times to accept the more complex social ideals, such as equality, equity, and justice. However, they too experienced identity growth, some expressed that this was the first time they saw themselves and were seen by others both as individuals and as members of a group.

IMPLICATIONS FOR SCHOOL PRACTICES

This study suggests the need to understand the relationship among friendships, achievement, and ethnic identity. It also confirms that students act deliberately and thoughtfully in chosen ways to reinforce their ethnic identity. In this case, students adapted competently with culturally mediated instruction (Hollins, 1996) in spite of past or concurrent damaging schooling experiences and societal problems. However, the most critical component in this educational experience was not the availability of classroom resources, but the perceived access and the equitable distribution of these resources.

REFERENCES

Agar, M. (1980). *The professional stranger.* New York: Academic Press.

Assor, A., & Connell, J. P. (1992). The validity of students' self-reports as measures of performance affecting self-appraisals. In D. H. Schunk & J. L. Meece (Eds.), *Student perceptions in the classroom* (pp. 25–50). Hillsdale, NJ: Lawrence Erlbaum Associates.

Azmitia, M., & Montgomery, R. (1993). Friendship, transactive dialogues, and the development of scientific reasoning. *Social Development, 2,* 202–221.

Branch, C. W. (1994). Ethnic identity as a variable in the learning equation. In E. R. Hollins, J. E. King, & W. G. Hayman (Eds.), *Teaching diverse populations: Formulating a knowledge base* (pp. 207–224). Albany: State University of New York Press.

Branch, C. W. (1999). Race and human development. In R. H. Sheets & E. R. Hollins (Eds.), *Racial and ethnic identity in school practices: Aspects of human development* (pp. 7–28). Mahwah, NJ: Lawrence Erlbaum Associates.

Brookins, C. C. (1996). Promoting ethnic identity development in African American youth: The role of rites of passage. *Journal of Black Psychology, 22*(3), 388–417.

Boykin, W. (1986). The triple quandary and the schooling of Afro-American children. In U. Neisser (Ed.), *The school achievement of minority children: New perspectives* (pp. 57–91). Hillsdale, NJ: Lawrence Erlbaum Associates.

Doll, B. (1996). Children without friends: Implications for practice and policy. *School Psychology Review, 25*(2), 165–183.

Ennett, S. T., & Bauman, K. E. (1996). Adolescent social networks: School, demographic, and longitudinal considerations. *Journal of Adolescent Research, 11*(2), 194–215.

Erikson, E. H. (1968). *Identity: Youth and crisis.* New York: Norton.

Filardo, E. K. (1996). Gender patterns in African American and White adolescent's social interactions in same-race, mixed-gender groups. *Journal of Personality and Social Psychology, 71*(1), 71–82.

Fine, G., & Sandstrom, K. (1988). *Knowing children: Participant observations with minors.* Newbury Park, CA: Sage.

Gay, G. (1987). Ethnic identity development and Black expressiveness. In G. Gay & W. L. Baber (Eds.), *Expressively Black: The cultural basis of ethnic identity* (pp. 35–74). New York: Praeger.

Gay, G. (1994a). *At the essence of learning: Multicultural education.* West Lafayette, IN: Kappa Delta Pi.

Gay, G. (1994b). Coming of age ethnically. *Theory into Practice, 33*(3), 149–155.

Gay, G. (1999). Ethnic identity development and multicultural education. In R. H. Sheets & E. R. Hollins (Eds.), *Racial and ethnic identity in school practices: Aspects of human development,* (pp. 195–212). Mahwah, NJ: Lawrence Erlbaum Associates.

Hartup, W. W. (1993). Adolescents and their friends. In B. Laursen (Ed.), *Close friendships in adolescence* (pp. 3–22). San Francisco: Jossey-Bass.

Hartup, W. W. (1996). The company they keep: Friendships and their developmental significance. *Child Development, 67*(1), 1–13.

Helms, J. E. (1990). *Black and White racial identity.* Westport, CT: Praeger.

Hollins, E. R. (1996). *Culture in school learning: Revealing the deep meaning.* Mahwah, NJ: Lawrence Erlbaum Associates.

Kich, G. K. (1992). The developmental process of asserting a biracial, bicultural identity. In M. P. P. Root (Ed.), *Racially mixed people in America* (pp. 304–320). Newbury Park, CA: Sage.

Kim, J. (1981). *The process of Asian-American identity development: A study of Japanese American women's perceptions of their struggle to achieve positive identities.* Doctoral dissertation, University of Massachusetts.

Lazarus, R. S., & Folkman, S. (1991). *Stress, appraisal and coping.* New York: Springer.

Lee, S. J. (1999). Are you chinese or what? Ethnic and racial identity among Asian Americans. In R. H. Sheets & E. R. Hollins (Eds.), *Racial and ethnic identity in school practices: Aspects of human development* (pp. 107–122). Mahwah, NJ: Lawrence Erlbaum Associates.

Marcia, J. E. (1981). Identity in adolescence. In J. Adelson (Ed.), *Handbook of adolescent psychology* (pp. 197–243). New York: Wiley.

Miles, M. B., & Huberman, A. M. (1984). *Qualitative data analysis: A source book of new methods*. London: Sage.

Newcomb, A. F., & Bagwell, C. (1995). Children's friendship relations: A meta-analytic review. *Psychological Bulletin, 117*, 306–347.

Phinney, J. S. (1993). A three-stage model of ethnic identity development in adolescence. In M. E. Bernal & G. P. Knight (Eds.), *Ethnic identity: Formation and transmission among Hispanics and other minorities* (pp. 61–80). Albany: State University of New York Press.

Ponterotto, J. G., & Pedersen, P. B. (1993). *Preventing prejudice: A guide for counselors and educators*. Newbury Park, CA: Sage.

Root, M. P. P. (Ed.). (1992). *Racially mixed people in America*. Newbury Park, CA: Sage.

Root, M. P. P. (Ed.). (1996). *The multiracial experience: Racial borders as the new frontier*. Newbury Park, CA: Sage.

Root, P. P. (1999). The biracial baby boom: Understanding ecological constructions of racial identity in the twenty-first century. In R. H. Sheets & E. R. Hollins (Eds.), *Racial and ethnic identity in school practices: Aspects of human development,* (pp. xxx–xxx). Mahwah, NJ: Lawrence Erlbaum Associates.

Rotheram, M. J., & Phinney, J. S. (1987). Introduction: Definitions and perspectives in the study of children's ethnic socialization. In J. S. Phinney & Rotheram, M. J. (Eds.), *Children's ethnic socialization: Pluralism and development* (pp. 10–31). Newbury Park, CA: Sage.

Schofield, J. W. (1982). *Black and White in school: Trust, tension, or tolerance?* New York: Praeger.

Schunk, D. H. (1987). Peer models and children's behavioral change. *Review of Educational Research, 57,* 149–174.

Seiffge-Krenke, I. (1995). *Stress, coping and relationships in adolescence*. Mahwah, NJ: Lawrence Erlbaum Associates.

Sheets, R. H. (1997, February). *Student perception of multiracial ethnic identity: Can friendships cross colors?* Paper presented at the Fourteenth Annual Teachers College Winter Roundtable on Cross-Cultural Psychology and Education, New York.

Silverman, D. (1993). *Interpreting qualitative data: Methods for analyzing talk, text, and interaction*. London: Sage.

III Challenges and Strategies for Multicultural Practices

In Part III, racial and ethnic identity theory and human developmental processes are united with multicultural education, curriculum and instruction, multicultural counseling, and educational leadership. This section speaks directly to frontline practitioners—administrators, counselors, school psychologists, teachers—and to those entrusted with their preparation, challenging them to create best practices in schools.

Hollins discusses the relationship between ethnic identity development and teachers' professional practice in chapter 10. She adapts her typology of teacher perspectives on culture and their conceptualization of school learning (Hollins, 1996) to incorporate Helms' (1990) developmental identity stage theory. Hollins identifies three positional perspectives: denying the importance of culture and ethnicity, recognizing culture and ethnicity as societal influences, and accepting and embracing culture and ethnicity as important factors in school learning. The discussion of these positional perspectives include the ways in which teachers might select instructional approaches, frame curriculum content, and create a social context for learning as well as the relationship between teacher perspectives and ethnic identity development.

Hollins concludes that teachers' practices based on their perspectives and position in their own ethnic identity development are likely to influence students' perspectives and ethnic identity development. Thus, a major purpose of this chapter is to initiate dialogue and propose directions for empirical research into the relationship among teacher perspectives, ethnic identity development, and teaching practices.

In chapter 11, Gay summarizes general principles of human growth and development, argues that one purpose of multicultural education should be to support the development of a positive and healthy ethnic identity, and provides examples of teaching techniques that support the development of a positive ethnic identity. Gay describes seven general principles of human growth and development relative to ethnic identity development: the principle of significance, the principle of mutability, the principle of continuous and progressional development, the principle of holism and dialecticism, the principle of integration, the principle of multiplicity, and the principle of process.

Gay discusses three techniques for supporting the development of a positive ethnic identity through multicultural education, case studies, ethnobibliotherapy, and modeling and mentoring. Case studies provide opportunities to examine situations indepth, including specific variables within the context and interactions and relationships among individuals and groups. Ethnobibliotherapy provides opportunities to read and examine stories of life experiences, revealing struggles in the development of a positive ethnic identity for persons from their own and different ethnic groups. Modeling and mentoring places an individual in direct contact with a member of his or her own ethnic group who has developed a positive ethnic identity.

Reynolds (chap. 12) focuses on ways to make multicultural counseling services in schools more responsive to racial, ethnic, and culturally diverse students. According to Reynolds, counselors must be aware of the cultural realities facing diverse students as well as understand that race is a critical component of student identity. Strategies for creating multicultural environments and ways of viewing and defining multicultural counseling are discussed.

To operationalize multicultural counseling, Reynolds focuses on six areas of competence: knowledge and understanding of cultural groups, knowledge about cultural concepts, self-awareness assessment of multicultural skills, culturally responsive interventions, awareness of the dynamics of a multicultural relationship, and deconstruction of cultural assumptions underlying the helping process. This chapter concludes with the changes needed in school counseling to enhance the multicultural competence of both professional and in-training counselors.

Critical inquiry as a method to explore critical consciousness and to develop cultural and racial identity in preservice school leaders is examined by Taylor in chapter 13. Taylor argues that the maturation of leadership skills must include a deep understanding of cultural identity and an unconditional willingness to begin the process of racial and ethnic identity development.

Taylor describes the process of aspiring school leaders experienced in the development of their racial, ethnic, and cultural identity. Because data supports the probability of racial and socioeconomic dissimilarity among school staff and students, Taylor describes the challenges he encounters as a Black professor with a majority of White students. This chapter presents critical inquiry as a theoretical framework to examine social structures (school) and value issues (social justice, freedom, equality, liberation) in ways that question previously held beliefs, assumptions, and actions. Taylor constructs a classroom climate that provides opportunities for personal reflection and competent communication as a way to bridge critical inquiry to practice. Student narratives illustrative of Helms' six-stage theory—Contact, Disintegration, Reintegration,

Pseudo-Independence, Immersion/Emersion, and Autonomy—document significant student movement from where they were first located.

10 Relating Ethnic and Racial Identity Development to Teaching

Etta R. Hollins
Wright State University

An important issue in the discussion of ethnic identity development is its relationship to teachers' professional practice. A central question is: How is a teacher's own position in ethnic identity development related to classroom practices, including the selection of learning experiences, the framing of curriculum content, and social interactions with students and colleagues?

It is apparent that teachers' perspectives guide their professional practice in classrooms and that these perspectives are derived from multiple sources including early socialization in the home, schooling experiences, and the professional preparation provided by colleges and universities. Certainly, in a race-conscious society, such as the United States, ethnic and racial identity development are implicit aspects of early socialization and schooling that are incorporated into adult perspectives. Because the process of ethnic and racial identity development is implicit rather than explicit, it is not well-understood. The purpose of this chapter is to initiate dialogue and propose directions for empirical research into the relationship between teacher perspectives, ethnic and racial identity development, and teaching practices.

In a recent study reported by Madsen and Hollins (1997), the ethnic and racial identity development of African American teachers, who taught in a predominately European American elementary school setting, was a salient factor in their relationships with the pupils they taught and their colleagues. The researchers in this study found that participants who expressed a strong sense of ethnic and racial identity were socialized within their own culture as children. This included attending public schools, where they were in the majority, and completing their teacher preparation at historically Black colleges. They also maintained active involvement in the African American community. These teachers drew on traditions from their own culture as a source of strength during crisis. The

183

teachers in this study, who expressed a strong sense of ethnic and racial identity, seemed to be more conscious of their own responses to European American colleagues than those who expressed an attenuated ethnic identity. They made deliberate choices about the manner and circumstances in which they interacted with colleagues. They were more sensitive and responsive to the needs of African American students than either their European American colleagues or African American teachers who did not express a strong ethnic identity.

In contrast, Madsen and Hollins (1997) found that African American teachers who expressed a more attenuated ethnic and racial identity were socialized outside of their own cultural group as youths and usually attended undergraduate school at a predominately European American college or university. This attenuated ethnic and racial identity appeared problematic in these teachers' relationships with peers and children from their own racial group as well as European American colleagues. For example, at times, one teacher seemed embarrassed by the presence of African American youngsters and tried to avoid being identified with them or showing any special sensitivity to them. One such teacher refused to join African American special interest groups and openly admitted having difficulty relating to other African Americans. The African American teachers in this study who expressed an attenuated ethnic and/or racial identity appeared more tolerant of racist behavior from European Americans than their colleagues who expressed a strong ethnic identity. At times, they seemed to emulate this racist behavior. These authors referred to this phenomenon as *codependent racism.*

Evidence from the Madsen and Hollins (1997) study, that there is a relationship between early socialization—especially early schooling experiences—and ethnic and/or racial identity development seems to suggest that children develop a perceptual schema, based on early experiences, that influences personal and group identity development, which subsequently frames adult behavior, learning, and perception. Educators and scholars should be concerned with the influence of such perceptual schemata on adult behavior, especially that of teachers. Also, there should be concern for better understanding the role of schooling in shaping identity development.

TEACHERS' PERSPECTIVES
AND ETHNIC IDENTITY DEVELOPMENT

One approach to investigating the influence of teachers' perspectives and ethnic and racial identity development on classroom practice is to collect enough preliminary data to construct a theory or typology that can direct further investigation. Hollins (1996) presented a typology showing the relationship between teachers' perspectives on culture and their conceptualization of school learning. An analysis of the categories in this typology reveals a kinship to theories concerned with ethnic and racial identity development. It is important to point out that the typology of teacher perspectives on culture was not intended as stage theory, however; there are similarities between the two frameworks when applied in the examination of teaching behaviors.

For the purposes of this discussion, the Hollins (1996) typology is adapted to incorporate racial identity development stage theory. In this discussion, Hollins' Type I—*Culture as Artifact and Behavior*—includes behaviors and perspectives associated with Helms' (1990) White racial identity development theory, Stage 1, Contact; Stage 2, Disintegration; and Stage 3, Reintegration. Hollins' Type II—*Culture as Social and Political Relations*—includes behaviors and perspectives associated with Helms Stage 4, Pseudo-Independence. Hollins' Type III—*Culture as Affect, Behavior, and Intellect*—includes behaviors and perspectives associated with Helms' Stage 5, Immersion/Emersion; and Stage 6, Autonomy. In analyzing Hollins' typology and Helms stage theory, three positional perspectives can be identified: denying the importance of culture and ethnicity; recognizing culture and ethnicity as societal influences; and accepting or embracing culture and ethnicity as important factors in school learning. These positional perspectives are discussed in relationship to ethnic and racial identity development.

DENYING THE IMPORTANCE OF CULTURE AND ETHNICITY

In Helms (1990) Stage 1 of White racial identity development, individuals deny the salience of race in their relationships with others, at the same stage in Black racial identity development (Cross, this volume), individuals tend to dissociate themselves from their own ethnic or racial group in preference for association with the majority group. Whites in this category have had limited contact with members of other ethnic and racial groups. The ethnic minorities with whom they have had contact were usually posturing European American behaviors and values. In Stage 2, White individuals question what they have been socialized to believe about people of color. Peer pressure can push them to Stage 3, Reintegration, the stage at which the myths of White superiority are accepted. These fluctuations in identity development are evident in the ambivalence in the positional perspectives Hollins (1996) described in the typology on teacher perspectives. This is especially evident when peer pressure is associated with maintaining a particular school culture.

Denial of the significance of culture and ethnicity is the central factor in Hollins' Type I and is translated to classroom practices by teachers at this stage of ethnic and racial identity development (discussed later in this chapter). Very few teachers openly admit to believing in White superiority, although there may be evidence of such in their classroom practices. In

Hollins' (1996) typology, teachers in Type I view culture in terms of artifacts, functions, and behaviors. In discussions about culture, these teachers tend to emphasize the quaint or exotic. Thus, in these teachers'
perspectives, culture has little significance in classroom instruction or in
explaining how children learn, although it may be included in the curriculum as objective content.

Type I teachers may have two seemingly opposing views of cultural differences among people. Some may believe that there are no substantial differences between people based on culture, ethnicity, or race. These
teachers are likely to contend that they do not see skin color among the
children they teach. Any discussions of racial differences may be dismissed
with such charges as, "We are all the same beneath the skin" or "We are
more alike than different." Social class is considered the only significant
factor that categorizes and separates people. That is, low-income ethnic
minorities are the same as low-income Whites. Children from low-income
groups are viewed as disadvantaged. Other teachers in this category may
argue that there are obvious differences among different racial and ethnic
groups. Knowing this, however, does not contribute to better understanding teaching and learning. In fact, teachers may argue that these differences interfere with learning and make teaching more difficult.
Knowledge of differences among students may not influence Type I teachers' selection of instructional approaches.

Selecting Instructional Approaches

Whether Type I teachers recognize ethnic and racial differences among
their students or view them as all the same, they tend to share a universalistic view of teaching and learning. They argue that "good teaching is good
teaching" and it is expected to have the same potential outcomes for all
children. In these teachers' classrooms, instruction is usually the same for
all children, except the gifted who are provided more autonomy and more
learning experiences requiring critical thinking. Teachers in Type I seem to
prefer a particular model, process, or plan for teaching regardless of the
background experiences, preferences, or competencies of the children they
teach.

Children who fail in school may be viewed as slow, lacking parental support in the home, or not putting forth sufficient effort to succeed. When
children from particular ethnic and racial backgrounds experience dispro-
portionate failure, some Type I teachers attribute their failure to deficits in
their culture or socialization at home. Regardless of the attribution of failure, remediation usually means smaller and less complex segments of instruction given at a slower pace.

Type I teachers support maintaining high and rigorous standards by
providing challenging instruction and assignments for their students.
They tend to rely on traditional methods of assessment for feedback on the

performance. Attempts at adjusting instruction to accommodate differences in how children learn, who come from culturally diverse backgrounds, is viewed as risking the high standards set for the children in their classrooms.

Framing Curriculum Content

Teachers in Type I tend to accept the traditional curriculum. They believe the curriculum does and should reflect the "American" culture. When questioned, these teachers may have difficulty explaining or describing what is meant by the "American" culture. They are not particularly concerned with including ethnic minority history or culture in the curriculum.

Type I teachers associate multicultural education with teaching about the separate cultures of the society at the expense of what they describe as the *common culture*. This, they claim, leads to ethnic preferences, such as a native language other than English, that interfere with or replace preparation for successful participation in the society as it exists. These teachers are convinced that the ethnic pride, resulting from multicultural education is divisive and should be resisted. Most of these teachers would agree, however, that the traditional curriculum should be expanded to include more ethnic minorities who have contributed to the *common culture*. The *common culture* refers to the European influenced dominant culture that presently exists in the United States.

Other discussions about culture from teachers in Type I are limited to cultural artifacts that are frequently treated as quaint or exotic and are restricted to the study of specific subjects in their classrooms. For example, children in the lower grades might learn about children in far away places in social studies. Their study might include an examination of the housing, food, clothing, music, and art of these children's culture. The information presented is often superficial and does not represent an authentic perspective from the cultural groups' studied that would provide insight into their particular worldview.

Creating a Social Context for Learning

Type I teachers are convinced that the teacher must be in control of the students at all times. Thus, most talk in the classroom is from the teacher to the students as a group or between the teacher and individual students. The interaction among students is teacher controlled and very limited. The teacher determines who speaks, to whom, when, and why. Usually, children complete their assignments individually and privately. Children direct all of their inquiries and responses to the teacher. Occasionally, students from the dominant group or those ethnic minorities who appear the most acculturated are allowed to display some authority as models for those who have not yet learned mainstream ways of thinking and behaving. These children may share their knowledge by tutoring "slow" children. However, the teacher is clearly in charge and strives to demonstrate "good classroom management" techniques.

RECOGNIZING CULTURE AND ETHNICITY
AS SOCIETAL INFLUENCES

In Helms' (1990) Stage 4 of White racial identity development, White individuals question stereotypes of people of color and reject notions of White superiority. At this stage, ethnic minorities develop a positive nonstereotypical ethnic identity. Members of both groups tend to recognize culture and ethnicity as important social forces that influence institutional practices, including schooling.

In Hollins' (1996) typology, teachers in Type II view culture as social and political relationships. These teachers tend to be strong advocates for multicultural education as an essential force in maintaining a free and democratic society. Type II teachers contend that ethnic and cultural pride and respect, as well as appreciation for cultural diversity, are central to the political unity of the nation and should be the primary goals of multicultural education. This perspective is reflected in selecting instructional approaches, framing curriculum, and creating a social context for learning.

Selecting Instructional Approaches

Type II teachers acknowledge and appreciate cultural uniqueness as well as cultural similarities. Doing so does not seem to have the anticipated impact on their thinking about teaching and learning. Rather than connecting knowledge about culture with how children learn, individuality is central in these teachers' thinking. That is, each child is thought of as an individual without conscious reference to his or her cultural background. The goal is to meet the needs of each individual child. These teachers are not wed to a particular model, process, or plan for teaching, but rather to what works. Thus, Type II teachers are somewhat spontaneous in their approach to instruction.

Type II teachers believe that differences in experiential backgrounds account for variation in academic performance in school. Children who fail in school are given individual help, such as peer tutoring or direct personal instruction by the teacher. Approaches to remediation take into account certain experiential factors. For example, a latchkey child may be viewed as not having proper parental attention to homework, which may have a negative effect on academic performance. These teachers are inclined to solve such problems by increased time on task, such as afterschool tutoring, or by spending more time in direct instruction on key skills and concepts. In other instances, the teacher might perceive some children as lacking the experiences necessary for learning certain content or skills. In such cases, the teacher attempts to provide the necessary background experiences and knowledge for the children.

Framing the Curriculum

Teachers in Hollins' Type II believe the school curriculum should be reframed to more accurately reflect the cultural diversity of the nation in both content and perspective. They believe the curriculum should be designed to promote social reform aimed at eliminating oppression and promoting a more just and equitable society.

Individuals in this category make serious effort to perceive and understand different cultures on their own terms, although they are at times hindered by their own cultural blinders. They are persistent in expanding their own knowledge and understanding of the culturally diverse groups that comprise their classrooms, schools, and the nation. New information about different cultures is integrated into curriculum content in meaningful ways.

Type II teachers do not necessarily connect experiential background with cultural values and practices. Instead, the curriculum is the standard against which the adequacy of a child's experiential background is measured. Children whose experiences do not support the existing curriculum are not viewed as culturally deficit, but rather as experientially deprived or disadvantaged.

Creating a Social Context for Learning

Type II teachers make every possible effort to ensure that all children in the classrooms feel comfortable and supported, especially ethnic minorities and children with special needs. A high value is placed on cross-cultural understanding and building children's self-esteem.

Type II teachers tend to be more relaxed in their classrooms than those in Type I. They contend that children need direction rather than control. Although these teachers tend to be spontaneous in finding what works for their students, they engage in careful planning that provides good direction for children to learn from and with their peers.

ACCEPTING AND EMBRACING CULTURE AND ETHNICITY AS IMPORTANT FACTORS IN SCHOOL LEARNING

In Helms' (1990) Stage 5 of White racial identity development, White individuals reject stereotypes about other groups, question their own personal and group identity, and seek accurate information about other groups. This new behavior helps individuals move to Stage 6, Autonomy, during which White individuals internalize a positive definition of Whiteness. In

Stage 6, the term *race* is replaced with concepts of *culture* and *ethnicity*. Ethnic minorities at this stage of racial development define the relevance of their own ethnic identity. There is a move toward personal control and internalizing one's own ethnicity. This deeper understanding of the centrality of culture and ethnicity in daily life is evident in teachers' selecting approaches to instruction, framing curriculum, and creating a social context for learning.

In Hollins' (1996) typology, teachers in Type III view culture as affect, behavior, and intellect. These individuals are comfortable with their own culture and understand how they fit into a culturally diverse society. They are comfortable with members of other cultures and do not feel personally or culturally threatened. Type III teachers understand the centrality of culture in our existence as human beings. They acknowledge cultural and individual uniqueness without perceiving them as exotic or quaint.

Type III teachers are strong advocates for multicultural education as a source for providing equitable and effective teaching and learning, as well as an essential force in maintaining a free and democratic society. These teachers contend that multicultural education means using knowledge about culture and cultural knowledge to promote academic learning and cultural understanding, appreciation, and harmony among diverse groups of people. Ethnic and cultural pride and respect, as well as appreciation for cultural diversity, are viewed as central to the political unity of the nation and are important goals for multicultural education.

Selecting Instructional Approaches

The indepth knowledge that Type III teachers have of culture and cultural knowledge contributes to their understanding of the relationship between the home culture of their students and how they learn in school. These teachers believe children are a product of their home culture. That is, how children perceive the world and how and what they learn is a product of cultural values, practices, and perceptions. Type III teachers alter the curriculum and instructional approaches as necessary to facilitate children's development into competent persons who can lead rich and productive lives.

These teachers' knowledge about culture supports a view of teaching and learning as contextual. How children approach a particular learning task is, in part, dependent on the present and past context of their experiences, the social relationships among students and between students and their teacher, the background knowledge of the teacher and the students, and the nature of the content or skill to be learned. How the teacher approaches instruction takes into consideration the present and past context. These teachers view each child as part of a cultural group, but also as personally unique.

These teachers believe that variations in academic performance in school results from uneven accommodation of children's home culture and experiential background. Thus, remediation means reviewing and reconnecting the learner's knowledge and experience with the new content. Remediation is much more than adjusting pacing and complexity. It requires the teacher to make careful and deliberate observations of the learner at work and in social settings, to examine the learner's previous work, and to engage in strategic conversation intended to provide insight into the nature of the disconnectedness between the learner's knowledge and skill and the task at hand. The teacher uses the information gained from this type of careful study to develop an approach to accommodating the needs of a particular learner. Type III teachers try to identify patterns in their students' approaches to learning. Some of the patterns they identify involve culture, some gender, and some yet other factors.

Framing Curriculum Content

Teachers in Type III believe the school curriculum should include knowledge about culture and cultural knowledge. Students should learn about their own culture as well as that of others. Students should also be able to apply the cultural knowledge they gain through their own socialization within the home culture to understand school knowledge. The school curriculum should be reformed to more accurately reflect the cultural diversity of the nation in both content and perspective. The curriculum should be designed to promote social reform aimed at eliminating oppression and promoting a more just and equitable society.

Type III teachers are persistent in expanding their own knowledge and understanding of the culturally diverse groups that comprise their own classrooms, schools, and the nation. New knowledge about cultures and cultural knowledge are integrated into the curriculum content in meaningful ways.

Creating a Social Context for Learning

Type III teachers make every possible effort to ensure that all children in the classroom feel comfortable and supported, especially ethnic minorities and exceptional children. A high value is placed on cross-cultural understanding.

Type III teachers work hard, are more relaxed, and seem to enjoy their teaching more than those in the other two groups. These teachers assume the roles of facilitator and primary resource for the students. They believe children need direction rather than control. They create a classroom context that is collaborative, purposeful, and supportive. Children learn a natural form of collaboration based on mutual interests and needs. These teachers engage in careful and systematic planning that provides good direction for children to learn from and with their peers.

IMPLICATIONS FOR SCHOOL PRACTICES

The foregoing discussion addressed teachers' practices based on their perspectives and position in their own ethnic identity development. However, teacher perspectives are influenced by prevailing ideology within the larger society. This ideology includes notions about ethnic and racial identity that are incorporated into all levels of schooling within the society. Hollins (1995) used two interdependent and overlapping categories labeled *essential schema* and *collateral schema* to analyze the influence of prevailing ideology. The *essential schema* refers to the economic, political, and social ideologies from which the purposes and practices of schooling are derived. The *collateral schema* refers to the research and theory supporting school practices and comprising the knowledge base for designing the curriculum, learning experiences (instructional methodology), assessment approaches, the social context within schools, and school–community relations. This interrelatedness of the essential and collateral schemas supports and perpetuates particular forms of ethnic and racial identity. One example is that presented by Adams (1988) describing the ideologies and purposes that formed the basis for Native American education from 1880 to 1900. Adams described fundamental ideologies as including Protestantism, capitalism, and republicanism, which appeared thematically as Protestantism, individualization, and Americanization. The primary purposes for providing formal education for Native Americans included acculturation, subordination, and dispossession of the land. The outcome of these practices was to eradicate or distort Native American ethnic identity.

Contemporary debates over the canon present an example of the interrelatedness of essential and collateral schemata. Both the multiculturalists and the traditionalists claim democracy as the undergirding ideology for their positions. However, the multiculturalists advocate cultural pluralism, whereas the traditionalists advocate a common culture. The multiculturalists contend that the school curriculum should include the culture and heritage of all ethnic and cultural groups (Banks, 1991/1992). The traditionalists argue that this is not the function of schools (Ravitch, 1991/1992). This debate brings to the forefront the interrelatedness of political ideology, the purpose of schooling, and school practices exemplified in curriculum content.

Finally, in order for teachers to promote a healthy identity for themselves and their pupils, they must begin with self-understanding. Hollins (1995) identified four approaches to self- understanding. Each approach examines self from a different perspective. First, the examination of the deep meaning of schooling in one's own development requires the careful recalling and documentation of as much of these experiences as possible. These experiences must be examined in relationship to the ideologies that undergirded them and that can be identified in one's own teaching practices. Second, examination of images of self as teacher requires recognizing how the role of teacher and teaching practices are influenced by past experiences and prevailing ideologies. Third, examination of one's own racial identity and that of others requires recognizing and acknowledging personal feelings and perceptions of one's own racial identity and ideas about other races. Fourth, the examination of cultural identity requires developing a functional definition of culture that encompasses a worldview that shapes thoughts and responses to people, events, situations, and phenomena.

REFERENCES

Adams, D. W. (1988). Fundamental considerations: The deep meaning of Native American Schooling, 1880–1900. *Harvard Educational Review, 58*(1), 1–28.

Banks, J. A. (1991/92). Multicultural education: For freedom's sake. *Educational Leadership, 49*(4), 32–36.

Helms, J. E. (1990). *Black and White racial identity.* New York: Greenwood.

Hollins, E. R. (1995, Spring). Revealing the deep meaning of culture in school learning. *Action in Teacher Education, 17*(1), 70–79.

Hollins, E. R. (1996). *Culture in school learning: Revealing the deep meaning.* Mahwah, NJ: Lawrence Erlbaum Associates.

Madsen, J., & Hollins, E. R. (1997, March). *Minority teachers in majority schools.* Paper presented at the American Educational Research Association Annual Meeting.

Ravitch, D. (1991/92). A culture in common. *Educational Leadership, 49*(4), 8–11.

11 Ethnic Identity Development and Multicultural Education

Geneva Gay
University of Washington

The self is learned. What is learned can be taught. What can be taught is fair game for the public schools. The question is not one of whether we approve of teaching for a positive self. ... We could not avoid affecting the self if we wanted to. We may ignore the self in our teaching [but] we cannot ... escape the fact of our influence upon the self or our responsibility with respect to whether the effects of schooling are positive or negative. (Combs, 1962a, p. 101)

Genuine acceptance of one's ethnicity is positively related to psychological well-being, interpersonal relations, social consciousness, and personal efficacy. These also are major priorities of multicultural education. Because these two areas of concern have many common goals and potential effects, they could easily be combined in the effort to find ways to better educate ethnically and culturally different students and to improve their academic, personal, and social achievement. The discussions in this chapter are based on these premises. They explore some of the specific features and trends in ethnic identity development and demonstrate conceptual and pragmatic connection to multicultural education.

This chapter is divided into three parts. The first section summarizes general principles about human growth and development based primarily on the thinking of perceptual, or *third force,* psychologists such as Abraham Maslow, Earl Kelley, Arthur Combs, and Carl Rogers. The second part of this chapter deals with salient features of the process of ethnic identity development gleaned from research in social psychology and cultural anthropology, such as those generated by Pai Young, William Cross, and George Spindler, and from personal experiences. These discussions are based on

195

the premise that ethnic identity is a powerful need and valuable resource that should be employed and facilitated by instructional leaders. The third part of this chapter builds a case for ethnic identity development and multicultural education being coterminous, conjoined, and reciprocal. Consequently, implementing one in classroom instruction can facilitate the development of the other. Some strategies are suggested for how this may be done.

GENERAL PRINCIPLES
OF HUMAN GROWTH AND DEVELOPMENT

The general principles that comprise the conceptual parameters for the discussion of ethnic identity development derive largely from psychological theories of ego and identity development and need gratification. Of particular significance are those that deal with what Erikson (1963, 1968) called *achieving identity clarification,* Kelley (1962) referred to as *being fully functioning,* Maslow (1954, 1962) characterized as *self- actualizing,* and Rogers (1961, 1962) described as *being and becoming.* Seven of these principles are briefly described in the following text.

The Principle of Significance

Identity clarification is a critical variable—a fundamental aspect—of human development. Different types of identity occur in tandem with other aspects of human growth, such as the intellectual, moral, social, and emotional development. Erikson (1963) explained that "only identity safely anchored in the 'patrimony' of a cultural identity can produce a workable psychosocial equilibrium" (p. 412). McAdoo (1993) agreed with Erikson and connected identity development specifically to ethnicity. She stated, "Our ethnicity is one of the most basic elements of our being. It reveals itself in the customs, rituals, values, attitudes, and personality types of individuals" (p. ix).

The Principle of Mutability

Like other aspects of a person's social psychology, a clarified, authentic identity is learned, and is, therefore, amenable to instructional intervention. A single sense of identity is not applicable to all times, places, and circumstances. As individuals travel through the lifecycle, they must learn different ways of *being* and *becoming* that are most suitable for changing stages of growth, experiences, conditions, and interactions (see Root, this volume).

The Principle of Continuous and Progressional Development

Human growth is persistent, and occurs in patterns of regularity and increasing complexity. These processes are *universal,* but not normative. Some common features of the growth process apply regardless of the race, culture, ethnicity, gender, or position of individuals. No one person's or group's specific timing, style, and success in moving through the patterns should be deemed the acceptable norm for everyone. Different aspects of human growth can be sequential without being invariant and linear, stable without being stagnant, orderly and regularized without being inflexible and intractable. Instead, they are dynamic ways of being that are continually growing, evolving, and reconfigurating. These developmental phases have spaces within and among them where further growth occurs.

The Principle of Holism and Dialecticism

Human development is a systemic and interactive process. All aspects of human growth occur simultaneously, although they are not initiated at once and do not unfold at the same rate. Intellectual, moral, physical, social, and psychological development affect and reflect each other as well as have their own discrete attributes. Thus, the various aspects of human development are correlational and dialectic, but not hierarchical and causal.

The Principle of Integration

As individuals become more psychologically mature, healthy, autonomous, and self-actualized, their psychological traits are unified into a well-balanced, cohesive, and harmonious personality construct. Maslow (1962) believed that when psychological integration occurs, "many dichotomies become resolved," and "work tends to be the same as play; vocation and avocation become the same thing" (p. 43). According to Combs (1962b), for those individuals who are psychologically integrated:

> Courage comes naturally. Indeed, behavior which seems courageous to their fellows often ... seems to be only the 'normal' thing ... they are less disturbed or upset by criticism. They can remain stable in the midst of stress and strain ... be effective without worrying about conformity or nonconformity ... behave in terms of what seems best to do, and let the chips fall where they may. ... [They] can risk taking chances ... without fear [of] the new, the untried and the unknown. This permits [them] to be creative, original and spontaneous. (pp. 51–53)

The Principle of Multiplicity

No aspect of development is monolithic or unidimensional; rather, all are pluralistic and multidimensional. Intellectual, social, psychological, physical, and identity development have many different sources, manifestations, and consequences. Therefore, a variety of diverse data sources, disciplinary perspectives, methodologies, and analytical techniques are needed to acquire an adequate understanding of them. The facilitation of all human development must likewise be interdisciplinary and multidimensional.

The Principle of Process

Human growth and development are neverending, but this continuous evolvement is not always in an uninterrupted positive direction. Individuals never reach a point where growth ceases if they are to be maximally healthy and functional. Rogers (1961) explained that being in *a stream of becoming* means that a person is not a fixed and static entity, not a block of solid material, nor a fixed quantity of traits, but "a continually changing constellation of potentialities" (p. 122). This process of becoming creates an image of people who are exploring, discovering, celebrating, sharing, responding, enjoying, and experiencing themselves and others.

PROCESS OF ETHNIC IDENTITY DEVELOPMENT

Ethnic identity development is grounded in the broader template of psychological growth as framed by the general conceptual principles summarized above. It is a unique case of a universal process, a specific example of a set of general patterns, the application of global theories to a localized context. The structural features of the process of ethnic identity development approximate those associated with becoming psychologically healthier, but their substance is fundamentally different.

Although ethnic identity and other types of psychological growth are approximate and may even be interactive to some degree, their relationship is not prerequisite, ordinal, or causal. That is, individuals do not necessarily need to have achieved a clarified gender, vocational, or familial role identity before they can become ethnically self-actualized, nor does having an internalized authentic ethnic identity lead automatically to the resolution of conflicts associated with one's political, physical, academic, professional, or sexual identities, concepts, and competencies.

Features of the process of ethnic identity development discussed here derive from two major sources. The first is thinking and research of social psychologists and educationalists such as William Cross, Jr., Janet Helms, Jean Phinney, Martha Bernal, George Knight, Beverly Tatum, Joseph

Ponterotto and others. The second source is a personal story, that is, the insights I have gained from my own experiences of going through the process of reclaiming, owning, embracing, and celebrating my ethnic identity as an African American.

Characteristics of the Development Process

Physiological traits are no more significant in constructing a positive ethnic identity than they are in creating healthy egos and self-concepts. They merely provide a biological cortex for a deeper, more significant psychological creation. This distinction is evident in the fact that, as individuals move through the construction process, the labels they use to self-reference their ethnicity become increasingly less descriptive and more figurative. Thus, being "Black" is not about skin pigmentation; it is a notation of cultural identity, ethnic affiliation, and political ideology. As Cross (1991) explained, "'Blackness' is a state of mind, not an inherited trait, and its acquisition often requires considerable effort" (p. 149). Feelings of historical connectedness, how they see themselves, and how they live their lives in relation to their cultural socialization are of more importance in determining Japanese American ethnic identity than national origins. Speaking Spanish, Vietnamese, or Navajo is not the only, or even the most important, measure of where members of these groups are on the scale of ethnic identity development. Genuine growth in this domain of functioning is a cognitive and affective process. Its achievement involves thoughts, feelings, emotions, values, and actions directed toward clarifying and changing how people perceive, value, embody, and affirm their ethnicity.

Conscientialization and transformation are necessary for the development of authentic ethnic identities. Individuals must be consciously aware of the need for, and very deliberate about making changes in, their ethnic perceptions, values, and behaviors. Sometimes the magnitude of the changes required to fully embrace one's ethnicity is so extensive that they constitute the birth or creation of a new psychological state of being. Cross (1991) likened the process to a metamorphosis of the ethnic self; Thomas (1971) made it analogous to recovery from a serious psychological illness of self-rejection; and Banks (1981) envisioned it as a release from psychological captivity or imprisonment. This altered sense of self permeates the totality of a person's being, believing, and behaving.

Ethnic identity, like other dimensions of human growth and development, is not achieved instantaneously. It requires time and nurturance. No part of the human canvas is ever completed with a single brush stroke, nor do masterpieces—but for the rare exceptional case—emerge from initial efforts. Most human creations require effort and skills, cultivated through growth and experience; they are not accomplished automatically or instantaneously. Such is the case with ethnic identity development. This is a very complex phenomenon, and some of its dimensions are incomprehensible during childhood and youth. The perceptual, intellectual, and moral maturity that comes from a wide range of living, learning, relating, and experiencing are necessary for their deeper meanings to be understood. However, when strong and authentic ethnic identity appears to be among youths, it is still immature and incomplete. It is not yet fully functioning or totally actualized. Children and adolescents have not had sufficient opportunities to completely experience all phases in the cycle of ethnic identity development.

Developmental age and maturity, then, are important variables in the ethnic identity process, but they do not guarantee its initiation or successful completion. This is especially true when the emphasis of the process is *reconstruction* or *reclamation*. That is, when individuals have to rid themselves of negative ethnic identities in order to build positive perceptions, as opposed to those who have positive perceptions of their ethnic self that continue to expand and deepen as they go through life.

Ethnic identity development is psychologically liberating and empowering. Moving through the process from preconscious, denigrating, or hegemonic notions of ethnicity toward critically clarified and accepting ones can cause individuals to become more centered with greater self-assurance, self-confidence, and self-determination. This disposition is a major source of personal power.

The achievement of a clarified or actualized ethnic identity does not immune individuals to the challenges of living in a society that is often hostile to ethnic and cultural diversity. Latino, Native, Asian, and African Americans can have genuinely positive perceptions of their ethnicity and still be subjected to prejudice, discrimination, and oppression. These positive ethnic identities do protect their psyches somewhat, even though they cannot prevent racism and other psychosocial attacks from occurring. This protection takes the form of being able to separate one's personal worth from the social problems encountered and to distinguish personal responsibilities from attempted impositions of blame by others.

Similarly, the need to counteract repeated occurrences of racism does not mean that one's own ethnic identity retrogresses or is any less authentic. Encounters with discrimination after achieving ethnic identity clarification and internalization do not necessarily cause a person to return to the preconscious, captivated, or searching stages. How people understand and deal with these attempts at denigration makes the difference. Recognizing and responding to them without internalizing their negative effects, or in any way feeling that they define one's personhood, are ethnic actualization responses.

The freedom that comes with self-ethnic clarification, while still having to contend with the mainstream societal inequities, illustrates the tension between *being* and *becoming*, identified by Kelley (1962) and Rogers (1962). Within the context of ethnic identity development, it is manifested as having to cope with racism while transcending the psychology of racial victimization. The latter is done, in part, through the creation of a strong ethnic selfhood. The *Children of the Dream,* whom Edwards and Polite (1992) wrote about, were able to do this. These highly successful professional African Americans demonstrated that however *success* is defined, it is "almost always the result of a peculiar kind of drama that gets played out first in the psyche" (p. 3). Part of this drama was being affirmed and empowered by a positive sense of their Blackness. These individuals fully understood that, despite high levels of social and economic achievement, they would encounter and have to deal with racial obstacles, prejudices, inequities, and exploitations. They placed the causes of these problems where they rightfully belong—on the perverse reactions of a racist society to their ethnic group, not on some personal deficiency within themselves. These "experts in the art of victory" clearly understood that:

> real success lies in who you become on the journey to achievement. The ability to not just overcome but to triumph in the face of obstacles, to make a way out of what appears to be no way, to wrest destiny from the seemingly arbitrary hands of fate, constitutes power that is transcendent, freedom that is supreme. (Edwards & Polite, 1992, p. 274)

Ethnic groups within the United States, especially those of color, share a similar pattern of ethnic identity development (Phinney, 1989; Phinney & Alipuria, 1990). Differences occur in its timing, focus, direction, and intensity. The groups least affected by racism and most represented in positions of sociopolitical power tend to begin their ethnic identity construction later and experience it less intently. Research (Helms, 1990; Phinney, 1989; Phinney & Alipuria, 1990; Tatum, 1992) indicates that this is the case with European Americans. They are less concerned about ethnicity and perceive it as an issue of little or no importance in their personal lives. This is one of those taken-for-granted features that Bowers and Flinders (1990) attribute to the privilege and power of the European American position of dominance in U.S. society.

Conversely, the ethnic identity clarification process appears to be more intense and begins earlier for groups of color (Phinney, 1989; Phinney & Alipuria, 1990). It is more challenging to construct an authentic ethnic identity starting from a negative and powerless position than from one of positiveness and power. This is true because of the lack of a supportive mainstream sociocultural infrastructure, the availability of limited resources, and the number of identity-related issues they have to negotiate. For some groups, the center of the identity process is weighted more toward race, class, language, religion, or ethnicity. For groups of color, these are so deeply interwoven that they are virtually inseparable in the construction of a healthy identity. For example, although upper class status may give European Americans greater license to be less concerned about their ethnicity, the same is not necessarily true for Asian, African, Native, and many Latino Americans. Their highly visible racial, and often linguistic, features make them more susceptible to others' negative racial attitudes, regardless of their social class, education, or gender status. This susceptibility intensifies the need for them to have a deeply grounded and more thoroughly clarified ethnic identity.

ETHNIC IDENTITY AND MULTICULTURAL EDUCATION

Ethnic identity development should be an explicit and critical component of multicultural education programs and practices implemented in kindergarten through college. Its inherent significance, and its close relationship to the overall mission and most of the goals of multicultural education, demand this kind of pedagogical attention. Furthermore, the multidimensional nature of the ethnic identity process requires instructional interventions that are comprehensive and varied in scope, type, and effects.

Interconnections

The most explicit connection between ethnic identity development and multicultural education is evident in the goal of helping students from different ethnic and cultural backgrounds develop positive self-concepts. This theme appears throughout multicultural education scholarship. Because of the continuing legacies of racism, exploitation, and cultural hegemony, perceptions of ethnicity are distorted to some extent. This distortion ranges from benign neglect to invisibility to ambivalence to inflated positivism to intense denigration. African, Asian, and Native Americans are still frequently seen as having made no worthy contributions to society, as criminal influences, as intellectually deficient, as physically unattractive, as people to be feared, as genetically inferior, and as lacking in leadership skills. Images of European Americans are often distorted in the opposite direction—as being the only significant cultural contributors, biologically superior, intellectually gifted, natural leaders, and otherwise better than everyone else (Smith, 1990). These perceptions permeate the entire fabric of society—media, politics, economics, education, religion, language, law, and personal relationships. Two very powerful ways in which messages are transmitted are through the placement and portrayal of different ethnic groups in the entertainment industry (e.g., television, newspapers, movies, and the performing arts), and educational programs. The negative consequences of these practices account, in part, for the prominence given to developing positive ethnic identities by advocates of multicultural education.

Imaging Ethnic Identity

Nieto (1996) shared some memories of negative educational experiences she encountered. Their consequences illustrate the need for this advocacy. She recalled her tenth-grade homeroom teacher asking if she was in a special English class after discovering that she spoke only Spanish when she began school in the first grade. Sonia responded, "Yes, I'm in Honors English." Reflecting on this experience many years later, she remembered feeling:

> fortunate that I was able to respond in this way. I had learned to feel somewhat ashamed of speaking Spanish and wanted to make it clear that I was intelligent in spite of it. Many students in similar circumstances who are in bilingual and ESL classes feel guilty and inferior to their peers.

> Those first experiences with society's responses to cultural differences did not, of course, convince me that something was wrong with the *responses*. Rather, I assumed, as many of my peers did, that there was something wrong with *us*. We learned to feel ashamed of who we were, how we spoke, what we ate, and everything else that was "different" about us. (p. 2)

Undoubtedly, some things have changed in the years since Nieto was a high-school student. The question is: How much and how real are the changes? Are they enough to reverse traditional practices of demeaning, ignoring, and devaluing the ethnic identity of people of color, while celebrating European Americans in educational programs and practices? Analyses of textbooks and other instructional materials suggest these changes should be more extensive. The most blatant ethnic and gender stereotypes (e.g., the "noble savage Indians," "the happy-go-lucky simpleton Blacks," the "lazy, uninspiring Mexican Americans," and the "helpless, decorative European American females") have been eliminated. Overall, more progress has been made for African Americans. Native Americans, Latinos, and Asian Americans remain largely invisible in textbooks, except for a few periodic events. Contemporary books still tend to sanitize content about ethnicity by avoiding most controversial issues; focusing on safe ethnic individuals who are nonthreatening to mainstream standards; emphasizing historical events over contemporary ones; not giving parity treatment to a wide range of ethnic groups; and restricting the content included largely to the margins of text narratives and the periphery of classroom instruction (Davis, Ponder, Burlaw, Garza-Lubeck & Moss, 1986; Wade, 1993).

Another arena in which the ethnic identities and self-concepts of people of color are vilified or valorized is literature that is used to supplement instructional materials. One graphic example is presented by Cullen (1970). He used the poem, "Incident," to show how one's ethnic identity can be violated in daily interactions. The poem tells the story of an 8-year-old African American boy being summarily dismissed, in the most derogatory way, by an European American boy of a similar age when he extended an overture of friendship toward him. While riding a bus on a visit to Baltimore, the Black boy saw the White boy looking at him. Assuming this was a friendly curiosity, he responded with a smile. The White boy reacted by sticking out his tongue, and calling the Black boy a "nigger." The long-term effects of these kinds of experiences on African American ethnic identity are indicated in the poem as the Black boy recalls, "I saw the whole of Baltimore from May to December; of all the things that happened there, that's all that I remember" (Cullen, 1970, p. 93).

Although Cullen's story is a poetic creation to raise a critical psychosocial issue, real incidents like it occur with frightening frequency today. In the Fall of 1996, the parents of a 10-year-old African American succeeded in getting the historical novel, *War Comes to Willy Freeman*, removed from classrooms in a suburban Chicago school district on the grounds that it was detrimental to the self-concepts of all students. This book repeatedly portrays the Black characters negatively and refers to them often as "niggers." After reading the book, the other students began calling these parents' son (the only African American in the class) "nigger," too. The opposing parents argued that this book was a primer "for the development of a full-blown, mature racist," and for the self-denigration of African Americans because:

A White child reading this [book] in the fifth grade could develop a mentality and attitude about Black people and women that could be damaging for the rest of his life. ... To Black children, it has the ability to diminish their self-image and devastate their self-esteem and sense of self-worth. ("Eric Johnson," 1996, pp. 23–24)

Other incidents depicted in the media and practices used routinely by mainstream institutions further document how the identities and self-concepts of some ethnic groups are regularly assaulted. Recently, a European American husband and wife were convicted of putting a noose around the neck of a preteen African American male, tying him to a tree, and shooting a gun at him, presumably to teach him a lesson against stealing. Similarly, for some Native Americans, federal government regulations requiring them to document the degree of their ethnic purity as a condition of legal recognition is a telling indication of deeply ingrained negative attitudes and evaluations. A Native American student in one of my classes expressed these sentiments in observing that, "No other group is routinely expected to declare its 'ethnic pedigree.' Anyway, pedigrees are something that is usually associated with showcase animals." African Americans, especially males, are sometimes referred to with language usually reserved for animals. They are the only group of people called "an endangered species." Asian Americans are largely invisible in nonprint mass media; when they do appear, they are portrayed in one-dimensional form—as quiet, industrious, and studious workers, high achievers, and genteel nontroublemakers. Even Asian American criminals in television and movies go about their illegal activities calmly, quietly, and with genteel dignity. This model minority stereotype is as unreal and burdensome for creating positive ethnic identities as the extremely negative ones ascribed to other ethnic groups.

Images made by and transmitted through mass media can affect ethnic identities and self-perceptions. These effects can be either positive or perilous, depending on whether the groups are validated or vilified. The example comes from a series of letters written by journalist Bob Teague to his son in the 1980s. It conveys a victimizing image and message. Teague (1989) pondered:

> I wonder how many of us have actually mapped the minefield of racism? From Square One, when a Black man leaves his sanctuary each morning, he is regarded and treated by perhaps most members of the ruling majority as an abnormality, a lower form of life. They see him as the potential perpetrator of the next violent crime to be reprised on the six o'clock news; a contaminated descendant of the African savages who invented sickle-cell anemia and probably AIDS; the primary cause of overcrowded prisons and urban blight; the most likely failure to eventually succeed as a pimp, crack dealer, or deadbeat. ... (p. 28)

Although Teague spoke specifically about males, females are included through implication and extension. After all, they are the males' mothers, sisters, daughters, spouses, friends, cousins, and ethnic kinfolk. What affects one affects the other. With hardly any stretch of the imagination, parallel negative caricatures can be evoked for Mexican Americans, Puerto Ricans, and Native Americans. Therefore, the burdens of racism and their ravages on ethnic self-perceptions are as consequential for females as males, and all ethnic groups, either directly or indirectly.

The images, roles, values, behaviors, and identities of ethnic groups transmitted through mass media can have significant impacts on the construction of ethnic identities. Therefore, students should be taught skills in how to critically analyze, deconstruct, and reconstruct them. These analyses might include determinations of positive and negative features; the extent to which media presentations cover a wide range of ethnic individuals and expressions; what stages of ethnic identity development are preferred by mass media in their presentations of ethnic groups and how these preferences are expressed in the promotion of issues, programs, and personalities.

These examples of ethnic representations in education and popular culture barely scratch the surface of a massive and pervasive iceberg of negativism that profoundly affects the development of ethnic identity. Students should be taught how to recognize these actions and their effects and to replace distortions of different ethnic groups' identities with more accurate portrayals. Other knowledge, values, and skills that buttress ethnic self-concepts and identities should be cultivated as well. They include teaching ethnic and cultural literacy and developing personal, social, and political consciousness, efficacy, and ethics. Together these constitute the empowerment agenda of multicultural education.

Teaching Strategies

Even if it is impossible to avoid the most difficult phases of the process when individuals are searching for alternate foundations to build a new ethnic identity, multicultural education can provide valuable assistance to students in working through these phases. In the haste to become ethnically reaffiliated, individuals can overemphasize ritualistic and superficial cultural features and romanticize or glorify their ethnic group. Multicultural education plays an equalizing function here by: teaching students accurate and significant information about the full range of their ethnic group's members, cultures, contributions, and experiences; affirming and valuing the ethnic heritages of all students; and promoting ethnic diversity as a personal and social reality, strength, and desirability.

Three pedagogical techniques are particularly appropriate for these purposes. One method, *case studies,* permits students to conduct indepth analyses of traits, events, individuals, and experiences that have contributed to the cultivation and dissemination of their own group's ethnic identity. Because students are searching for their ethnic and cultural roots, self-ethnic group studies are imperative. Thus, European American students examine how incidents and individuals of European heritage (e.g., Anglo Saxons, German, and Irish) are grappling with recentering their ethnic identity away from cultural superiority, imperialism, and hegemony. Different Asian Americans (e.g., Chinese, Cambodian, Filipino, and Vietnamese) explore their own specific ethnic groups' struggles and successes with creating self-determined ethnic identities, and so on. These inquiries should cover a variety of groups, experiences, and perspectives within different ethnic families or clusters. Therefore, tribal groups (e.g., Cherokee, Sioux, Navajo, and Colville) in various regions of the country, in urban, rural, and reservation settings, and in historical and contemporary times are included in the case studies of Native American ethnicity. Mexican, Puerto Rican, Cuban, South American, Caribbean, and other Spanish origin variations are incorporated in studies of the development of Latino ethnic identity.

The second instructional technique to use in assisting individuals through the search for alternative sources of ethnic identity is a variation of bibliotheraphy. It uses ethnic literature that deals with ethnic identity development. These include personal accounts across a wide range of literary genre: novels, real and fictional autobiographies, essays, poetry, short stories, personal interviews, and song lyrics. The intent is for students to gain feelings of affiliation and learn some techniques for dealing with their own identity issues from the situations and characters portrayed in the literature. For these reasons, this instructional technique is appropriately called *ethnobibliotheraphy*.

Literature is a window to the soul. It allows the writer to render meaningful the self that is deep within so that others can see it embodied in structure, content, and form. It is second in value and effect only to direct personal experiences for encountering significant intraethnic and interethnic interactions and finding ethnic affirmation. Speaking specifically about African American poets, Melhem (1990) said their works "inscribe a dual conception and need; the self and the self-in-society," (p. 4) and are continually "inventing, reinventing, discovering, and creating their own dazzling identities" (p. 5). Authors who use their cultural experiences and voices to tell their individual and communal stories are seeking to name themselves, to create themselves in language, to become self-authenticating, to reveal their whole consummate being. When their culturally centered literary voice is heard, their identity is vindicated (Jones, 1991).

Gates (1991) recognized the power and potential of ethnic literature in the creation of self-identities and as a means for rendering these visible and accessible to others. He spoke eloquently about how, throughout history and oppression, African Americans have used autobiography, as a literary technique, for self-creation and presentation:

> The ultimate form of protest, certainly, was to register in print the existence of a "black self" that had transcended the limitations and restrictions that racism had placed on the personal development of the Black individual. ... The will to power for black Americans was the will to write; and the predominant mode that this writing would assume was the shaping of a black self in words ... the impulse to testify, to chart the peculiar contours of the individual protagonist on the road to becoming, clearly undergirds even the fictional tradition of black letters, as the predominance of the first-person form attests ... the African American [literary] tradition, more clearly and directly than most, traces its lineage ... in the act of declaring the existence of a surviving, enduring ethnic self—to this impulse of autobiography.

> The connection among language, memory, and the self has been of single importance to African Americans, intent as they have had to be upon demonstrating ... that their "selves" were, somehow, as whole, integral, educable, and as noble as were those of any other American ethnic group. (p. 3–7)

In their literary traditions, African Americans and other ethnic groups are continually constructing their self-ethnic identity. The "I" these writers speak of is both personal and symbolic—a representation of their individual self-creations and the collective construction of their ethnic group's identity. In these presentations, they deal with multiple dimensions of the self-creation process and what it generates. Their ethnic identity becomes exalted as they explore and declare: "I was; I am not; I can; I do; I think; I believe; I will; I won't; I may; I be; I am." This impulse to self-creation in literary forms other than the autobiography genre per se brings to mind such powerful examples as "I am Joaquin" by Corky Gonzales (1972), "Still I Rise" by Maya Angelou (1986), "If You Want to Know What We Are" by Carlos Bulosan (1976), and "Ego-Tripping" by Nikki Giovanni (1973). These self-creations provide invaluable knowledge, skills, guidance, affirmation, and motivation for students in their own ethnic identity development processes.

The third teaching technique for creating, reclaiming, and reconstructing ethnic identity is *modeling and mentoring.* It is especially appropriate for individuals who are approaching ethnic clarification. Students in this phase may study the personal profiles of people from a variety of ethnic groups and participate in relationships with them. Individuals selected to be mentors should be ethnically actualized and able to make the techniques and experiences they used in clarifying their ethnic identity available for others to see, analyze, and emulate. Their developmental progressions and ways of being serve as points of reference for students in the construction of their own ethnic identities. Thus, these individuals function as *process models and mentors.*

Students and adults with clarified ethnic identities can also be helpful in classrooms as peer tutors and coteachers. Their progression through stages of identity development gives them a perspective on the process that can be a valuable teaching tool. It allows them to be sensitive, caring, empathetic, and supportive of others who have not yet completed their identity formation, without feeling the need to solve their dilemmas. Their best assistance is being available to commiserate if the need arises, to be an anchor in times of uncertainty, and to be tangible images of what ethnic identity clarification looks, feels, sounds, and acts like embodied in actual human behavior. Being ethnic, according to their own standards that these individuals exhibit, equals self-definition, self-control, self-direction, and self-evaluation—the epitome of personal autonomy, efficacy, and empowerment. They make themselves available to assist, on request, in the similar empowerment of others.

This kind of characterization, collaboration, and caring among persons in different phases of ethnic identity development appeals to and employs many of the other salient features of multicultural education. Among them are cooperative learning, personal experiences, comparative and multiple perspectives, values clarification, ethical actions, self-determination, and intraethnic and interethnic community building. Consequently, ethnic identity development is simultaneously a mission, content, outcome, and quality measure of multicultural education.

IMPLICATIONS FOR SCHOOL PRACTICES

Multicultural education is a useful tool to facilitate the ethnic identity aspect of human growth and development. When advocates insist that educational institutions include in their programs and practices accurate representations of diverse ethnic groups' members, cultures, experiences, and contributions, they are, in essence, making a case for ethnic identity development. Explicit statements about the need for and right of all students to have access to positive images about their ethnic groups, to accept themselves, and to be proud of who they are permeate multicultural education theory. So do persistent references to developing positive self-concepts. Ethnic identity is one of the many self-concepts that a person has. Like others, such as gender, race, intellect, physicality, and vocation, it should be a centerpiece of educational programs and should be taught directly and deliberately.

What has been missing thus far is sufficient explication of the natural and unavoidable relationship between ethnic identity development and multicultural education. This oversight may have occurred because the connection seems so obvious as to require no explanation. Another reason could be the absence, until relatively recently, of any systematic ways to think about how ethnic identity evolves. This is no longer the case. Research and theory in social psychology and multicultural counseling are generating a rich pool of ethnic and racial identity development models, paradigms, and diagnostic techniques. Now it is possible to demonstrate how multicultural education can systematically facilitate ethnic identity development. The suggestions made in this chapter are a mere beginning in this undertaking. Hopefully, they open the way for many others to follow, each with increasing conceptual clarity and greater pedagogical praxis.

REFERENCES

Angelou, M. (1986). And still I rise. In M. Angelou, *Poems* (pp. 154–155). New York: Bantam.

Banks, J. A. (1981). *Multiethnic education: Theory and practice*. Boston: Allyn & Bacon.

Bowers, C. A., & Flinders, D. J. (1990). *Responsive teaching: An ecological approach to classroom patterns of language, culture, and thought*. New York: Teachers College Press.

Bulosan, C. (1976). If you want to know what we are. In E. San Juan, Jr. (Ed.), *Carlos Bulosan and the imagination of the class struggle* (pp. 86–88). New York: Oriole Editions.

Combs, A. W. (Ed.). (1962a). *Perceiving, behaving, becoming: A new focus for education*. Washington, DC: Association for Supervision and Curriculum Development.

Combs, A. W. (1962b). A perceptual view of the adequate personality. In A. W. Combs (Ed.), *Perceiving, behaving, becoming: A new focus for education* (pp. 50–64). Washington, DC: Association for Supervision and Curriculum Development.

Cross, W. E., Jr. (1991). *Shades of Black: Diversity in African-American identity.* Philadelphia: Temple University Press.

Cullen, C. (1970). Incident. In A. Murray & R. Thomas (Eds.), *The Journey* (p. 93). New York: Scholastic.

Davis, O. L., Jr., Ponder, G., Burlaw, L. M., Garza-Lubeck, M., & Moss, A. (1986). *Looking at history: A review of major U.S. history textbooks.* Washington, DC: People of the American Way.

Edwards, A., & Polite, C. K. (1992). *Children of the dream: The psychology of Black success.* Garden City, NY: Doubleday.

Eric Johnson, President/CEO Baldwin Ice Cream, forces school district in Chicago suburb to remove book containing racial slurs. (1996, December), *Jet, 91*(3), 23–24.

Erikson, E. H. (1963). *Childhood and society* (2nd ed.). New York: Norton.

Erikson, E. H. (1968). *Identity: Youth and crisis.* New York: Norton.

Gates, H. L., Jr. (Ed.). (1991). *Bearing witness: Selections from African-American autobiography in the twentieth century.* New York: Pantheon.

Giovanni, N. (1973). Ego-tripping. In N. Giovanni, *Ego-tripping and other poems for young people* (pp. 3–5). New York: Lawrence Hill.

Gonzales, R. (1972). *I am Joaquin: An epic poem.* New York: Bantam.

Helms, J. (1990). *Black and White racial identity: Theory, research, and practice.* New York: Greenwood.

Jones, G. (1991). *Liberating voices: Oral tradition in African American literature.* Cambridge, MA: Harvard University Press.

Kelley, E. C. (1962). The fully functioning self. In A. W. Combs (Ed.), *Perceiving, behaving, becoming: A new focus for education* (pp. 9–20). Washington, DC: Association for Supervision and Curriculum Development.

Maslow, A. H. (1954). *Motivation and personality.* New York: Harper & Row.

Maslow, A. H. (1962). Some basic propositions of a growth and self-actualization psychology. In A. W. Combs (Ed.), *Perceiving, behaving, becoming: A new focus for education* (pp. 34–49). Washington, DC: Association for Supervision and Curriculum Development.

McAdoo, H. P. (1993). Introduction. In H. P. McAdoo (Ed.), *Family ethnicity: Strength in diversity* (pp. ix–xv). Newbury Park, CA: Sage.

Melhem, D. H. (1990). *Heroism in the new Black poetry: Introduction & interviews.* Lexington: The University Press of Kentucky.

Nieto, S. (1996). *Affirming diversity: The sociopolitical context of multicultural education* (2nd ed.). White Plains, NY: Longman.

Phinney, J. S. (1989). Stages of ethnic identity development in minority group adolescents. *Journal of Early Adolescence, 9*(1–2), 34–49.

Phinney, J. S., & Alipuria, L. (1990). Ethnic identity in college students from four ethnic groups. *Journal of Adolescence, 13*(2), 171–183.

Rogers, C. R. (1961). *On becoming a person: A therapist's view of psychotherapy.* Boston: Houghton Mifflin.

Rogers, C. R. (1962). Toward becoming a fully functioning person. In A. W. Combs (Ed.), *Perceiving, behaving, becoming: A new focus for education* (pp. 21–33). Washington, DC: Association for Supervision and Curriculum Development.

Root, P. P. (1999). The biracial baby boom: Understanding ecological constructions of racial identity in the twenty-first century. In R. H. Sheets & E. R. Hollins (Eds.), *Racial and ethnic identity in school practices: Aspects of human development,* (pp. 67–90). Mahwah, NJ: Lawrence Erlbaum Associates.

Smith, T. W. (1990, December). *Ethnic images.* Unpublished GSS Topical Report No. 19, University of Chicago, National Opinion Research Center, Chicago.

Tatum, B. D. (1992). Talking about race, learning about racism: The application of racial identity development theory in the classroom. *Harvard Educational Review, 62*(1), 1–24.

Teague, B. (1989). *The flip side of soul: Letters to my son.* New York: Morrow.

Thomas, C. (1971). *Boys no more.* Beverly Hills, CA: Glencoe Press.

Wade, R. C. (1993). Content analysis of social studies textbooks: A review of ten years of research. *Theory and Research in Social Education, 21*(3), 232–256.

12 Working With Children and Adolescents in the Schools: Multicultural Counseling Implications

Amy L. Reynolds
Fordham University

The demographic transformation of the United States has been increasingly highlighted as the 21st century approaches. Locke (1992) stated that more than one third of the U.S. population will consist of people of color, and others point out that native-born Whites will become just another group within the diverse racial and ethnic peoples living in the United States (Cox, 1993; Jamieson & O'Mara, 1991; Wittmer, 1992). According to Johnson (1995), "schools serve as a barometer for measuring the demographic changes taking place in the society at large" (p. 103). In recent years, schools have reported rising numbers of students of color, biracial, and immigrant students (Johnson, 1995; Kopala, Esquivel, & Baptiste, 1994; Nishimura, 1995; see Taylor, chap. 13, this volume). Unfortunately, many schools are not prepared or well-equipped to address the needs of this growing group of students. Many of these students experience difficulties in the schools. Immigrant children and their families often have limited support systems (Esquivel & Keitel, 1990) and typically do not utilize available support services (Acosta, Yamamoto, & Evans, 1982). Dropout rates among many students of color, especially in urban environments, are alarmingly high and many students report feeling disempowered and disenfranchised in their schools (Cummins, 1990). There are also increasing incidents of violence, some of which are racially biased, committed by elementary, middle, and secondary school-aged students (Ferrara, 1992).

These conflicts and difficulties threaten the ability of all students, not just students of color, to succeed in school and develop emotionally and psychologically because they create tense, hostile, and unwelcoming environments. All students, regardless of their racial or ethnic background, need a safe and affirming environment, where diversity is valued, in order

213

to learn and grow. Students are dependent on school personnel, such as principals, teachers, and counselors, to facilitate their growth and development.

The purpose of this chapter is to explore the implications for utilizing multicultural counseling in the schools. More specifically, the goals are to: heighten the awareness of students of color and their issues among those working in schools, especially school counselors; increase readers' knowledge and awareness of effective and necessary strategies to enhance the increasingly diverse environment in the schools; strengthen understanding and implementation of multicultural counseling in a school context; and highlight changes necessary in the profession, schools, and communities in order to create multiculturally competent and sensitive school counselors.

According to Johnson (1995), "as the human development specialist within the school system, whose mission is to facilitate the educational, social, psychological, and career development of all students, the school counselor is in an instrumental position to cultivate such an environment" (p. 103). Although school counselors are increasingly working with students of color, unfortunately, "many school counselors are inadequately trained in multicultural counseling" (Hobson & Kanitz, 1996, p. 246). Hobson and Kanitz identified this lack of training as a significant ethical issue because some school counselors are working outside their level of competence and may, in fact, be serving students in a culturally insensitive or inappropriate manner.

CULTURAL AND DEVELOPMENTAL
REALITIES FOR STUDENTS OF COLOR

Before exploring what school counselors can do to enhance their multicultural competence and what strategies can be implemented to increase the responsiveness and effectiveness of schools to address the developmental and cultural realities of students of color, it is important to briefly examine some of the realities for these students. According to Nishimura (1995), "identity development is a key factor in the overall developmental process of children, therefore unresolved identity issues have potential for creating difficulties that negatively affect a child's educational experience" (p. 54). Without specific opportunities to develop positive perceptions or self-images, all students, particularly students of color, will lack the exposure necessary to develop positive self-esteem (Nishimura, 1995). Such exposure can take place in terms of positive role models in and out of school, beneficial experiences and relationships with peers who are culturally different from them, and participation in programs and interventions that celebrate and affirm all aspects of diversity.

It is important that children and adolescents be seen as whole individuals with their race and ethnicity being part of who they are. It is important that children and adolescents of color receive constant and positive messages about their race and ethnicity. According to Phinney (1989), adolescents of color who have a fuller appreciation and understanding of their ethnicity perform better on measures of family relations, sense of mastery, self-evaluation, and social and peer interactions. Immigrant children and adolescents, regardless of their race or ethnicity, have the additional burden of mastering the acculturation and language development process, which can create additional stressors and barriers to their growth and development (Kopala et al., 1994). It is also important to realize that young people understand and cope with their ethnicity differently, depending on their age and developmental level (Phinney & Rothman, 1987).

STRATEGIES FOR CREATING MULTICULTURAL ENVIRONMENTS

With an understanding of this important information about students of color, school counselors are in a position to make a difference in creating positive and affirming school climates that embrace diversity. According to Shertzer and Stone (1981), school counselors serve a range of roles and functions across the following areas: counseling individuals and groups, planning educational programs, consulting with parents and staff, interpreting tests, making appropriate referrals, and acting as a liaison among home, school, and community. Kaplan and Geoffroy (1990) further emphasized the potential for school counselors to become change agents and take an active role in the school environment. By using diverse roles—advocate, expert, trainer, alternative identifier, collaborator, process specialist, factfinder, reflector—school counselors help build positive school environments. Thus, school counselors can serve as leaders and catalysts in their schools and profession.

Some strategies and solutions for change require an individual approach or effort, whereas others demand an institutional perspective or effort. Johnson (1995) surveyed 100 guidance directors in suburban New York and found that few schools implemented any type of ongoing, programmatic, or institutionalized multicultural awareness activities. According to Johnson, school counselors must support the notion that in order to enhance multicultural sensitivity and create profound and longlasting change, efforts must be:

> multifaceted (entailing varied activity and service approaches), inclusionary (engaging students, teachers, pupil personnel, administrators, parents, and community members), developmental (proactive rather than reactive in nature), continuous (featuring ongoing and successive efforts), and district-supported (if not districtwide). (p. 104)

Similar findings have become increasingly evident in the multicultural literature in student affairs and higher education. Pope (1995) and others

(Barr & Strong, 1989; Manning & Coleman-Boatwright, 1991) stress the need for multicultural change efforts to occur at the institutional level in systematic and systemic ways. Pope (1995) identified three primary areas for multicultural efforts—assessment, strategic planning, and curriculum transformation. Focusing on these three areas can create a multifaceted approach similar to the one proposed by Johnson (1995).

Johnson's (1995) research identifies a framework for multicultural initiatives for the schools. This framework consists of four phases: formulate an integrated plan (with goals, objectives, and strategies), conduct a needs assessment, design and implement program interventions, and conduct ongoing assessment. He recommended the creation of a diverse and dynamic Multicultural Advisory Council, which can identify and prioritize issues needing attention in the schools. Once this council has received the support and backing of the school district and leadership, the development of a comprehensive needs assessment strategy is essential. Evaluating the perceptions, expectations, and experiences of all members of the school environment is crucial to meaningful goal setting. Although many of the target areas identified by the needs assessment may not be within school counselors' roles or responsibilities, they can still act as catalysts for change (Johnson, 1995). Possible assessment approaches, tools, or strategies have been proposed by Boyer (1983), Carey, Boscardin, and Fontes (1994), and Pope (1995).

Guidance directors surveyed by Johnson (1995) identified 10 areas of possible intervention that could be included in any multicultural initiative and supported by school counselors. These areas include:

1. Culturally responsive counseling.

2. Human relations training.

3. Orientation and transitional services for newcomer students.

4. Conflict resolution and peer mediation programs.

5. Small group counseling.

6. Bibliotherapy.

7. Classroom guidance.

8. In-service training.

9. Evaluation appraisal and advisement material.

10. Parent education.

Within the higher education literature, there are some developmental models that describe the change process and suggest possible strategies and interventions for creating multicultural change (Katz, 1989; Manning & Coleman-Boatwright, 1991; Pope, 1995).

Finally, once various strategies or interventions have been implemented, it is important to participate in ongoing assessment and evaluation of those efforts. Without such information, it is not possible to know which efforts are successful and which are not. King, Lyons Morris, and Taylor Fitz-Gibbon (1987) offered helpful suggestions for program evaluation.

Developing effective multicultural counseling skills is an important strategy for creating multiculturally sensitive environments that are within the immediate roles and responsibilities of school counselors (Johnson, 1995). According to Coleman (1995), "school counselors need to be constantly assessing the manner in which cultural realities are being created within their schools and their offices" (p. 185). Before describing specific multicultural counseling competencies, it is important to define multicultural counseling, because one's definition of multicultural counseling affects how one perceives the necessary competencies and the field of multicultural counseling as a whole.

DEFINITIONS OF MULTICULTURAL COUNSELING

There are many ways to define and conceptualize *multicultural counseling* and the competencies counselors need to work effectively and ethically across cultural groups. Some persons in the counseling profession may believe that universality is more relevant and significant than multiculturalism (Patterson, 1985), whereas others may feel that cultural differences are overemphasized. The discussion becomes even more complex as various multicultural counseling experts debate "what client characteristics should be the focus of efforts to enhance counselors' multicultural competence" (Helms & Richardson, 1996, p. 61).

There are some who define *multiculturalism* exclusively around racial issues and fear that broader definitions weaken the efforts to eradicate racism (Carter, 1995; Carter & Qureshi, 1995; Helms, 1994; Helms & Richardson, 1996; Locke, 1990). Other scholars adopt a broader definition that expands the definition to include gender, socioeconomic status, sexual orientation, and national origin (Fukuyama, 1990; Pedersen, 1988; Speight, Myers, Cox, & Highlen, 1991). The difficulty in having one word—*multiculturalism*—that means different things to different people increases the definitional problem. Carter and Qureshi (1995) maintained that there is some confusion in mental health training programs regarding the meaning of culture. According to Helms and Richardson (1996), "the controversy stems in part from the lack of precise psychological conceptualizations of multiculturalism and related terms as well as the absence of relevant theoretical models for interpreting the role of such factors in the counseling process" (p. 61). Although this definition problem may be key to the debate about what constitutes multicultural counseling, Carter and Qureshi (1995) identified a more central component. That is, for many researchers and practitioners, "definitions are driven by a number of unstated philosophical assumptions about the meaning of difference" (p.

240). Carter and Qureshi (1995) created a typology or classification system of philosophical assumptions for five distinct multicultural training approaches: Universal, Ubiquitous, Traditional, Race-based, and Pannational. Their belief is that these assumptions affect the content, strategies, and interventions used to prepare individuals to be multiculturally competent.

According to Reynolds (1995), there are two different ways of viewing or defining *multicultural counseling*: the culturally distinct perspective and the universal point of view. *Counseling*, from the culturally distinct perspective, requires specific knowledge of a given cultural group and may involve indigenous practices and treatments. The universal view of *multicultural counseling* emphasizes the similarity among people and maintains that within-group differences are greater than between-group differences. Counseling from the universal worldview requires an awareness of core human dimensions and experiences and typically involves universal treatments and practices. A universal point of view is more likely to include a broader discussion of difference (e.g., race, sexual orientation, gender, and ability).

These two perspectives create a false dichotomy, and the reality of diverse perspectives and definitions is probably closer to the complexity of Carter and Qureshi's (1995) typology. Regardless of how one ultimately defines multicultural counseling, two important items are worthy of mention. First, as Carter and Qureshi (1995) recommended, it is vital that counselors be clear about their underlying assumptions and beliefs about difference. Second, one's definition and understanding of multiculturalism should be complex, dynamic, and multifaceted, allowing for the reality of individual and cultural similarities and differences, as well as universal dimensions, to coexist.

MULTICULTURAL COUNSELING COMPETENCIES IN SCHOOLS

How one defines multicultural counseling often determines the type of multicultural competencies one believes are needed to effectively counsel students in the schools. According to Helms and Richardson (1996), "most contemporary conceptualizations of multicultural competence come from a seminal paper originally proffered by Sue et al., (1982) and later updated by Sue, Arredondo, and McDavis (1992)" (p. 69). They offered a view of multicultural competence that incorporated three primary areas: multicultural awareness, knowledge, and skills. Many multicultural experts maintain that multicultural competence is a necessary prerequisite to effective, affirming, and ethical work in counseling. *Multicultural counseling competence* may be defined as the awareness, knowledge, and skills necessary to counsel effectively and ethically across cultural differences. Awareness of these diverse components can allow counseling professionals to assess the development of their own multicultural competencies and/or the awareness, knowledge, and skills of someone they are supervising (Pope & Reynolds, in press).

Although describing multicultural competence in terms of the tripartite model—awareness, knowledge, and skills—has been vitally important to the multicultural counseling field, such conceptualization lacks the specificity and heuristic value that more detailed conceptualization models offer. Reynolds (1995) identified six core competencies necessary to effectively counsel across differences. Although it is possible to view these differences broadly (e.g., gender, class, and sexual orientation), this chapter primarily focuses on race and ethnicity, which profoundly affect the counseling process. The six competencies are:

1. Acquiring appreciation, knowledge, and understanding of cultural groups, especially those individuals and communities that have been historically underserved and/or underrepresented by the counseling profession.

2. Increasing content knowledge about important culturally related terms and concepts such as racial identity, acculturation, worldview.

3. Enhancing awareness of one's own biases and cultural assumptions, and assessing one's own multicultural skills and comfort level.

4. Developing the ability to use that knowledge and self-awareness to make more culturally sensitive and appropriate interventions.

5. Developing an awareness of the interpersonal dynamics that occur within a multicultural dyad.

6. Deconstructing the cultural assumptions underlying the counseling process.

Acquiring Knowledge and Understanding of Cultural Groups

Gaining knowledge about the history, traditions, current needs, strengths, resources, and concerns of the various underserved racial and ethnic groups in the schools is vital to effectively meeting their needs. This knowledge should include an appreciation for and understanding of the experiences and culture of those groups, especially their experiences in the schools. Without this important information, school counselors may make assumptions and lack empathy for the culture, experiences, and feelings of those individuals.

For example, a first generation, college-bound, Latina high-school student, concerned about her college applications, makes an appointment with her school counselor. Although she is aware that her SAT scores are low and that her senior grades are substantially below what she and her counselor had expected, other important issues affecting her include feeling uneasy about leaving her parents, siblings, and friends; worrying about the money needed for college; and questioning her ability to succeed academically in college and survive alone away from home. A counselor who focuses only on test scores and grades may not acknowledge or appreciate the fears and conflict that might be generated by this student's educational goals and her home values, even though her family and friends may express support to continue her education. To be effective the counselor would need some understanding of the cultural dynamics that could be affecting this client. Without an understanding of the complexity of this student's feelings and concerns, the school counselor might not conceptualize the student's issues in a culturally affirming manner or even know what questions to ask to fully understand her situation. Counselors who have inaccurate, incomplete, or biased knowledge about their clients' cultures must correct or complete that information base before their multicultural development can proceed.

Increasing Knowledge About Cultural Concepts

Obtaining knowledge about important cultural concepts is vital for school counselors to fully appreciate students who are culturally different. Learning about constructs, such as acculturation and racial identity, are important first steps to working with students who may be struggling to fit into multiple cultures. Failure to consider within-group psychological differences, such as racial identity or acculturation, increases the likelihood that counselors will assume that all students of color have identical attitudes, beliefs, and perceptions about themselves and the world around them (Carter, 1995). Such assumptions interfere with counselors' abilities to meet individual and cultural needs of their clients and to be sensitive to their concerns.

Understanding racial and ethnic identity theories as part of human development allows counselors to address and understand the cultural context of students of color. Counselors must also be able to apply their understanding of these concepts to themselves. Counselors who have an awareness of their own racial and ethnic identity and how these dimensions of self affect their perception of themselves and others are able to work more effectively with students who are culturally different from them.

Self-Awareness Assessment of Multicultural Skills

Multicultural awareness consists of the attitudes, beliefs, values, assumptions, and self-awareness necessary to counsel students who are culturally different from oneself (Pedersen, 1988). School counselors may have an inaccurate or inappropriate awareness of culture (e.g., stereotypes and biases) and those false attitudes and assumptions must be changed before counselors can effectively meet the needs of culturally different clients (Pedersen, 1988; Pope-Davis & Dings, 1995; Sue et al., 1982). Counselors need to make a commitment to looking within and addressing the assumptions and stereotypes they may carry about other racial and ethnic groups. All individuals, regardless of their race and ethnicity, have been exposed to misinformation and cultural biases about various groups.

One of the most important steps to preventing cultural miscommunication is continual self-assessment. Rather than assume they can work effectively with all students, counselors should gather information about their level of effectiveness with various racial and ethnic groups. This ongoing assessment might include observing which students do not approach them or disclose personal information. According to Reynolds (1995), "while no one likes to believe s/he has biases or lacks skills to work with others, unless the questions are asked, the skills never will be developed or enhanced" (p. 164). Gathering this type of knowledge requires that counselors frequently monitor their behaviors and outcomes of their sessions, as well as ask others, including students who are different from them, for feedback about their multicultural communication and counseling skills. Such honest self-appraisal allows counselors to seek out additional training and supervision as necessary.

Imagine a Chinese American school counselor's inability to understand why she feels uncomfortable with increasing numbers of Chinese American immigrant children. Her lack of attention to her own racial or ethnic identity contributes to this problem. Likewise, imagine a White counselor who perceives himself to be culturally sensitive and responsive to students of color, who on reflecting on his personal life, realizes that he has never had significant relationships with people of color. He might need to explore what has blocked him from translating his beliefs into action in his life. Unless counselors understand these types of biases and examine these skill limitations, they will have a negative effect on their relationships with students as well as be limited in their ability to meet the needs of culturally different students.

Culturally Responsive Interventions

Once counselors have content wisdom and personal insight into the various cultural groups with whom they work, they must next learn how to apply that knowledge and self-awareness in culturally affirming ways. Such skills could include knowing what questions to ask, being aware of when one's biases are interfering and discerning when one does not have the multicultural knowledge or ability to work effectively with a particular student or group of students. An important multicultural skill is the willingness and ability to seek consultation to work with various students, including the use of cultural brokers or individuals who can help mediate a cultural or family system. Utilizing a previous example, instead of merely challenging the Latina student to bring up her grades and perform to expectations, a culturally sensitive counselor would ask the student to talk about her family, her culture, and what they mean to her. That does not mean the counselor should assume that her culture or her family is interfering with her plans and dreams to graduate from college; instead, the counselor must understand that her knowledge and application of Eurocentric developmental and counseling theories may be causing her to make inappropriate assumptions or conclusions about her client's behavior.

Dynamics of a Multicultural Relationship

It is important for counselors to remember that all multicultural relationships, in which there are both similarities and differences, are rich with potential and are an opportunity for both the school counselor and the students to better understand themselves and others. Counselors need to develop an appreciation for the interpersonal process and dynamics that occur when working with students who are culturally different from them. According to Reynolds (1995), "cultural differences can have a profound effect on the communication and relationship development process" (p. 165). Without an awareness of how culture can affect communication, counselors are likely to make assumptions that inhibit the development of these relationships.

If school counselors do not know how students from other cultures and countries communicate differently (e.g., physical space and eye contact), they may misinterpret the students' actions or act in inappropriate ways that make it difficult to build meaningful relationships. For example, a very affectionate elementary school counselor who often hugs all students may not realize that such physical contact may not always be a culturally appropriate behavior. Her relationships with some students could become strained if such physical contact is unwelcome.

Cultural Assumptions Underlying the Helping Process

The final area of multicultural competence necessary for effective counseling is an awareness of the cultural assumptions underlying the counseling process. According to Katz (1985), the values of counseling, as historically and traditionally defined, are based on White middle-class values. Deconstructing those underlying and often hidden values is vital before one can make counseling more accessible and relevant to some people of color and other individuals who may not subscribe to White middle-class values.

For example, it is often assumed that counseling can only occur in a private office and that effective counselors must be somewhat detached from their clients. However, this model may be unfamiliar to many people of color who gain support and assistance from family and friends. For some, talking with a stranger about personal or family difficulties often feels inappropriate, disloyal, and uncomfortable. It might be far more effective for school counselors to spend some informal time with students playing chess, shooting hoops, or just hanging out. School counselors need to uncover these underlying values and assess their impact on clients as well as assess whether they are causing some students to avoid coming for counseling and support altogether. Discovering these value differences can lead to a deeper appreciation of the more subtle and invisible barriers and challenges to working with students who are culturally different.

Although there has been increasing attention focused on multicultural counseling competence, according to Pope-Davis and Dings (1995), "what is lacking in this discussion is the important role that counselor training must play if multicultural competencies are to become a permanent part of the profession" (p. 288). There are many changes individuals, organizations, and the professions must make if the counseling profession is to move beyond maintaining and reinforcing the status quo. Allowing insensitivity, discrimination, and lack of preparation to interfere with working with individuals who are culturally different from the counselor maintains the status quo. School counselors, with the increasingly diverse student body, need to pay special attention to these issues and possible solutions.

IMPLICATIONS FOR SCHOOL PRACTICES

Counseling across cultures is a core competency that all school counselors need to develop in order to work effectively with students who are culturally different. Because it is becoming increasingly clear that "many school counselors cannot expect to practice without coming into contact with diverse clients" (Hobson & Kanitz, 1996, p. 246), it is essential that school counselors pursue the training necessary to become multiculturally competent. As an integral member of the school community, school counselors, who attempt to enhance their multicultural competencies and implement initiatives as described earlier, send an important message to students, faculty, and other staff and administrators.

It is important to acknowledge that as school counselors attempt to make these changes, both individually and within an existing system, there may be resistance (Napierkowski & Parsons, 1995). This resistance may come from several fronts. The first area of reluctance involves the increasingly administrative role that many school counselors are playing. Because of staffing needs and limited resources, schools often do not contribute the necessary human and monetary resources to allow counselors to fully implement a counseling agenda (Moles, 1991). However, according to Napierkowski and Parsons, one of the most significant barriers to change is the overall inertia within a school system; "schools, like most organizations, resist change and operate out of a culture of maintenance" (p. 365). Finally, many organizations and institutions are known to specifically resist multicultural initiatives because they challenge the core values and assumptions of the system (Manning & Coleman-Boatwright, 1991).

Napierkowski and Parsons (1995) offered some principles and suggestions on how to break the cycle of resistance and create change. Borrowing heavily from the literature on diffusion of power and innovation (cf., Meyers, Parsons, & Martin, 1979; Piersel & Gutkin, 1983; Rogers & Shoemaker, 1971; Sarason, 1971), they offered advice to counselors on how to "break out of their limiting roles and employ the skills and knowledge that they have been trained to use" (p. 365). In terms of multicultural counseling, this might entail skills and knowledge that many school counselors use or need to develop.

Napierkowski and Parson (1995) identified five principles:

1. Keep innovation culturally compatible.

2. Focus on the person, not the theory or concept.

3. Align innovation with opinion leaders.

4. Demonstrate value to the system.

5. Move in a crisis.

In this context, the term *culture* refers to the body of knowledge that identifies the underlying culture within organizations and institutions. This culture is made up of the assumed and underlying values, beliefs, norms, and the structures that support them. The belief is that, to create change, the transformation must appear compatible with the underlying values and structures of the system. Therefore, it is essential that school counselors understand the school culture and determine how multicultural values fit within and support that system. For example, it is important to remember that a goal of education is to prepare students to live, learn, and work effectively as responsible and caring citizens (Nishimura, 1995). Because the workforce and our communities are becoming increasingly diverse, it is important that educational institutions take a leadership role in preparing the next generation to participate effectively within that diversity.

The second principle—focus on the person, not theory or concept—means making the ideas accessible and meaningful on a personal and applied level, rather than promoting an abstract idea or value or concept to which all people should subscribe. In other words, how will a more multiculturally sensitive environment enhance everyone's life? Will there be less racial tension or violence? School counselors need to listen to the issues and concerns of students, faculty, and staff to find the points of agreement and to become sensitive to multicultural issues and concerns. Keeping one's rationales and ideas concrete and simple is often appealing to the individuals who may ultimately implement them.

Align innovation with opinion leaders is the third principle. Most of the writings in organization development and the multicultural literature in higher education point out the need to create change from the top down (Katz, 1989; Manning & Coleman-Boatwright, 1991). School counselors must invest in building relationships with the opinion leaders in their schools who may or may not be the formal leaders (Napierkowski & Parsons, 1995). Building connections and alliances with these leaders may help change efforts to succeed.

The fourth principle emphasizes the need for school counselors to "demonstrate their value to the system by using power bases available to them" (Napierkowski & Parsons, 1995, p. 367). Offering strategies or ideas of value to the system and demonstrating one's competence and expertise are just two ways that school counselors can enhance their power base and increase opportunities for successful multicultural interventions. In schools where there has been a suicide or another type of violence, many school counselors have been able to assist the school personnel as well as students, their families, and community members to cope more effectively with the crisis, thus demonstrating their value and competence to the school.

The final principle—move in a crisis—emphasizes the need for school counselors to have initiatives and strategies in mind and be ready to implement them even when the system is not ready for them. When a crisis occurs, the system will be open to new ideas and innovations as a way of coping with the problem. Some multicultural programs or initiatives begin as a result of a cultural conflict or some other public event (e.g., racial violence and inappropriate behavior of a teacher or administrator) that accentuates the need for improved multicultural relations. Once the crisis diminishes, there may be ongoing support for any new programs or strategies that were successful during the crisis.

These five principles offered by Napierkowski and Parsons (1995) are only one means of creating change. There are many ways for school counselors to conceptualize how to have an important impact on their environments. In addition to changing their immediate school environment, school counselors can also attempt to influence their profession and the community. Although many professional associations, such as the American Counseling Association (ACA) and the American Psychological Association (APA), have recognized the importance of multicultural standards for the past two decades, their actions have not always demonstrated their commitment to these important issues (D'Andrea & Daniels, 1995). From an ethical perspective, it is the responsibility of professional associations to take a leadership role in enhancing the multicultural competence of counselors currently in the field as well as those in training (Hobson & Kanitz, 1996).

Finally, by helping the school build bridges with the surrounding community, the school counselor can ensure that all relevant parties are involved in the change effort. Creating community boards or action committees that include parents and community leaders, schools can take an important leadership role in the creation of multiculturally sensitive and responsive environments. Creating multicultural change cannot occur in a piecemeal fashion. It must be part of a deliberate, focused, and multifaceted effort that involves as many diverse constituencies as possible. Commitment to students and the betterment of their lives must be an unswerving pledge that brings all of us closer to a truly affirming, democratic community where the voices of all citizens matter.

The efforts of the multicultural counseling movement toward incorporating and affirming multicultural values, assumptions, and tools into the counseling profession offer an important and exciting avenue toward creating better experiences and opportunities for youth in our schools. According to Sue (1995), "it is precisely our ability to influence organizational dynamics that represents the next multicultural counseling frontier" (p. 474). Although the field of multicultural counseling continues to grow and develop and many would agree that it is no longer in its infancy (Rowe, Behrens, & Leach, 1995), there is still much work to be done. Expanding our multicultural theory base, as well as tools available for individual and organizational change, are necessary steps to instituting true and lasting change. At the very root of all of these change efforts must be an expansion of our awareness of the assumptions and worldviews that affect our work with others who are both culturally similar and different from us. Carter (1995) and others acknowledged the importance of understanding race and racial identity as prerequisites to understanding our own and others' worldviews. Jones (1990) argued that one way to prevent misunderstanding and misinterpretion of developmental and other core psychological theories that inform our work as counselors is to incorporate racial identity theory into our understanding of the differences that exist within racial groups. Racial and ethnic identity theory and research are both the historical roots and the future of the multicultural counseling movement. Such theory and research must inform our practice as counselors to ensure effective work with all students.

REFERENCES

Acosta, F., Yamamoto, J., & Evans, L. A. (1982). *Effective psychotherapy for low income and minority patients.* New York: Plenum.

Barr, D. J., & Strong, L. J. (1989). Embracing multiculturalism: The existing contradictions. *NASPA Journal, 26*(2), 85–90.

Boyer, J. (1983). *Multicultural education: From product to process.* Washington, DC: National Institute of Education (ERIC Document Reproduction Service No. ED 240 224).

Carey, J. C., Boscardin, M. L., & Fontes, L. (1994). Improving the multicultural effectiveness of your school. In P. Pedersen & J. C. Carey (Eds.), *Multicultural counseling in schools* (pp. 239–249). Boston: Allyn & Bacon.

Carter, R. T. (1995). *The influence of race and racial identity in psychotherapy: Toward a racially inclusive model.* New York: Wiley.

Carter, R. T., & Qureshi, A. (1995). A typology of philosophical assumptions in multiculturalism counseling and training. In J. G. Ponterotto, J. M. Casas, L. A. Suzuki, & C. M. Alexander (Eds.), *Handbook of multicultural counseling* (pp. 239–262). Thousand Oaks, CA: Sage.

Coleman, H. L. K. (1995). Cultural factors and the counseling process: Implications for school counselors. *The School Counselor, 42,* 180–185.

Cox, T. (1993). *Cultural diversity in organizations: Theory, research, and practice.* San Francisco: Berrett-Koehler.

Cummins, J. (1990). Empowering minority students: A framework for intervention. In N. M. Hidalgo, C. L. McDowell, & E. V. Siddle (Eds.), *Facing racism in education* (pp. 50–68). Cambridge, MA: Harvard Educational Review.

D'Andrea, M., & Daniels, J. (1995). Promoting multiculturalism and organizational change in the counseling profession: A case study. In J. G. Ponterotto, J. M. Casas, L. A. Suzuki, & C. M. Alexander (Eds.), *Handbook of multicultural counseling* (pp. 17–33). Thousand Oaks, CA: Sage.

Esquivel, G. B., & Keitel, M. A. (1990). Counseling immigrant children in the schools. *Elementary School Guidance & Counseling, 24*(3), 213–221.

Ferrara, M. L. (1992). *Group counseling with juvenile delinquents.* Newbury Park, CA: Sage.

Fukuyama, M. A. (1990). Taking an universal approach to multicultural counseling. *Counselor Education and Supervision, 30*(1), 6–17.

Helms, J. E. (1994). How multiculturalism obscures racial factors in the therapy process: Comment on Ridley et al. (1994), Sodowsky et al. (1994), Ottavi et al (1994), & Thompson et al. (1994). *Journal of Counseling Psychology, 41*(2), 162–165.

Helms, J. E., & Richardson, T. Q. (1996). How "Multiculturalism" obscures race and culture as differential aspects of counseling competency. In D. B. Pope-Davis & H. L. K. Coleman (Eds.), *Multicultural counseling competencies: Assessment, education and training, and supervision* (pp. 60–82). Thousand Oaks, CA: Sage.

Hobson, S. M., & Kanitz, H. M. (1996). Multicultural counseling: An ethical issue for school counselors. *The School Counselor, 43*(4), 245–255.

Jamieson, D., & O'Mara, J. (1991). *Managing workforce 2000: Gaining the diversity advantage.* San Francisco: Jossey-Bass.

Johnson, L. S. (1995). Enhancing multicultural relations: Intervention strategies for the school counselor. *The School Counselor, 43*(2), 103–113.

Jones, W. T. (1990). Perspectives on ethnicity. In L. V. Moore (Ed.), *Evolving theoretical perspectives on students* (pp. 59–72). San Francisco: Jossey Bass.

Kaplan, L. S., & Geoffroy, K. E. (1990). Enhancing the school climate: New opportunities for the counselor. *The School Counselor, 38*(1), 7–12.

Katz, J. H. (1985). The sociopolitical nature of counseling. *The Counseling Psychologist, 13,* 615–624.

Katz, J. H. (1989). The challenges of diversity. In C. Woolbright (Ed.), *Valuing diversity on campus: A multicultural approach* (pp. 1–21). Bloomington, IN: Association of College Unions-International.

King, J. A., Lyons Morris, L., & Taylor Fitz-Gibbon, C. (1987). *How to assess program implementation.* Newbury Park, CA: Sage.

Kopala, M., Esquivel, G., & Baptiste, L. (1994). Counseling approaches for immigrant children: Facilitating the acculturative process. *The School Counselor, 41*(5), 352–359.

Locke, D. C. (1990). A not so provincial view of multicultural counseling. *Counselor Education and Supervision, 30*(1), 18–25.

Locke, D. C. (1992). *Increasing multicultural understanding.* Newbury Park, CA: Sage.

Manning, K., & Coleman-Boatwright, P. (1991). Student affairs initiatives toward a multicultural university. *Journal of College Student Development, 32*(4), 367–374.

Meyers, J., Parsons, R. D., & Martin, R. (1979). *Mental health consultation in the schools.* San Francisco: Jossey-Bass.

Moles, O. C. (1991). Guidance programs in American high schools: A descriptive portrait. *The School Counselor, 38*(3), 163–177.

Napierkowski, C. M., & Parsons, R. D. (1995). Diffusion of innovation: Implementing changes in school counselor roles and functions. *The School Counselor, 42*(5), 364–369.

Nishimura, N. J. (1995). Addressing the needs of biracial children: An issue for counselors in a multicultural school environment. *The School Counselor, 43*(1), 52–57.

Patterson, C. H. (1985). The therapeutic relationship: *Foundations for an eclectic psychotherapy.* Monterey, CA: Brooks/Cole.

Pedersen, P. (1988). *A handbook for developing multicultural awareness.* Alexandria, VA: American Association for Counseling and Development.

Phinney, J. S. (1989). Stages of ethnic identity development in minority group adolescents. *Journal of Early Adolescence, 9*(1–2), 34–49.

Phinney, J. S., & Rothman, M. J. (Eds.). (1987). *Children's ethnic socialization: Pluralism and development.* Newbury Park, CA: Sage.

Piersel, W. C., & Gutkin, T. B. (1983). Resistance to school-based consultation: A behavioral analysis of the problem. *Psychology in the Schools, 20*(3), 311–320.

Pope, R. L. (1995). Multicultural organizational development: Implications and applications in student affairs. In J. Fried (Ed.), *Shifting paradigms in student affairs: A cultural perspective* (pp. 233–249). Washington, DC: ACPA Media.

Pope, R. L., & Reynolds, A. L. (1997). Student affairs core competencies: Integrating multicultural awareness, knowledge, and skills. *Journal of College Student Development, 38*(3), 266–277.

Pope-Davis, D. B., & Dings, J. G. (1995). The assessment of multicultural counseling competencies. In J. G. Ponterotto, J. M. Casas, L. A. Suzuki, & C. M. Alexander (Eds.), *Handbook of multicultural counseling* (pp. 287–311). Thousand Oaks, CA: Sage.

Reynolds, A. L. (1995). Multiculturalism in counseling and advising. In J. Fried (Ed.), *Shifting paradigms in student affairs: Culture, context, teaching, and learning* (pp. 155–170). Washington, DC: ACPA Media.

Rogers, E. M., & Shoemaker, F. E. A. (1971). *Communication of innovation*. New York: The Free Press.

Rowe, W., Behrens, J. T., & Leach, M. M. (1995). Racial/ethnic identity and racial consciousness. In J. G. Ponterotto, J. M. Casas, L. A. Suzuki, & C. M. Alexander (Eds.), *Handbook of multicultural counseling* (pp. 218–235). Thousand Oaks, CA: Sage.

Sarason, S. B. (1971). *The culture of the school and the problem*. Boston: Allyn & Bacon.

Shertzer, B., & Stone, S. C. (Eds.). (1981). *Fundamentals of guidance* (4th ed.). Boston: Houghton Mifflin.

Speight, S. L., Myers, L. J., Cox, C. I., & Highlen, P. S. (1991). A redefinition of multicultural counseling. *Journal of Counseling and Development, 70*(1), 29–36.

Sue, D. W. (1995). Multicultural organization development: Implications for the counseling profession. In J. G. Ponterotto, J. M. Casas, L. A. Suzuki, & C. M. Alexander (Eds.), *Handbook of multicultural counseling* (pp. 474–492). Thousand Oaks, CA: Sage.

Sue, D. W., Arredondo, P., & McDavis, R. J. (1992). Multicultural counseling competencies and standards: A call to the profession. *Journal of Counseling and Development, 70*(4), 477–486.

Sue, D. W., Bernier, J. E., Durran, A., Feinberg, L., Pedersen, P., Smith, E. J., & Vasquez-Nuttall, E. (1982). Position paper: Cross-cultural counseling competencies. *Counseling Psychologist, 10*(2), 45–52.

Wittmer, J. (1992). *Valuing diversity and similarity: Bridging the gap through interpersonal skills*. Minneapolis: Educational Media Corporation.

13 Lessons for Leaders: Using Critical Inquiry to Promote Identity Development

Edward Taylor
University of Washington

its late an I dont know what time it is but I kno its late. . .
day breakin
sun comin up
the bird in the tre soun like a blu bird
sky blu blu mr wigin
good by mr. wigin tell them im strong tell them im a man good
by mr wigin ...

(Gaines, 1993, p. 234)

In his award-winning novel, *A Lesson Before Dying,* Ernest J. Gaines (1993) described the relationship between Jefferson, a young Black man who is sentenced to die in the electric chair, and Grant Wiggins, who has returned to his small Cajun community to teach in the plantation school. Grant's aunt and Jefferson's godmother want him to teach Jefferson to become a man before his execution. An incredulous Grant asks, "What do you want me to do? What can I do? It's only a matter of weeks, a couple of months, maybe. What can I do that you haven't done the past twenty-one years?" His aunt only offers, "You the teacher" (p. 13).

In this richly textured account of the relationship between teacher and student, we become privy to the essence of relationships—the raw power of words, the urgency of communication, and the development and awakening of critical awareness and consciousness of both the teacher and the student. Similarly, at the heart of the education and development of school leaders is their willingness and capacity to develop a critical awareness of themselves in relation to their school, staff, students, and the communities they serve.

231

This chapter illustrates the use of critical inquiry as a method to urge consciousness and cultural identity development among school leaders, including principals and administrators. *Cultural identity* is defined as one's understanding of the multilayered, interdependent, and nonsynchronous interaction of social status, language, race, ethnicity, values, and behaviors that permeate and influence nearly all aspects of our lives. A central tenant of this chapter is that the process of leadership development, inevitably, is nurtured by a deep understanding of the dynamic and complex nature of the factors that influence one's cultural identity; a critical aspect of this process includes a willingness to move through the stages of racial identity development.

When Grant Wiggins began to visit the prisoner who had been called "as dumb as a hog," he struggled with the questions all teachers face: What is the language with which we can communicate? What am I supposed to teach? To what end? What do I need to know about myself in order to do this? These questions illuminate the essence of what it means to become a critical and reflective leader.

As I entered my second year teaching a year-long course on race, gender, and class issues to aspiring school leaders, I too struggled with some important questions: How can we talk? What conditions will enable our discourse? What are we to talk about and why? What roadmap can I use to foster students' cultural identity development? Like Grant Wiggins, I am left with a prodigious subject matter and the daunting task of deciding what to teach and how to teach in a limited amount of time. How the students and I are situated in the program is of consequence. As a Black male, will my views be construed as dogmatic? Will I be seen as representative of all Black people? My students are White. What do these aspiring school leaders need to know about their race, ethnicity, and culture in order to be culturally responsive school leaders? Such leadership must be built on a foundation of self-awareness, critical consciousness, and reflective inquiry and practice. Thus, critical inquiry, as a method, is one way to advance identity development among school leaders. Educational leadership preparation programs should provide opportunities for aspiring leaders to reflect on their own schooling, culture, and social circumstances as a precursor to becoming responsive educators in a multicultural world.

The purpose of this chapter is threefold: to situate the training of school leaders in current demographic trends, to review critical approaches and views of leadership, including Freire's (1970) rejection of bureaucratic ways of thinking and Sirotnik's (1991) paradigm for the praxis of critical inquiry, and how critical inquiry, as a method, was utilized in my classroom to promote racial identity development among White aspiring principals and administrators.

RECONCILING DIFFERENCE

When Grant Wiggins was given the task of educating Jefferson, the young man sentenced to death, his first recognition was how little he had in common with his student. As a result, there were extraordinary burdens placed on his teaching task. My challenge as a Black professor teaching European American students appeared equally formidable. Although the races may be reversed, sociocultural dissimilarity between teachers and students is a common phenomenon in educational institutions in the United States. Many of our school leaders are White; increasing numbers of the population under their guardianship are not.

The number of racial and ethnic minority students has increased dramatically during the last few decades, with Latinos being the fastest growing group. Although the following data suggests that racial and/or ethnic categories are an objective and measurable fact, considerable debate exists about the limits of this demographic information. For example, Black and White people are the only ones counted by race. The Hispanic category does not count racial or ethnic groups per se, rather it attempts to homogenize individuals with Spanish cultural roots. This practice suggests a uniform population, despite substantial social and economic differences between and among Mexican, Puerto Rican, Cuban, and Central and South American subgroups representing substantially different experiences in schools. Definitions for *Asians* vary, and may or may not include Pacific Islanders. Although membership in a tribal group for Native Americans is determined by individual tribes, it is defined by *blood quantum*; that is, the degree of Indian ancestry expressed in fractions such as one-half or three-sixteenths (Wilson, 1992). Multiracial persons are not recognized, although there is increasing pressure to do so (Yanow, 1996). With these caveats in mind, consider the following: Currently, 34% of children attending public elementary and secondary schools are children of color—16.6% African American; 12.7% Hispanic, 3.6% Asian or Pacific Islander, 1.1% American Indian (NCES, 1995). Census projections suggest that by 2050, Whites will account for 53% of the population (down from 74% today); Hispanics will make up 24.5%; African Americans will remain fairly stable at 13.6%; and Asians will make up 8.2% (Holmes, 1996).

Dramatic demographic shifts have not occurred in the ranks of teachers. Instead, increasing numbers of educators are White, middle-class, and reside in suburban communities. As of 1994, 86.5% of elementary and secondary school teachers were White; 7.4% African American, 4.2% Hispanic, 1.1% Asian, and .08% American Indian (NCES, 1995). Similar racial imbalances occur in the distribution of school principals—84.3% were White; 10.1% African American, 4.1% Hispanic; and, less than 1% were Asian or American Indian (NCES, 1995).

Education in a multiracial, multiethnic, and multilingual democracy comes with special challenges. Accordingly, as a nation that has viewed itself as committed to *e pluribus unum* since its inception, *pluribus* values of freedom, individualism, and diversity live in constant tension with *unum* values of commonality and community (Cortes, 1991). One of the ways this tension is resolved is by entrusting our schools with the "fashioning and refashioning of a democratic polity" (Gates, 1992, p. 176). Unfortunately, our school leaders do not know how to accomplish this.

Taylor (1994) contended that human identity is shaped, in part, by consciousness and recognition of one's racial and ethnic identity, or the lack thereof. When significant sociocultural differences exist in schools, the risk of misunderstanding and stereotyping is present. Confining or demeaning pictures of students are formed; this can potentially inflict considerable harm and impose a form of oppression by forcing students into a false and superficial mode of being. In the absence of prior knowledge of or experience with discrimination, bias, prejudice, and other forms of oppression, White school leaders may misinterpret or fail to recognize problems. Leaders who have experienced some form of oppression, or recognize their own position of privilege, are more likely to recognize and take action against domination and oppression.

In view of current demographics and future demographic changes, principals and administrators must have the capacity and commitment to reconcile and bridge racial, social, cultural, and linguistic gaps between themselves and their students. Preparation programs must incorporate specific goals and intentions for students; these are as follows:

- Understanding of theories and frameworks relevant to serving underrepresented populations.

- Enhanced understanding of the power, potential, and limits of schools and school leadership toward substantially improving the living, learning, and development of all students.

- Advancement of leadership that understands the cultural landscape of the schools and students they serve.

- Examination of the personal strengths, limits, and potential in becoming culturally responsive leaders.

- Incorporation of critical reflection, dialogue, and inquiry as a means to enhance self-awareness and identity development.

CRITICAL VIEWS OF EDUCATION, LEADERSHIP, AND INQUIRY

Critical inquiry is a theoretical framework and method that critiques and examines social structures, like schooling and educational leadership, by addressing internal and external value tensions and issues of social justice, freedom, equity, and liberation (Foster, 1986; Sirotnik, 1989). Such inquiry questions the fundamental way things are and sets how things ought to be. Leadership preparation, informed by critical inquiry, demands a confrontation with human interest in political, social, and economic contexts. The role of criticism in education and leadership has a distinguished history, including the works of Dewey (1916), Hegel (1900), Marx (1932), and Freire (1970).

Freire (1970) urged the abandonment of rigidly formalistic, bureaucratic ways of thinking and relating to achieve true human liberation or "conscientization" (p. 225). This arousing of critical awareness is indispensable to the inquiry process, leader identity development, and ultimately social action. Freire wrote "For apart from inquiry, apart from praxis, men cannot be truly human. Knowledge emerges only through invention and re-invention, through the restless, impatient, continuing, hopeful inquiry men pursue in the world, with the world, and with each other" (p. 58). Conscientization requires more than awareness of oppression; it must be "a permanent critical approach to reality in order to discover it and discover the myths that deceive us and help to maintain oppressing dehumanizing structures" (Freire, 1976, p. 225).

Leadership preparation, informed by critical inquiry, is egalitarian, nonauthoritarian, and activist. The activist component is conceptualized as *praxis*—the recognition that in order for theory to be relevant in improving the human condition, it must eventually be located in human activity (Foster, 1986). This occurs when all members of the community culture are legitimized and able to engage in acts of leadership that incorporate participative, democratic, and collaborative principles. Leadership, in this sense, is located in actions and interactions, not in positions or titles.

For Greene (1973), *praxis* involves the ability of school leaders to engage in a mode of knowing that involves posing and solving problems in their social context. Grob (1984) suggested that leadership must always be a critical practice and explicitly stated that leadership training must be grounded in the awareness of one's life:

> In pointing to the critical spirit as the ground of all leadership, my intent has been to argue that without that willingness to examine one's life, alleged leaders in any and all areas of human endeavor must, of necessity, become identified with their purposes, purposes which inevitably congeal into fixed doctrines or dogma. In short, potential leaders *without this ground* find themselves in the service of fixed ideas or causes, and thus agents of the use of power in their behalf. *No longer nourished by a wellspring of critical processes at its center, leadership dries up and becomes, finally, the mere wielding of power on behalf of static ideals.* (p. 270)

Foster (1986) further developed the intent of self-examination for leaders. He stated that praxis-oriented leadership preparation creates an environment in which people can explore the historical circumstances of their conditions, such as the influences of birthright (e.g., race, gender, and class) and the ways in which cultural heritage influences opportunities.

Leadership preparation, then, involves a willingness to engage in difficult and challenging dialogue. To examine one's self often requires the posing of disturbing questions. It requires, as Greene (1973) stated, the ability "to look through new perspectives upon the familiar life-world. It should involve, wherever possible, an examination of cultural assumptions" (p.

185). For educators, particularly those in the majority racial group, it means examining one's positionality (see Tetreault, 1993; see also Code, 1991, for further explication of positionality) or the ways in which race, ethnicity, gender, language, nationality, social class, religion, sexual orientation, and ability work together to fashion the lens through which people view the world. It is not enough for well-intentioned leaders to empathize or commiserate with students different from themselves. Nor is it enough to take a scenic tour through the history of oppression endured by racial minority groups. The far more difficult task is to create conditions that facilitate and promote an honest, serious look inward.

Effective leadership will not automatically ensure when school leaders examine their positions or engage in self-examination. Rather, a heightened consciousness of their positions, beliefs, and roles can lead to changes in those worlds.

As a method, *critical inquiry* is analytical, dialogical, communicative, and purposeful (Sirotnik, 1991). The focal points of this method center on institutions and individuals. The process is rigorous and ongoing. To be *critical,* inquiry must challenge individually held beliefs, values, assumptions, and behaviors. Critical and reflective inquiry is a powerful method that enables prospective school leaders to explore their cultural identity by examining their racial identity development. This inquiry is an essential step toward understanding and meeting the needs of their diverse students.

CRITICAL INQUIRY: FROM THEORY TO PRACTICE

The practice of critical and reflective inquiry in the leadership preparation classroom relies on certain conditions for both personal reflection and effective communication. Fewer things, however, are more challenging than the honest and productive exchange of ideas, particularly on value-laden issues such as race, culture, and gender.

For Sirotnik (1991) and Habermas (1970), competent communication occurs under certain conditions: (a) *comprehensibility*—the clarification of misinterpretation and misunderstanding; (b) *sincerity*—good faith efforts to create an atmosphere of honesty and trust; (c) *fidelity*—the critical evaluation of information and the pursuit of truthfulness; (d) *justifiability*—dialogue mutually regarded as appropriate for all parties; and (e) *fairness*—an equal opportunity to express opinions and to refute others. Ultimately, competent communication can occur only in a classroom environment of mutual trust and honesty.

Once these conditions have been approximated in the classroom, critical inquiry can begin. Sirotnik (1991) described a process of critical and reflective inquiry as follows: First, problems have to be considered in their current context. Participants in a critical inquiry must agree that certain conflicts or problems exist at a broad level—delinquency, low standards, assessment, etc. They must agree that dilemmas also exist at an interpersonal level—bias, stereotyping, and barriers to understanding, "How are things being done now?" or more personally, "What do I believe now?" Second, problems have a history and they need to be understood in this context. "How did things come to be this way?" or "How did my beliefs and values come to be this way?" Third, inquiry must assess the impact of how deeply held beliefs and actions affect targeted populations. The operant question here is, "Whose interests are served or not served by the way things are now?" "Do my core values reflect a commitment to social justice and equity?" Fourth, knowledge about the issues is imperative. Information from all sources—personal experience, reflection, research studies, journal articles, etc.—informs the process. Finally, critical inquiry must impact practice, "How can what I've learned or come to realize impact my classroom or school?" The goal here is to translate insights into action.

In my attempt to undertake critical reflective inquiry as a method of discourse, reflection, and action to advance self-reflection and identity development, I asked my students—all experienced teachers aspiring to become principals—to write about the origins of their sense of racial identity. The intent of the assignment was to encourage students to explore their own identity as a means of better understanding the racial, cultural, and gender status of their students. In effect, they were to interrogate their own cultural heritage by examining the role of race in the consequential events and people in their lives—the circumstances and relationships—that helped to shape their ideas, behaviors, beliefs, and values.

As a starting point, we discussed ways of understanding culture. Although there is no single definition that social scientists agree on, most believe that *culture* includes symbolic, ideational, and intangible aspects of human societies. In the context of schooling, *cultures* are often viewed as being monolithic, static and predictable; for example, African American culture and American Indian culture often lend themselves to misleading explanations of groups and perpetuating stereotypes of poverty, disinterest, or lowered academic expectations (Banks, 1988).

It is easy to overlook, negate, or underemphasize the variations within a national culture or the variations between a larger culture. Banks (1988) defined the national, or shared culture, the *macroculture,* and the smaller cultures within the larger community, *microcultures.* Thus, whereas every nation's macroculture has overarching symbols, mores, and values, microcultures may interpret, perceive, or experience these overarching symbols differently.

What, then, are the components of a school culture? How do groups of students, particularly racial minorities, fit into the macroculture? How do school leaders fit within and promote a school culture that avoids marginilization and stereotyping? What impediments exist that may prohibit the healthy functioning of persons and organizations?

In response to these questions rasied in our discussion, Eric (pseudonym), a White male student, stated that he understood our charge as it related to racial minority students, teachers, and staff. However, he did not see how his own race or culture fit: "I'm not saying there is anything wrong with my culture not being present within such frameworks. I just don't clearly see where I fit in this picture."

This question is rooted in common, widely held assumptions by the majority population. The first is that Whites in the United States do not share a culture with a common history, social standing, and similar experiences. The second assumption is that leadership and education that are responsive to racial minority youth are developed by people of color and intended only for students of color. Eric's question provided an opening to start the process of self-examination. What is your culture? What experiences set you apart from other groups? In what ways has your family influenced your sense of identity? What experiences have you had with other racial and cultural groups?

Initial responses admitted that this assignment was much harder than had been anticipated:

> This is my third attempt at this essay. My first effort bogged down in general reflections on racial and ethnic diversity. That's no surprise considering my majority background. ... My second effort was personal, strongly worded and outside the traditional realm of ethnicity and race. Unfortunately, as I was unleashing some raw personal issues, my computer shut down—erasing my document. (Joel, White male)

> For months, this assignment has simmered in my thoughts ... questions keep surfacing. What is really the essence of what makes me feel/think the way I do today? How much do I want to share? How can I best express the core of my personal cultural experience? (Susan, White female)

Another interesting result was the way in which students defined culture, particularly the ways in which they felt different or set apart from other Whites. Although their responses did not directly address identity development, I found their thoughtfulness to be disarming and an important step in interrogating positionality. These particular events and their aftermath created a permanent sense of loss and marginalization. For one young man, it was divorce:

> My experiences as a child of divorced parents has bonded me with other people, who in other ways are entirely different from me, but this powerful shared experience draws us together, separates us from the general public, and provides us with a sense of camaraderie and understanding that is uniquely cultural. ... Without question, nothing has had a greater impact on my life. (Michael, White male)

For another, facing adulthood without the possibility of reproducing:

> As a young man in the middle of a "practical" marriage, I came to an easy decision not to have children and had a vasectomy. ... I was confronted with

the idea of children when I remarried six years ago ... [but] I am in the position of being unable to father children. I'm the end of my line, though I usually don't think of having children in those kinds of terms. It's largely a feeling of wondering what it would have been like to have a child, coupled with a twinge of sadness. (Bill, White male)

From this starting point of self-reflection, I introduced the impact of race, family, and class on personal identity. As students grappled with describing those defining incidents or situations that shaped their sense of self, the framework of racial identity development theory was helpful for understanding the evolution and impact of their experiences.

RACIAL IDENTITY DEVELOPMENT

As defined by Helms (1990), *racial identity development* for Whites consists of two major developmental tasks—the abandonment of individual racism and opposition to institutional and cultural racism—and six stages (see Richardson & Silvestri, chap. 3, this volume). Importantly, these stages are rarely stepwise but more like a spiral staircase (Tatum, 1992, 1994). As a person climbs up a spiral staircase, he may stop and look down and see where he was, but the vantagepoint has changed. As people move between stages, their perspective on previously held views is inevitably altered.

Contact

This first stage is one of minimal awareness of racial group membership in which people usually see themselves as *normal* and generally describe themselves as free from stereotyping or racial prejudice. Challenges to this stage may result in denial or demonstration of a superficial grasp of the issues as illustrated:

I know that society defines me and that I often define myself as a heterosexual, White male. I practically define the cultural norm. (Phil, White male)

Another feels he already understands the difficulties racial minorities face because he has already experienced painless prejudice:

In the field of education, Republicans are in the minority. According to our poll, I was the only one. ... I have noticed a definite tendency by professors and students to favor a Democratic perspective. Actually, I do not see it as a negative thing, because it has allowed me to painlessly experience prejudice in an "institutionalized" setting. (Ralph, White male)

Another student described some of the advantages he enjoyed and recognized growing up as a male. He wrote, "I enjoyed being lucky, I was

White ... and just as important, I was a boy, which I also know was better than being a girl in 1968."

This student went on to describe the transformation he underwent when he no longer felt lucky:

[When I was a little boy], I flunked a hearing test, and have been flunking them ever since, and will continue flunking them in the future. At first, I didn't know hearing had anything to do with culture. ... Although I realize I am different, I recognized I have not been exposed to the kind of oppression and discrimination that others have endured. (Allan, White male)

Disintegration

Characterized by increasing awareness of the ways in which their lives have been affected by their race, and the ways in which others have been negatively impacted, this stage often causes discomfort. If students have believed that our culture is meritocratic, realization of the social impact of race and ethnicity can be insightful. As my students continue:

I am able to go about my day, comfortably with little awareness of my color, physical attributes, or sex. When I am downtown, or in a mall, I am not stared at or followed, no one cowers in the elevator when I enter it, and I have never heard anyone mutter anything under their breath because of my attire or skin color. (Ron, White male)

My vision has not always been on the "individual." I catch myself faltering. The beat of my heart if a Black man approaches me on the street, not confronting a peer at a social gathering for a racial joke, quickening my pace when passing odd looking teens or passing without responding to someone who is begging on the street. Not recognizing another's humanity does not make me proud. (Andy, White female)

Reintegration

A common response to the guilt and cognitive dissonance resulting from the disintegration stage is to explain racism as a result of the inferior qualities and attributes of minorities. Previously held views are often justified by anecdotal evidence. By blaming the victim, guilt and responsibility are therefore avoided. Given the social pressures to either ignore or accept racism, this stage is particularly challenging and critical. One respondent defended her dissapproval of interracial relationship by reciting the following story:

Unfortunately, everything my mom was worried about that could happen if I dated a Black man, happened. It didn't happen to me, but it did happen to my parents' best friend's daughter, who dated Jim. They got pregnant. She did not graduate with her class. He deserted her. He ended up at the penitentiary for forgery and burglary. She lived in poverty when she did not live with her parents and was responsible for raising the child alone. (Stacy, White female)

Pseudo-Independence

Attempting to distance themselves from earlier stages that are now seen as problematic, the individual may move away from earlier relationships and seek to establish new ones with racial minorities or with others who are antiracist. Success at building these bridges depend, in part, on the stage of racial identity of the new-found friends. At this point, formation of a positive sense of one's Whiteness is fragile. Efforts to forge new friendships, however, are sincere, as the following illustrates:

[I now take time to] sit down with Pauline, the African American principal, and share our commonality as women in our fifties with grown children and a passion for educating all children; time to sit down at lunch with children whose cultures, languages, and experiences are very different from mine and begin talking and laughing with them. (Carol, White female)

Immersion/Emersion

Efforts to create a positive definition of Whiteness are focused and productive. Identification with antiracist Whites, such as Morris Dees and Bill Bradley, may occur. People begin to feel a sense of excitement as they begin to conceive of themselves as able to work to end oppression and racism. Realization that they can unlearn their own racism and begin to affect change is often empowering.

I definitely realize how privileged I am to have been born a White male in this society. My only "minority status," being Jewish, is something that I can usually hide or not share if I so choose. ... with my privileged background I can continue on the life path I have begun while still supporting ideas such as affirmative action and other social programs which attempt to "level the playing field." I went into education without a clear reason for doing so ... now I realize that with my choice I am able to reach children at a young age. (Robert, White male)

Autonomy

This final stage consists of the internalization of one's Whiteness. At this point of comfort and acceptance of a positive sense of one's race, other forms of oppression can now be recognized and worked against. Interest in other races, cultures, and issues broadens.

This level of racial identity was not exhibited by my students over the timeframe of one class. Responses tended to be clustered in the earlier stages, suggesting that, at least for these students, a sense of racial identity was just beginning.

IMPLICATIONS FOR SCHOOL PRACTICES

The students in this class made numerous advancements. First, the conditions for dialogue across difference and critical inquiry were established. Most importantly, these conditions were determined by the students themselves. This meant recognizing different styles of respectfully interacting with one another. This also meant providing a forum in which participants could be heard and differences could be recognized and discussed. A second accomplishment was exploring and understanding the various racial communities that the students will serve. A third major accomplishment was the students' interrogation of their own racial and cultural heritage. They explored their own experiences of privilege, oppression, loneliness, hegemony, power, and powerlessness, as well as the perpetration of discrimination and the experience of being discriminated against. They also acknowledged and addressed the ways in which their culture influenced their beliefs and actions toward others.

It is imperative that school leaders understand cultural and racial identity development as it relates to self, their school, and community because these leaders are clearly in positions of power and bring their knowledge and experience to bear on their interactions with their community. Nurturing aspiring leaders' capacity and willingness to explore the ways in which they are alike and different from their community is a first step toward culturally responsible and responsive leadership.

What should a school leader know about issues of race, class, and gender? I have concluded that there is no easy answer; indeed, the scope of the problems are complex and nonsynchronous. In our classroom, however, critical inquiry proved a valuable roadmap as we made our way through the process of racial identity development. To the degree that this helps prospective school leaders understand leadership as an inquiry driven process that will better serve changing educational communities, these methods will enhance the development and preparation of future school leaders for a multiracial, multiethnic, and multicultural world.

REFERENCES

Banks, J. A. (1988). *Multiethnic education: Theory and practice* (2nd ed.). Boston: Allyn & Bacon.

Code, L. (1991). *What can she know? Feminist theory and the construction of knowledge.* Ithaca, NY: Cornell University Press.

Cortes, C. E. (1991). Through media literacy: An approach. In C. E. Sleeter (Ed.), *Through education* (pp. 143–157). Albany: State University of New York Press.

Dewey, J. (1916). *Democracy and education.* New York: Macmillan.

Foster, W. P. (1986). *Paradigms and promises: New approaches to educational administration.* New York: Prometheus Books.

Freire, P. (1970). *Pedagogy of the oppressed.* New York: Seabird Press.

Freire, P. (1976). A few notions about the word "conscientization." In R. Dale, G. Esland, & M. MacDonald (Eds.), *Schooling and capitalism: A sociological reader* (pp. 224–227). London: The Open University Press.

Gaines, E. J. (1993). *A lesson before dying.* New York: Vintage Books.

Gates, H. L. (1992). *Loose canons.* New York: Oxford University Press.

Greene, M. (1973). The matter of justice. *Teachers College Record, 75*(2), 54–67.

Grob, L. (1984). Leadership: The Socratic model, In B. Kellerman (Ed.), *Leadership: Multidisciplinary perspectives* (pp. 263–280). Englewood Cliffs, NJ: Prentice-Hall.

Habermas, J. (1970). Towards a theory of communicative competence. *Inquiry, 13,* 360–375.

Hegel, G. W. F. (1900). *Philosophy of history.* New York: Cooperative Publication Society.

Helms, J. E. (Ed.). (1990). *Black and White racial identity: Theory, research, and practice.* New York: Greenwood.

Holmes, S. A. (1996, March 14). Census sees a profound ethnic shift in U.S. *The New York Times,* p. A8.

Marx, K. (1932). *Capital.* Chicago: Charles H. Kerr.

National Center for Education Statistics (1995). *Digest of education statistics, 1995* (NCES 95–029). Washington, DC: U.S. Government Printing Office.

Richardson, T. Q, & Silvestri, T. (1999). White identity formation: A developmental process. In R. H. Sheets & E. R. Hollins (Eds.), *Racial and ethnic identity in school practices: Aspects of human development,* (pp. 49–66). Mahwah, NJ: Lawrence Erlbaum Associates.

Sirotnik, K. A. (1989). The school as the center of change. In T. J. Sergiovanni & J. H. Moore (Eds.), *Schooling for tomorrow: Directing reforms to issues that count* (pp. 89–113). Boston: Allyn & Bacon.

Sirotnik, K. A. (1991). Critical inquiry: A paradigm for praxis. In E. C. Short (Ed.), *Forms of curriculum inquiry.* New York: State University of New York Press.

Tatum, B. V. (1992). Talking about race, learning about racism: An application of racial identity development theory in the classroom. *Harvard Educational Review, 62,* 1–24.

Tatum, B. V. (1994). Teaching White students about racism: The search for White allies and the restoration of hope. *Teachers College Record, 95*(4), 462–476.

Taylor, C. (1994). *Multiculturalism: Examining the politics of recognition.* Princeton, NJ: Princeton University Press.

Tetreault, M. K. T. (1993). Classrooms for diversity: Rethinking curriculum and pedagogy. In J. A. Banks & C. A. M. Banks (Eds.), *Multicultural education: Issues and perspectives* (2nd ed., pp. 129–148). Boston: Allyn & Bacon.

Wilson, T. P. (1992). Blood quantum: Native American mixed bloods. In M. M. Root (Ed.), *Racially mixed people in America* (pp. 108–125). Newbury Park, CA: Sage.

Yanow, D. (1996). American ethnogenesis and public administration. *Administration & Society, 27*(4), 483–500.

About the Contributors

Rosa Hernández Sheets is assistant professor at San Francisco State University. Her experience in higher education include teaching courses in social foundations, multicultural education, and supervising student teachers. She is coeditor of *Starting Small: Teaching Tolerance in Preschool and the Early Grades,* a research project of Teaching Tolerance, Southern Poverty Law Center in Montgomery, Alabama. This book won the 1998 Excellence in Educational Publishing Award. Her work in progress includes a book titled: *Classroom Discipline: Understanding Racial, Ethnic, and Cultural Dimensions* (Lawrence Erlbaum Associates).

Etta R. Hollins is professor and associate dean for Teacher Education at Wright State University. Her experiences in higher education include teaching courses in social foundations, curriculum development, multicultural education, and supervising student teachers. She is author of *Culture in School Learning* (Lawrence Erlbaum Associates), editor of *Transforming Curriculum for a Culturally Diverse Society* (Lawrence Erlbaum Associates), senior editor of *Teaching Diverse Populations: Formulating a Knowledge Base* (State University of New York Press), and *Pathways to Success in School* (Lawrence Erlbaum Associates), and coeditor of *Preparing Teachers for Cultural Diversity* (Teachers College Press). She is the recipient of the 1997 American Association of Colleges' of Teacher Education outstanding writing award for her book *Culture in School Learning.* This book also received the critics choice award.

Curtis W. Branch, a clinical psychologist by training, is currently a researcher at New York State Psychiatric Institute/Columbia University. He is interested in issues of race and ethnicity as they impact human development across the lifespan. Specific issues addressed in his scholarly and clinical writings include ethnic identity development among young African American children as a function of parental attitudes and adolescent identity transformations in the areas of ethnic and racial identity. His most recent works, *Clinical Interventions With Gang Adolescents and Their Families* (Westview) and *Adolescent Gangs: Old Issues, New Approaches* (Taylor & Francis), apply developmental theory and clinical axioms to working with gang affiliated adolescents.

William E. Cross, Jr. is professor and chairperson for the Department of Student Development and Pupil Personnel Services in the School of Education at the University of Massachusetts, Amherst. Dr. Cross is considered one of the leading experts in the study of African American identity, and his text, *Shades of Black; Diversity in African-American Identity* (Temple University Press) is considered a classic.

Donna Deyhle is associate professor in the Departments of Educational Studies and Ethnic Studies at the University of Utah. Her major professional interests focus on anthropology and education, cultural conflict, and the education of American Indians and Navajos. She received a Spencer Foundation Fellowship and two Spencer research awards for her research on Navajos and Karaja Indians in Brazil. She is the author of numerous publications and awards.

Peony Fhagen-Smith is a doctoral student in development psychology at Pennsylvania State University, University Park. Her major research interest is self- and racial identity development among Black and biracial children, adolescents, and young adults as it relates to social–emotional development, psychological well-being, and family socialization.

Geneva Gay is professor of Education at the University of Washington, Seattle. Her specialties are general curriculum theory and multicultural education. She is internationally known for her scholarship in curriculum design, staff development, and classroom instruction for ethnic and cultural diversity. She is particularly interested in the interactions of culture, ethnicity, and identity, and how these affect the values, attitudes, and behaviors of students and teachers in school settings. She is the coeditor of *Expressively Black: The Cultural Basis of Ethnic Identity* (Praeger) and the author of *At the Essence of Learning: Multicultural Education* (Kappa Delta Pi).

Maurice Korman is the Elizabeth H. Penn professor of Clinical Psychology and chair of the Psychology Division at the University of Texas Southwestern Medical Center at Dallas. He has directed the institution's doctoral program in clinical psychology for more than 30 years and more recently assumed the chair of the Department of Rehabilitation Science. His research activities in Texas and Mexico have focused on the use of inhalants and comparative studies of middle class families.

Stacey J. Lee is an associate professor of Educational Policy Studies at the University of Wisconsin, Madison. Her research interests include ethnic and racial identity among Asian Americans, minority student achievement, and interracial relationships between Asians and nonAsians. She is the author of *Unraveling the "Model Minority" Stereotype: Listening to Asian American Youth* (Teachers College).

Margaret LeCompte is associate professor at the University of Colorado, Boulder. Her research interests include ethnographic methods, school reform, and the academic careers of at-risk students, including the culturally and linguistically different and artistically gifted. She is coauthor of *The Way Schools Work: A Sociological Analysis Of Education* (3rd Ed., Longman), *Giving Up On School* (Corwin Press), and *Ethnography and Qualitative Design in Educational Research* (2nd Ed., Academic Press). She is coeditor of *The Handbook of Qualitative Research in Education* (Academic Press). In her latest work, she serves as coeditor of *The Seven Volume, The Ethnographer's Toolkit* (Altamira Press).

Manuel Ramirez III is a professor of Psychology at the University of Texas, Austin. His areas of research specialization are in ethnopsychology and cross-cultural psychology. He has been named Distinguished Minority Researcher by the American Educational Research Association. Dr. Ramirez is the author of *Psychotherapy and Counseling With Minorities: A Cognitive Approach to Individual and Cultural Differences* (Allyn & Bacon) and of the forthcoming book, *Multicultural/Multiracial Psychology* (Jason Aronson).

Amy L. Reynolds is assistant professor of Counseling Psychology at Fordham University, Lincoln Center. She received her doctorate in Counseling Psychology from Ohio State University. Her research interests and publications emphasize multicultural counseling, training, and supervision; lesbian, gay, and bisexual issues; and feminist psychology.

Tina Q. Richardson is an associate professor of Counseling Psychology in the Department of Education and Human Services at Lehigh University. Her research interests include multicultural issues in counselor training, racial identity development, gender identity development, health psychology, and alternative healing practices. Currently, she is president-elect for the Delaware Valley chapter of the Association of Black Psychologists and a member of the Board of the African Psychology Institute. She has received awards for outstanding teaching and community service.

Norma Rodriquez is assistant professor of Psychology and Chicano Studies at Pitzer College. Her research interests include the study of psychosocial and sociocultural factors associated with Latino academic achievement and adjustment to college.

Maria P. P. Root is associate professor in American Ethnic Studies and adjunct associate professor in Psychology and Women's Studies at the University of Washington, Seattle. Her most recent edited books are *Filipino Americans: Transformation and Identity* (Sage) and *The Multiracial Experience: Racial Borders as the New Frontier* (Sage). Root has been the recipient of distinguished career and service awards for her work in minority mental health with women and in the area of racial identity. Her edited book *Racially Mixed People In America* (1992) was the recipient of the Gustavus Myers Center Outstanding Book for Human Rights in 1993. She was awarded the 1997 APA Distinguished Contributions to Psychology in the Public Interest Early Career Award.

Timothy J. Silvestri is a doctoral student in Counseling Psychology at Lehigh University. He has also been employed for the past four years at St. Luke's Hospital, Bethlehem, PA as an adjunct therapist running groups on a diversity of issues ranging from anxiety, PTSD, and self-esteem. His research interests include White racial identity, multicultural counseling, and the historical and contemporary roots of racism.

Linda Strauss is currently completing her doctorate in social psychology at Pennsylvania State University, University Park. Her research focuses on the functions of racial identity, providing empirical confirmation for the Nigrescence theory of racial identity development.

Edward Taylor is an assistant professor at the University of Washington, Seattle, in the area of Educational Leadership and Policy Studies. His areas of interest and specialization are higher education and the social and cultural issues that influence policy, practice, and critical race theory. He has published in the areas of multicultural education and knowledge construction, leadership theory, and student ethnic identity development.

Author Index

A

Abell, P. K., 92, *99*
Aberle, D. P., *138,* 138*n*
Aboud, F. E., 19, 20, *25,* 94, *99,* 110, *119*
Acosta, F., 213, *226*
Adams, D. W., 192, *193*
Adams, G. R., 13, *25,* 27, 53, *63*
Agar, M., 158, *176*
Aguilar, R., 81, *86*
Akbar, N., 29, *46*
Alba, R. D., 95, *99*
Alipuria, L., 52, 53, *64,* 201, *210*
Allen, J., 13, *26*
Allen, V., 8, *25*
Allen, W. R., 18, *28,* 40, 47
Allman, K. M., 77, 78, *85*
Allport, G., 74, 75, *85*
American Psychological Association, 146, *154*
Anderson, A., 40, *46*
Anderson, J., 40, *46*
Angelou, M., 208, *209*
Antoni, M., 17, *28*
Anzaldúa, G., 83, *85*
Arce, C. H., 78, *85*
Ardila, R., 141, *154*
Arredondo, P., 218, *229*
Asher, S., 8, *25*
Assor, A., 159, *176*
Atkinson, D. R., 3, *5,* 49, 51, *65,* 72, *86*
Atwater, E., 11, *25*
Azmitia, M., 157, 169, *176*

B

Bagwell, C., 157, 169, *177*
Baldwin, J., 9, *25*
Bandura, A., 91, *99*

Banks, J. A., 19, *25,* 119, *119,* 192, *193,* 199, *209,* 237, *242*
Baptiste, L., 213, 215, *228*
Barr, D. J., 216, *226*
Barsham, R., 17, *28*
Barth, F., 94, *99,* 109, 114, *119*
Bauman, K. E., 169, *177*
Begay, S. M., *138,* 138*n*
Begay, W., *138,* 138*n*
Behrens, J. T., 226, *229*
Bennett, S. K., 3, *5,* 49, 51, *65*
Bennion, L., 13, *25*
Bentley, G. C., 97, *99*
Bernal, M. E., 18, *25,* 94, *99*
Bernier, J. E., 218, 221, *229*
Berry, J., 108, *119*
Berzonsky, M., 13, *26*
Betancourt, H., 141, 143, 151, 152, *154*
Bird, C., 8, *26*
Blake, R., 8, *26*
Bondi, J., 127, 130, *139*
Borodovsky, L. G., 49, *65*
Boscardin, M. L., 216, *226*
Bowers, C. A., 201, *209*
Boyd-Franklin, N., 36, *46*
Boyer, J., 216, *226*
Boykin, W., 169, *176*
Branch, C. W., 8, 10, 13, 14, 18, 20, 22, *26,* 91, 93, 94, 95, 98, *99,* 157, *176*
Breningstall, O., 135, 136, *138*
Bronfenbrenner, U., 34, *46*
Brookins, C. C., 169, *176*
Brookins, G. K., 18, *28,* 40, 47
Brooks-Gunn, J., 14, *26*
Brown, N. G., 84, *86*
Bruer, H., 13, *26*
Bulosan, C., 208, *209*

249

Subject Index